PALACE OF DARKNESS

TRACY L. HIGLEY

THOMAS NELSON
Since 1798

NASHVILLE   MEXICO CITY   RIO DE JANEIRO

Published in Nashville, Tennessee, by Thomas Nelson. Thomas Nelson is a registered trademark of HarperCollins Christian Publishing, Inc.

Thomas Nelson, Inc., titles may be purchased in bulk for educational, business, fund-raising, or sales promotional use. For information, please e-mail SpecialMarkets@ThomasNelson.com.

Publisher's Note: This novel is a work of fiction. Names, characters, places, and incidents are either products of the author's imagination or used fictitiously. All characters are fictional, and any similarity to people living or dead is purely coincidental.

Library of Congress Cataloging-in-Publication Data

Higley, T. L.
  Palace of darkness : a novel of Petra / Tracy L. Higley.
    pages cm
  ISBN 978-1-4016-8750-2 (paperback)
1. Petra (Extinct city)--Fiction. 2. Civilization, Ancient--Fiction. I. Title.
PS3608.I375P35 2014
  813'.6--dc23

                                       2014011027

Printed in the United States of America

14 15 16 17 18 19 RRD 6 5 4 3 2 1

*To the three men who have served God as
my pastors during my adult life:
Jeffrey Hartman
Mike Otto
Bob Sloan
Each of you has faithfully preached the freedom of the gospel,
prayerfully opened the Scriptures to me,
and given yourself to the work of the Kingdom.
Thank you for your ministry in my heart
and the hearts of so many others.*

WORD LIST

————◆————

betyl—a sacred stone, often in the form of a block

Cardo Maximus—the main thoroughfare of a city

cavea—seating area in a Roman arena or amphitheatre

cella—inner chamber of a temple

contubernium—the smallest organized unit of soldiers in the Roman army

cunei—wedge-shaped sections that divided the amphitheatre vertically, separated by stairs

denarii—small silver coin in Roman currency, most common coin

gladius—short sword

mina—a unit of weight equal to sixty shekels, monetary unit

pilum—javelin

scanae—the scene building behind the stage

sestarii—small unit of money

shekel—a unit of weight equal to about half an ounce, monetary unit

tessera—stone tile worn around the neck and used as a ticket

triclinium—dining room containing a dining table with couches along three sides

velarium—type of awning stretched over the seating area

ONE

———◆———

Rome, AD 106

THE STREETS OF ROME LAY BARREN AND EMPTY, SUCKED
dry by the colossal Flavian Amphitheatre that had swallowed seventy-
five thousand Roman citizens in a single gulp, and would hold each
one captive until they enjoyed the horrors Julian now raced to prevent.

More time. I need more time. Already the crowd inside the four-
story rim of stone cheered for the first event.

Julian's sandals smacked the black basalt road that led toward the
amphitheatre. The blistering Roman sun pounded the moisture from
his skin and left him panting. He had run most of the way, since an
old servant in Vita's house had pointed a gnarled finger toward the
east, toward the Forum, toward the arena of death.

Eighty arches ringed the outside of the theatre on each of its first
three stories. The bottom arches provided access to the public, and
the second story's niches held statues of the gods and emperors, who
now looked down on Julian as he sprinted across the large travertine
slabs that paved the arena's edge.

He ran toward one of the four main entrances and fumbled for the *tessera*, the stone tile he wore around his neck. The *designatores* at the entrance would insist on examining it, to see the sector, row, and seat to which he was assigned.

Indeed, the usher at this entrance was full of his own importance and held a palm to Julian's oncoming rush as though he could stop him with only the force of his arm.

"Too long in your bed this morning, eh?" His smug smile took in Julian's hastily wrapped toga and sweat-dampened hair.

Julian thrust the *tessera* before the man's gaze. "Here, here, look at it."

Still the amused smile. The usher opened his mouth to speak again.

"Look at it!"

Daunted, the man let his gaze travel over the tile, then took a tiny breath and stepped back. His grin faded to a look of regret, and he bowed his head. As if that were not enough, he bowed at the waist and extended a hand to invite Julian to enter.

Julian did not wait for an apology. He pushed past the usher and under the vaulted entrance, then straight through the arena's outer corridor and up a ramp that led to the *cavea*, the wedge-shaped sections of marble seats. This main entrance led directly to the central boxes reserved for the elite.

He exploded from the dimly lit ramp onto the terrace. The morning sun slashed across half the seats, the height of the amphitheatre leaving the other half in shade. The red canvas *velarium*, the awning used to shade the spectators, would be raised before it got much hotter, but for now, thousands of bleached togas on white marble blinded the eye and the smell of the masses assaulted the nose.

Julian crossed the terrace in two strides, slammed against the waist-high wall that separated him from the arena. A figure dashed at him from the shadows.

His mother's hands were on his arms in an instant. "Julian, what are you doing?" Her words were as clipped and terror-filled as his every movement.

"They have Vita, Mother!"

She wrenched his body to face her. Julian stood nearly a cubit taller than his mother, but Ariella had retained all the strength of her youth, along with the beauty. "There is nothing that can be done, my son."

He yanked his arms from her grasp. "Do not say that!" Julian searched the *cavea* behind him, full to overflowing with the purple-edged togas of senators. "Where is Father? Is he here?"

"Julian, think! You must think." Her voice was urgent and low, and her clutching fingers again slowed Julian's restlessness. "You will bring more harm—"

"I do not care!" He fought to harden his feelings into action. "I must end this."

"You cannot, son."

He turned flaming eyes on Ariella. "Do you not understand? I should be down in those cages."

Ariella's eyes misted. "I would not lose both my son and his betrothed on the same day."

Betrothed. The word washed more guilt over Julian's stricken soul.

A senator, one of his father's friends, walked past and paused to hold out an arm in greeting to Julian. "Fine day for the games, is it not?"

Julian straightened at once, resuming the noble bearing trained into him since childhood, and returned the man's grip. He nodded once but did not speak. The senator moved on, and Julian dropped his shoulders, ashamed he had not made a statement.

Ariella seemed to read his thoughts. Her dark gaze held his own. "It will take more than a day to change the Empire."

Julian looked out over the yellow sand of the arena. "But this day,

3

Mother, this day we must!" He slapped a hand against the top of the marble wall. "I am going to find Father."

"Julian, you know he can do nothing—"

He spun on her. "No. I am tired of both of you, always moving about your circles quietly, behind closed doors, the truth spoken only in whispers." He lifted his own voice as an example. "There is a time to speak!"

Ariella's nostrils flared but she said nothing. Turning from her, Julian stalked to the nearest break in the seating and ascended the tiers alongside his father's section. Here the nobility did not sit on wooden planks as the rest of the citizens but were given cushions or even chairs for comfort. He scanned the rows of seats for his father's graying head and instead met his dark gray eyes.

Julian shook his head and opened his mouth to shout across the intervening seats, but his father held up a hand, then stood and excused himself from his colleagues. He slid along in front of a dozen other senators and emerged at the end of the row beside Julian.

Quietly, he spoke into his son's ear. "I have just now heard. It is outrageous."

Julian's hands balled into fists at his side. "You must do something."

"What can I do, Julian? The emperor has ruled, and Trajan is not a man to be defied."

Across the arena, Julian watched as a trapdoor slid upward and a huddled band of men and women were prodded onto the sand at the end of Roman spears. Julian's heart pounded with the shortness of the time left and he turned to his father. "She is out there, Father!"

But his father's eyes held only grief, not the fiery anger that could change the future, even now.

Julian pushed past him, down the steps. If his parents would do nothing from their positions of influence, then he would stop this madness from a position of strength.

It had been his fault, all of it. Trajan had made his stance clear. As long as they kept to themselves, did not flaunt their disagreement with imperial policy, did not take a public stand, they would be left alone. But that had not been enough for Julian. Passionate about the truth, eager to show himself a leader, and foolish enough to believe himself invincible, he had spoken too loudly in too many places.

And now this. Vita and the others arrested, convicted, and sentenced without his knowledge. Julian had brought this on them all, but he had escaped their fate.

At the terrace level he circled the arena toward the imperial box. The amphitheatre was one of the few places where the public had access to the divine emperor. Julian grasped at the thin hope that he could get near enough to plead for Vita's life.

He had not loved her. Not like he should, though he tried. He had never known a more virtuous woman. The arranged match between them was a good one. But Julian never felt more than the flame of admiration and respect for her, and he saw nothing but the same in her eyes. Still, they would have been married.

We will be married.

The foot-stomps of the crowd rose around him like a hundred thousand drumbeats. The cadence resonated in his chest and pushed him forward. He knew that sound. It was the sound of a mob hungry for blood.

Terror drove his footsteps. He could not look to the arena. Not even when he heard more trapdoors rise and the low growl of beasts begin.

The crowd screamed as one, and their shouts lifted to the pale-blue sky like a puff of evil smoke from the underworld. Julian's bones seemed to turn to water. He raced on. The emperor's raised box was in sight.

But then they were beside him again, both his parents this time, grasping at his arms, pulling him backward.

"It is too late, son." His mother's voice held the grief of both the present and the past, for she had seen much sorrow in the arena in her day.

His father turned him to the wall to face the sand. "You must say good-bye, Julian. You must say good-bye."

He let his parents hold him there at the marble wall. He scraped his hands across the top, then gripped the white stone.

Lions. Six of them. Circling, circling the knot of friends in the center of the bright-yellow sand brought from one of the hills of Rome and spread on wooden planking to soak up the blood of gladiator, beast, and the condemned.

The lions charged at once, but for Julian, the moment stretched out like a thread of silk spun from a slow-turning wheel, and though the crowd still bellowed, in his head all had gone silent and he saw only his group of friends, crumpling in on themselves like sand flowing into a sinkhole.

The lions must have roared before they pounced, though Julian heard nothing, felt only the relentless scraping of his own hands across the stone wall. He scraped until his hands were torn and bloody, wanting to bleed with her, wanting to bleed with all of them as he should have.

The sun had risen to pour its rays into the center of the arena, and the yellow sand beneath them turned to molten gold in the light, an oval of liquid gold with Vita and the others drowning in the center of it. He saw her face for a moment, lifted to heaven.

His mind disconnected and drifted strangely, then, to the words at the end of the apostle John's Revelation and his vision of the New Jerusalem with its streets of pure gold.

Would Vita fall asleep in this golden sand and wake to streets of gold?

The beasts did their job well and quickly, and when it was over and the mutilated bodies of his friends lay scattered across the sand, Julian woke from his stupor. The weight of every lost life bore down on him as though the stones around him had collapsed on his head. Bile rose in his throat, and he turned away from the wall to retch onto the paving stones.

His parents held his arms as he emptied the contents of his stomach. He heard the jeers directed toward him. When he stood, the tear-streaked faces of both his parents matched his own.

But he found no solace in their shared grief. They did not have to bear the guilt of it as he did. As he always would. He pulled from their embrace and escaped the amphitheatre, running back the way he had come, running like a haunted man.

When his grief had hardened into bitter anger, he tried once again to change the minds and policies of the Roman government. But in the end he brought only more disgrace, and more danger, upon his family.

In the cool of the evening three days after Vita's death, he stood at the terrace wall of his father's lavish villa in the Roman countryside, looking down into the flowered gardens his mother had commissioned and listening to the fountain that trickled night and day into the central pool. He inhaled deeply of the night air, dragging in the scent of roses.

His guilt over Vita's death had not abated, and he had added to it with his actions in the days since. His brazen words in the Senate House, and later the Forum, had identified him as one who should have also met his death in the arena that day.

Perhaps that was his wish. To be arrested himself, to be thrown before the gaping maw of a dozen lions, to be given what he deserved.

But his family. He had not wanted the same for his family. His only brother, long since stationed in some military outpost, had never embraced the family's beliefs, but even he could be reached by the long arm of the Empire and brought back to face condemnation with the rest.

Behind him slaves stirred to prepare the evening meal and lit torches on the veranda. His parents would appear soon, and they would all pretend their privileged life continued.

But Julian had made a decision. His life in Rome was over. To protect his family, he must disappear.

He thought of his brother's stories of the provinces that lay at the edges of the Empire. Of Britannia, of Judea. But even there the Roman army could search out a man. No, he must go farther east than even Judea.

There was a place, a hidden city he had heard tales of since he was a boy. Stories that sparked his imagination and gave him the desire to travel across the desert sand to discover the city tucked between the rock cliffs of Arabia.

Petra. Capital of the Nabataean kingdom, wealthy center of the east-west trade route, and beyond even the Roman Empire's reach.

Julian rubbed his hands together, palms still raw from being torn open the day Vita had died. Yes, it was a good plan.

He would flee to Petra.

TWO

———◆———

CASSIA STOOD AT THE WINDOW OF HER DAMASCUS HOME, the bronze mirror that gave evidence of Aretas's violent affection for her still clutched in her hand.

How long until the brute returns?

The afternoon sun slanted into their tiny stone home, but it told her nothing. Aretas did not keep the regular hours of a merchant, nor the respectable schedule of a farmer.

She touched the purple flesh around her left eye and winced, then pressed her fingers against the angry bruise until she could no longer bear the pain. But she welcomed the pain today, let it feed her fury, let it harden her hatred. The vows she had whispered into the night, as Aretas slept off his wine, had been only words.

The languid summer air inside the house, weighted with the heady scent from the platter of dates she had set out, dizzied her, and Cassia went to the front door, in need of a fresh breeze.

From her open doorway she glanced left and right down their narrow alley, watching for Aretas's swagger. Instead, she spotted another figure, dear to her heart, approaching.

The small boy walked with head down and his feet dragged.

"Alexander?" His head lifted and she expected his sunny smile, but it was absent.

Even from this distance, the uncanny ability she'd always had to see into others' hearts exposed his hurt. Her feet carried her to him of their own accord. She saw before many steps that tears tracked across his grimy, little-boy face.

She did not speak, and the boy was silent as well but buried his sweet head against her abdomen and sniffed.

"Come home, Alexander." She reached out a hand. "We will talk there." He let her take his hand and lead him home.

Inside, they curled up together on a collection of red floor cushions placed against the wall. Cassia had surrounded this niche with clay pots of her favorite plants, and the effect created by the privacy lent itself to the whispering of secrets and hidden hurts. At six years old, Alexander was nearly too big to crawl onto her lap, but thankfully, he did not realize it. With the boy's head against her chest, she stroked his hair, damp with the heat of the afternoon.

"I thought you were going to play with Kelaya until nightfall."

"He did not want to play."

"No? Did his mother have too many chores for him?"

"He wanted to go to the river with the older boys. They said I could not come."

"Ah, but you will be older soon too." She felt Alexander shake his head against her, and she smiled. "Before you know it—"

"They said they would not allow the son of a bandit."

At her sharp intake of breath, the precious child looked up into her eyes. "Is my father a bandit?"

She held a hand against his smooth cheek. With his sandy hair and light eyes, the boy was more his father's than hers, but his sweet, puppy-like enthusiasm for life came from the gods themselves. "We will have more fun here, anyway." She hid her anger. "I need your special touch to prepare for the harvest feast."

He leaned his head against her once more and nodded, just a small dip of his head that bespoke hurt and shame. And the rejection of his playmates was like an injury to herself, a sharp stab of pain in her soul as real as any blow she'd ever received at the hand of Aretas. She added this new wound to the last.

Never again.

Refusing to let Alexander dwell on his disappointment, Cassia spun out one of her silly stories for him until his tears turned to giggles, aided by her tickling fingers.

"Come." She lifted the boy from her lap. "You can lay out the palm fronds." She pointed to a large orange pot standing beside the door, stuffed with green fronds she had gathered this morning from the outskirts of town, where date palms ringed the oasis that fed all of the Syrian city of Damascus. She decorated for the meal because it pleased her. Aretas would take no notice.

"Like this." She took a handful of fronds and scattered them like a green carpet.

"Kelaya's mother says you have more green things inside the house than outside. She says it is unnatchel."

Cassia laughed. "Unnatural?" She ran a palm branch through her fingers. "How can anything living be unnatural? Besides"—she handed him more palms—"it is a tradition to lay a palm carpet for the date harvest celebration."

Tradition. There had been none of it in her shortened childhood, so she had tried to build a life of tradition and ritual for Alex, hoping it would be a secure foundation in spite of the tentative life Aretas provided. How had she let them come so far?

When the palms were laid, she sent Alex to the back of the room to sit on a three-legged stool and practice his lyre. "For your papa. It will please him to hear you strum for our celebration."

Alexander shrugged. "Yesterday he told me to be quiet."

She bit back a slur on Aretas's manhood and shifted the platter of bloodred dates on the table. "He was tired, shekel. Tonight he will love to hear you play."

"Why do you call me *shekel* still, Mama?" He plucked a few strings on the lyre. "I must be at least a mina by now."

Cassia laughed again. Perhaps he was aware, after all, of how big he had grown. "I don't care if you are as big as fifty minas." She pointed a finger. "You will always be my bright, shiny shekel."

Alexander began his practice, and Cassia took a date from the platter, cut it in half with a sharp knife, and absently examined its wrinkly skin. She bit into it, her glance on the door once more. How long did they have? And what mood would be upon Aretas when he returned? It would depend on the success of his day—how many he had swindled and for how much. The sweetness puckered her cheeks. She went to Alex and held out the rest of the date to him. He grinned and opened his mouth.

"How are those two teeth?" She popped the fruit between his lips.

"Still wiggly." He demonstrated by wobbling his two front teeth back and forth with a small forefinger.

She laughed. "Chew your date."

He crooked his finger at her, indicating she should bend down to him. She brought her face close to his and he whispered into her ear.

"I like you best." He kissed her cheek.

She exhaled and pulled him against her shoulder, unwilling to let him see the emotion pooled in her eyes. "And you are my very favorite boy in all the world." She turned away before he could ask why he had made her sad.

A knock sounded at the door, then a cheerful voice. "Cassia?" The door opened and her neighbor Magdala entered with Alexander's playmate, Kelaya, in tow. "You weren't at the market this morning—" Magdala's voice choked off when she saw Cassia's face. She crossed the room and put her arms around Cassia, then removed her arms and put both hands on Cassia's shoulders, turning her toward herself. Magdala studied Cassia's eyes until Cassia had to look away. "How bad?"

Cassia drew a breath, shrugged one shoulder, and grinned at Magdala. "I will not soon win any footraces."

Magdala clucked her tongue and pulled Cassia toward her in another careful embrace, which smelled of jasmine and honey. "When are you going to leave?" she whispered.

"I have nothing, Magdala. No money. No family. I must first have a good plan."

Magdala's bright-red dress and the matching linen wrapped around her head and shoulders offset Cassia's aged white tunic, and clearly conveyed Magdala would never understand Cassia's lack of finances.

Her neighbor's hand on her back was gentle and warm. "You are strong, Cassia, even if you do not believe it for yourself. Most in your place would have given up on life by now. You *can* raise that boy. You can make a life for yourself without Aretas. And you will!"

Cassia only nodded at her friend.

"What about Aretas's family?" Magdala's lip curled. "That man comes from money. It's written all over him. Why don't you at least find them and let them help take care of you and Alexander?"

"Aretas never speaks of his family. And he gets angry whenever I ask." She pushed Magdala toward the door. "You both must go. He will be home soon, and you know how he feels about my friendship with you."

"That man would be threatened by a stray pup if it befriended you. He hoards your beauty like he hoards his dishonest wages." Magdala beckoned to her son.

"Ah, perhaps he will toss me into a sack of coins one day, and I'll find the money I need to flee this place." Cassia smiled and gave Magdala another painful embrace before closing the door behind them both.

She went to the cushions once more and propped herself there to listen to Alex play. There was nothing left to prepare. There was only the waiting, no different from any night. The uncertain waiting. Tonight would Aretas's touch be angry or sweet? Would he find her entertaining or simply bothersome? She sent up a simple prayer to the gods that she would not kill him while he slept, though she always doubted they listened to anyone but the temple priests.

The sun carved a yellow line across the floor, cutting an advancing path through the room, until at last there came a scratching in the dust outside the front door. Cassia stood and Alex's music ceased as though his hand had been slapped from the instrument.

The door flew open and Aretas stumbled across the threshold, outlined by the setting sun.

Cassia went to him, anger flooding her. He was clearly drunk.

Aretas grinned and kicked the door shut. He held a worn leather pouch in one hand, tied shut with a dirty woven cord. Even slightly bent, he towered over Cassia, and he wrapped a muscular arm around her shoulder. The pouch he carried bumped against her upper arm, heavy and rough.

"Alexander the Great!" he yelled, using the title given to the boy's conquering namesake four centuries earlier. "How high can you count?" He was still yelling, and Cassia led him, stumbling across the room, to the cushions where he collapsed. "Let's see if all that learning your mama's been giving you is working." He tossed the pouch at the boy's feet, and it landed with a harsh jingle of coins. "Count that!"

His words huffed out as though he were in pain, and he used the back of his hand to swipe at his windblown black hair. He had the smell of drink on him, along with the ordinary smell of sweat, which he seemed to acquire in spite of his aversion to hard work.

And then she saw it. The reddening gash across the front of his tunic.

"You are bleeding!" She reached for the torn edges of the tunic, but he slapped her hand.

"Count the money!"

Bleed to death, then, stubborn fool.

She moved across the room to Alex and together they dumped the coins on the floor.

"So many!" Alex's eyes widened. "What did you sell to get these, Papa?"

Aretas laughed, a scornful laugh that dug into Cassia's heart the way her gardening trowel attacked the hard desert soil.

"Just count, Alex." Without looking over her shoulder at Aretas, she said, "How bad is it?"

There was no answer, and she glanced back. Aretas's eyes were closed and the stain on his tunic had spread. She left Alex to the counting and went to him, compassion taking over. There had been a time when she found Aretas, and the danger he brought with him, irresistible. Long ago. Before Alexander.

His eyes fluttered open. "How much?" His voice did not seem so strong as it had when he staggered in.

"We are not finished yet."

He grinned, closing his eyes. "That is good."

She reached for the injury again, and he did not push her away. "One day all of this will catch up with you, Aretas." She pulled at the torn tunic and he grunted.

"Perhaps today."

The cut was not deep, only wide. As though someone had slashed at him as he ran, catching more tunic than skin. Who was the attacker? An honest tradesman yielding to a moment of temper? Or one of the unsavory merchants who passed through town and was usually on the cheating end of deals, who did not easily play the victim?

She wiped the blood from the cut.

"Aaahhh!" Aretas arched his back. "Easy, woman! I am not one of your goats!"

"Sorry." Cassia bit her lip to hide a smile.

Across the room, Alex dropped the last coin onto the pile. "Thirty-two denarii, Papa!"

Aretas propped himself on two elbows and scowled at the boy. "Are you certain? There must be more."

Alex lowered his eyes. "I will count again."

She shifted to stand, but Aretas caught her wrist. "Why so serious, Cassia? Aren't you proud of me?" He squeezed her arm until it tingled. "Do I not provide well for you both? Better than you deserve?"

She forced a cold smile. She had been with Aretas all six of Alexander's years, since she herself was only sixteen. She could wait a little longer. "I worry about you, that is all."

He released her. "I can handle myself. You would do better to worry about your own skin. A trading caravan is on the horizon. Tomorrow we work together."

Cassia's stomach hardened. "No, Aretas. It is not safe for Alexander."

Aretas glanced at the boy, still counting and oblivious to their conversation. "Of course it is safe. Do you think I would ever endanger my boy?"

She stood and moved to the table, and the palm fronds crunched under her feet. "As you said, you provide well for us yourself. You do not need us."

The sun dipped below the horizon at last, and the house descended into gloom. Cassia brought a plate of dates and a small loaf of bread to Aretas.

"No, I do not need you." He took the food from her hand. "But it does not serve to play the same game every day. You and Alex vary the game."

Cassia lowered her voice to a hiss. "I am sick of helping you cheat people. And it *is* dangerous for Alex. Play your own foolish games."

Aretas's eyes bore into hers, and he tossed the plate to the blanketed floor, spilling the fruit.

She had provoked him purposely, even though she keenly sensed the direction of his mood. She knew he would hit her. *One more time, to strengthen my heart. Then never again.*

"It is still thirty-two denarii, Papa." Alex held up the pouch and shook it to jingle the coins.

Aretas did not take his eyes from Cassia. "That is good, Alexander the Great. You are a very smart boy. But it is time for sleep now."

"But the festival—"

"To your bed, Alexander!" Aretas's voice was iron, ready to strike.

The boy's face fell and Cassia's hands formed fists at her sides. She despised Aretas when he hurt Alexander's feelings. The boy came to her and hugged her waist. She bent her head to him. "Where are my ten kisses?"

"A hundred kisses!" He pecked her cheek in their nightly ritual.

"A thousand kisses," she whispered as always, then nudged him to the back room. She gathered the dates from the floor, replaced them on the plate, and considered her choices as Aretas came at her.

She could leave until morning. But it would be worse when she returned.

She could leave now, forever. But he would never let her take Alexander.

She could not leave alone.

No, she must wait. Wait for her chance. She thought of Aretas's insistence that she and Alex help swindle the traders passing through Damascus. He would give her money as part of the game they played. She toyed with a possibility, turning it over in her mind like a new gold coin.

The gash in his side must not have pained Aretas too much, at least not enough to soften the blow to her ribs. *Don't cry out. Focus on tomorrow. Our last chance.*

She dodged his fists and focused on her pot of caraway. *A little brown on the tips of the leaves. More water, perhaps.* Caraway was a sensitive plant.

Aretas soon tired and left her alone. She wiped the sweat from her brow and blood from her mouth. The beatings never lasted long when he had been drinking. He was asleep within minutes, one arm thrown over his forehead, mouth dropped open and snoring. But Cassia did not sleep, not for many hours. Tomorrow was too important.

When she did at last drift off, it was with the comforting thought that although her ribs burned like fire, her heart had at last turned to ice.

She had been weak for too long. It was time for action.

THREE

THE EARLY-MORNING LIGHT, WATERY AND COOL, FILTERED into the front room and woke Cassia from her uneasy sleep. She lifted herself from the cushions, wincing at the stab in her side. But she would not give in to self-pity today.

Across the room, Aretas sat cross-legged on the floor, readying what he called their "merchandise."

Nothing more than powder and lies.

"Paid too much for this alabaster," he muttered, pouring powdered resin through a small funnel into the mouth of a tiny pearl-white jar.

"It is beautiful." Cassia crossed the room and knelt beside him to stroke the smooth surface of the jar. Aretas knew all about luxuries such as alabaster. He had never brought her anything so fine.

Aretas set the jar on the floor and picked up a small clay jar. He pulled the stopper from it and, in an uncommon gesture of goodwill, held it to Cassia to let her smell.

She breathed deeply of the cloying scent of myrrh.

"The trick is to mix it just right." Aretas sniffed it himself.

Cassia said nothing. Aretas always enjoyed explaining his schemes to her.

"A few pinches in the jar"—he let the amber-yellow powder drift into the jar's mouth—"then a generous coating on the rim and the stopper." He finished his preparation of the jar, then held it out to her to smell again.

She took a sniff and nodded. "Smells the same. As strong as the pure myrrh."

Aretas grinned. "Though worth a fraction of the price."

Cassia tried to match his smile, but her stomach knotted and she felt her expression darken. Aretas did not miss the change, but he mistook her resolve for fear.

"You will play your part well." He left no room for argument. "It grows late. You two get dressed." He reached for another small jar to repeat his villainous process.

Cassia crossed the room to a wooden box he had placed on the table. Inside lay the dress, the sumptuous silk robe she was only allowed to wear on these occasions. She lifted the pale-yellow silk from its soft folds and let it fall before her.

"Alex," she called to the back room. "Get dressed in your linen tunic."

She stripped her dirty tunic and let the yellow silk wrap her in softness. In the bottom of the box lay two delicate sandals, and she slipped these on as well, then turned for Aretas's approval.

He looked up, nodded once, and then returned to his work. "Better powder that eye."

She found some of the white lead powder and brushed it across the bruised flesh.

Alexander emerged as Aretas packed his jars between layers of linen in a large pouch and lifted the strap over his head and shoulder. "You look pretty, Mama."

Cassia straightened his belt. "And you look like a young prince."

Aretas held out a short dagger. "Here, hide this under your robe."

Cassia lifted her hands, palms out. "No weapons. You know how I feel."

He swore and tossed the weapon on the table. "We will walk together until we reach the edge of the traders' market." And then the small pouch he had brought back last night, with more added besides, was in her hands at last. She hid a smile. Today was the day.

She forced them to walk slowly out of town, to keep the dust down and the yellow silk clean. Aretas grew impatient as Alexander kept darting off to investigate stray goats, wild foxes, shy badgers. Cassia kept him moving, but the boy could not pass an animal without stopping to talk to it. Friends hailed him as they passed, and Cassia smiled to hear other boys call his name. Somehow he had won hearts here in spite of everyone knowing what kind of man his father was.

"Do we really need Alexander?" Cassia asked Aretas. "I can do this without him. Let him stay with his friends."

Aretas stalked on ahead. "The boy makes you respectable." He left her behind to ponder the deeper truth of his words.

She slowed even more, knowing she had sufficient time to linger. Aretas had work to do.

"Come, Alexander." She held out a hand to the boy and he bounded to her, placing his small hand in hers.

"Did you see that fox, Mama? It had big eyes."

"Perhaps it was a magical fox, eh?" She tugged at his hand.

Caravan traders arrived in Damascus several times each week from faraway places like Egypt and India, Persia and China. They came with loaded camels, snorting and jingling with treasures, and gathered at the edge of town, where they camped and waited for other traders to arrive and make deals. When they left in a few days, it would be with new purchases. And hopefully, with one small woman and an even smaller boy.

Ahead, a series of small tents, nothing more than blankets propped on sticks pushed into the dirt, dotted the horizon. These men had been at the edge of Damascus for a few days, but the new caravan approaching in clouds of dust brought new treasures and fresh opportunities. Aretas had timed his arrival perfectly so he could mingle with the resident traders and those arriving, with neither group realizing he did not belong. He had even let his face go unshaven for several days to better fit in with the travelers.

It was her task to stay close enough to arrive at the right time herself, without being seen too soon.

She kept her attention trained on Aretas's tall figure and muscular arms, watching him move through the crowd as though at home. And then he had begun to engage some of them. No business yet. Just conversation. She heard his booming laugh and saw him slap a trader on the back.

The new caravan, with its red-tasseled camels and loaded packs, blended with the first group, and Cassia lost sight of Aretas.

"Do you see your father?" she asked Alex. His hand had grown sweaty in hers.

The boy shielded his eyes with the other hand. "There he is!" He pointed.

Aretas had pulled away from the crowd a bit and had taken two traders with him.

It begins.

Alex wriggled his hand from hers. "You are hurting me, Mama."

She clutched him to her side. "I am sorry, shekel." She tipped his face up to look at her. "Do you remember what you must do?"

He nodded, his tongue playing with his loose teeth. "Stay quiet. Always quiet."

She smiled. "Good boy."

She looked back to Aretas. Was it time? Her mouth went dry. She must finish the game he played, then she would be free to move among the traders and complete the true task that drew her today.

Now.

"Come, Alex." She led him forward, forcing a casual smile to her lips. Within a few minutes they had reached the traders. She tried to make it look as though they wandered but kept her steps headed for Aretas. A trickle of sweat ran down the center of her back, and she regretted the yellow silk would absorb it. She read the language of the lead traveler's body. Interested. Not yet sold.

She watched from the corner of her eye as Aretas wielded his winning smile and spoke with the traders as though he were the prince of the land, all grace and charm.

The first trader, clearly the spokesman, had a weasely look about him, beady-eyed with a pointy nose. She hoped Alexander would not point out this fact. The second stood behind him, like a wall of intimidation, wide-chested and a vacant look in his eyes.

They began to move away. A flick of Aretas's eyes signaled her.

She strode up to him, smiling.

"Ah, here you are." She spoke loudly enough to be heard by the retreating traders. "I have been searching for you."

As they always did, the traders stopped and turned at the sound of a woman's voice, an uncommon occurrence in caravan camps.

Aretas held out both arms and grinned. "My best customer, and most beautiful." His voice dripped with flattery. To the two men he nodded and winked. "Here's a lady who knows quality and where to find it."

"Indeed." Cassia smoothed the yellow silk over herself and smiled at the traders. "Those cheats in the town market would try to sell me their wives' wash water if I let them, eh?" She waited for a returning smile. "I know where to come."

The larger of the two men sidled back toward them. "Smelled rather weak to me," he grunted. But she could sense his interest. The other one leaned into the conversation, clearly trying to gain Cassia's attention. "We can do better in Petra."

Beside her, she felt Aretas's body straighten at the mention of Petra. The feeling lasted only a moment, then he held out one of his alabaster jars to Cassia. She removed the red clay stopper and waved the jar under her nose. "Oh, you must not be familiar with the subtler scent of Anatolian myrrh. It does not overpower yet is finer than any Egypt can produce." She smiled and nodded to Aretas. "I will take it."

He named an outrageous price, and she argued him down a bit but then glanced at the traders and shrugged prettily. "One must pay for quality." She pulled a few coins from her pouch, flashing the sum conspicuously.

Aretas took her money, then bowed over her hand and kissed it. The gallant gesture brought her a jolt of the attraction that had first brought them together, and she couldn't help but smile. She did not miss the elbow jab and wink the big trader gave his friend. "Too bad she's got her boy with her, eh?" he said to Aretas.

"I must move on." Cassia gathered her dress around her. "I have more to purchase. But I will see you again, I am sure."

Aretas bowed again and she drifted away, with Alexander following. He had played his silent part well.

Behind her, she heard the trader say, "You won't take me for the lady's price, so let's make it fair."

She realized she'd been holding her breath and forced her heart to slow. They had succeeded.

Now to find an honest-looking trader who would take a few coins in exchange for a promise of safe passage to anywhere for Alex and her.

She could not go far. The jingle of coins changing hands meant

Aretas would be leaving soon, before the traders could inspect their purchases too closely. She would need to be close behind or he would suspect.

Another of the newly arrived traders tried to interest her in a sack of fabrics tied to his camel. She released Alexander's hand to run her fingers through it. When she looked up to use her special sight to read his heart and his character, Alex had disappeared.

She turned a frantic circle, not wanting to cry out and draw attention. Ah, but there he was, heading back to Aretas.

No, Alex.

She moved toward the small group. The traders were packing away their myrrh and Aretas was pocketing his "earnings."

Alex skipped to Aretas's side. As far as she was from them, Cassia still heard his voice ring out, and the words drained the courage from her.

"Papa! I forgot to show you my loose teeth!"

The big man, who had been slinging his pouch over his camel's back, stopped in midair and eyed Alex.

Cassia's hand fluttered at her chest, betraying her nerves. Should she retrieve her son or let Aretas handle the situation?

"Papa?" the burly man repeated. "The boy is yours?"

Aretas opened his mouth, exhaled, then closed it again and glanced at Cassia.

She tried to mask her horror, but it was too late. Understanding flickered in the eyes of the trader as he looked from her to Aretas. Her temples throbbed at the murder she read in his eyes.

She watched, rooted to the ground, as Aretas secured his money pouch to his belt, grabbed Alexander's hand, and spoke only one word to the boy.

"Run!"

FOUR

———◆———

I never should have let him bring Alex.

Cassia sprinted behind Aretas and her son as they took to the open field between the caravan camp and the town. Long grasses slashed at her thighs and grabbed at the yellow silk as though they knew it was too fine for her.

Behind them, the two foreign traders rained curses down on them. No doubt they were securing their goods and camels so they could give chase. The fugitives did not have long.

Aretas still held Alexander's hand as they ran. Cassia strained forward, trying to take the boy's hand from Aretas, but she could not reach them. Alex stumbled once, then again, and Aretas yanked his arm upward to set him on his feet. He cried out in pain and fear.

"He can't run as fast as you!" Cassia yelled at Aretas's back.

"He'd better!"

Cassia's breath came in short gasps now, but she risked a look over her shoulder. Across the field, the two traders had started their pursuit.

"They are coming!"

She hated open spaces. She felt vulnerable, exposed as they ran.

As if their pursuers could stop them simply by pointing a finger across the expanse.

But the town loomed, and they were soon within its limits. Aretas turned into a narrow street lined on either side with small, mud-brick houses. They ran through the street speckled with greenish horse dung. Aretas pulled Alex against a wall and let the boy catch his breath. Cassia lowered herself until her face was even with her son's.

"Are you well, shekel?"

He panted but nodded. Tears had channeled down his cheeks and already dried to white streaks.

Aretas paced. "Is he well? He's the reason we're in trouble. And he's going to get us caught!"

Cassia spun on him, her jaw tight. "Then go on alone! We'll be fine without you!"

Aretas's eyes went dark and his hand fisted. He swallowed hard, then shook his head. "We must keep going."

They outpaced the traders somehow, losing them in the close-packed streets of Damascus. They returned to the house, and Cassia placed Alexander on a chair to wipe the grime from his body.

Aretas growled. "The boy deserves a whipping, not gentleness."

Cassia's lips tightened and her breath shallowed.

Aretas was not finished. "One of these days he's—"

"Stop!"

Alexander jumped at the sharpness of her voice.

"Not another word, Aretas." She turned on him, protecting her son with body and words. "You pulled us into your trickery when we wanted no part of it. I warned you it would be dangerous for us, but you did not care. So do not speak another word of blame to me!"

She sensed his tension. Like a snake coiled to strike. But she had venom in her as well.

Later, when Alexander had been given his thousand kisses and tucked into his bedding and the day's take sat fat and heavy in a pouch beside the boy's lyre, Cassia lay tense and angry beside Aretas.

"Those traders"—she hesitated, then pushed forward—"when they spoke of being in Petra—"

Aretas cut her off. "It was my home."

"You never speak of it."

"For good reason."

In the darkness she could not see his face, but she could read him easily. Regret, perhaps bitterness, soured his voice. In all their years together, she had only learned bits and pieces of his early life. "Have you no one there anymore?"

He did not answer at once, and when he did speak, his voice was thick. "They are there. But they do not want me back."

"But perhaps Alexander . . ."

Aretas rolled to his side, away from her. She had seen all she would see through that small window. He was asleep long before her, his breathing steady and untroubled, even after the frightening day.

But sleep again did not favor Cassia. Today's plan had been shattered. A new plan was needed.

Sleep did come, eventually. But sometime in the early watches of the morning, a pounding came at the door. Cassia bolted upright, her heartbeat matching the clamor.

Aretas was on his feet. Alexander appeared in the doorway behind her. He clutched a tiny carved lion, his bedtime companion. Cassia went to him and turned as the door burst inward.

She gathered her son behind her and faced the two intruders. She recognized them in an instant.

"We want no trouble here." Aretas wore a light tunic only and had no weapon. In that moment he seemed quite weak.

The trader Aretas had swindled took in the room with a glance.

"We want what's ours," the man said through clenched teeth. "And then *you* will be the one who pays." His gaze drifted to Alexander and her, and the throbbing in her head warned her of danger.

This was it, then. The day she had known would come since she had first tied her fate to Aretas's, somehow believing she could love him into respectability, create out of him a man worth having, who would love her in return in the way she yearned for. She had stayed with him, had borne him a son. Somehow she had believed her own commitment would foster his. And yet some part of her had always known that Aretas's past or his present would someday find him.

Now all that remained was to see if he would destroy her and Alex as well. She pushed the boy behind her and held his arm with her own slick hand, willing him to stay as unseen as possible.

But it was *not* possible. Perhaps it was the scent of gold at the boy's feet.

It happened in an instant, and yet slowly. The weasel-man flashed a knife and lunged for Aretas. The beefy man lumbered toward Alex and her, where they stood with the coins beside their sandals. His hands were outstretched, and his fingers were fat and clubbed, like greasy sausages in the market.

There was no time to react before he knocked them both aside with one sweep of his massive arm. They fell together, and Cassia heard Alex's lyre fall to the floor with a crack. The boy had landed on the instrument. She felt an illogical jolt of sadness at the loss, as though something much greater was not at stake.

Cassia reached for Alexander. The boy held his hand to his mouth, as he often did when trying not to cry.

Behind them Aretas screamed, and Cassia turned to see the little man pull his knife from Aretas's stomach.

Her own insides turned to water then, with the ponderous dread that comes when one's entire world is about to change.

Alex lay upon the money pouch. Cassia turned back as the fat man kicked her little boy in the stomach to push him aside. The air whooshed from his lungs. His light eyes widened in terror and fixed upon her as his only hope. "Mama!"

Aretas was in trouble, but the protective fierceness that rose up in her was only for Alex. She pulled him away from the scattered coins. His attacker bent to scrabble in the dirt.

The bitter taste of fear and anger rose in her chest. She glanced around her, saw the heavy pot of caraway, and wrapped her hands around the cool weight of the terra-cotta. She scrambled to her feet, hefted the pot over her head, and smashed it down with a furious yell onto the fat man's bent head. The clay cracked and the soil spilled over him like a dirty anointing, and he went down with a groan and lay still.

On shaking legs, Cassia turned to the other, smaller man. He faced her, bloody knife in hand.

Alex whimpered at her feet, and one glance at him revealed a bloody mouth. The two wiggly front teeth had been knocked out.

Somehow the injury to her boy, though slight, raised a fury in her like she had never known, not even when Aretas would shove him aside in impatience and neglect.

She took two rapid steps to the table, still laid from yesterday's holiday celebration, and grabbed up the knife she'd left there while cutting dates. She spun to her attacker, who clearly debated whether to lunge for her first or the boy.

She gripped the hilt of the knife in sweaty palms and forced the tremor from her voice. "Go into the back room, shekel." She did not take her eyes from the intruder.

The beady-eyed man started forward as soon as Alex moved— he intended to kill the boy. The realization nearly suffocated her, but she could not succumb to the fear. She moved like summer lightning between her son and him. If he killed her first, no one would be left to save Alex. Aretas lay moaning on the cushions and could not save them.

They faced off, with Alex somewhere behind her. She prayed he had escaped the room.

She pierced the little man with her gaze and held the knife toward him at her waist. It took only an instant to read him. Greed drove him, not revenge. "Aretas has stolen from you, and you have retrieved your money. Now take it and your friend, and go. There is justice in taking what is yours. But no one will forgive you the needless deaths of a woman and child." Her voice was like hard steel, surprising even her.

His eyelids fluttered with indecision.

The big man on the floor groaned again and struggled to his knees.

"Take your money and go!" she shouted.

The man on the ground was scooping the coins and dumping them into the pouch.

The little man waved the knife to his friend. "We have what we came for. Leave them."

And then they were gone, and the house was silent like the grave, and just as still.

Cassia stood in the center of the room, breathing heavily and gripping the knife, unable to take her gaze from the door still swinging on its hinges.

It was not Aretas's moans that brought her to her senses, but Alexander's quiet cry. She turned slowly to see him there with his crushed lyre and his bleeding mouth. Her sweet shekel.

But Aretas's blood also drew her attention and she went to him on the floor. She ripped away his tunic. His stomach was covered in the purple-red of smashed dates, she thought, her mind oddly disconnected from the truth. All those smashed dates, reminding her of the festival she had planned last night.

Aretas gripped her arms with surprising strength, and she looked into his eyes.

These were their last moments together. She searched for the right words. Nothing came.

"You could have stopped him," Aretas hissed. "If you hadn't been shielding that cursed boy."

It was strange, this feeling she had. As though Aretas spoke to her from the other end of a dark tunnel, and each moment receded from her farther, until she could see his lips moving but heard nothing, felt nothing.

And then his mouth stopped moving and his eyes focused on the roof above them and then focused not at all and his grip loosened and he was gone.

Cassia moved backward on her knees, backward until she bumped against something. Alexander. She reached for him and pulled him into an embrace.

And they cried together there on the floor, though Cassia did not know exactly why she cried.

For more than anything else, more than grief or fear or even shock, and even with all that was now unknown about their future, what Cassia felt was a sickening, betraying, yet welcome sort of relief.

⚜

Two days later Cassia buried Aretas in a poor man's grave outside the city limits of Damascus. No rock-cut tomb where his embalmed body could be left for the requisite year before moving his bones to an ossuary. Rock tombs were for rich men, for men with families. *Respectable men.*

Instead, she stood on the barren plateau, with the desert air blowing in from the east, and stared at the rock pile that covered Aretas's body. Alexander stood beside her. He clutched her hand in his own and leaned his head against her side, above her hip. It seemed to her the boy had not released her for two days.

She had hoped to give him a good childhood with his father. Her own father had abandoned her so early, and she still felt the pain.

She smelled of myrrh. There had been little money to purchase the other embalming spices, but it was only right to wrap his body traditionally, and she had used some of his treasured supply.

Magdala was there, and her son, Kelaya. She had followed behind Cassia and Alexander as though part of a larger mourning party, and Cassia was grateful for the support, however pitiable. A few drops of water on parched ground.

"You are better off without him."

Her friend's words were true, but she raised her eyes to the distant trunks of palm trees, outlined against the wavering heat of the orange-tan sand, and hoped for Alex's sake Magdala would not continue.

"You are a strong woman, Cassia. You can survive alone. Raise that boy alone. Teach him what's right, instead of—"

"Thank you, Magdala." Cassia gripped Alex's hand. "Thank you for coming." She smiled at the woman, whose bony-sharp features matched her words.

"What will you do?"

Cassia voiced the thought that had come to her on the heels of Aretas's death. "Petra."

Alexander looked up at her with curious eyes, and she put a hand on his shoulder. Their time had come at last.

"Aretas came from Petra, he told me. His family, *Alexander's* family, must still be there."

"Family?" Alex spoke the word as though it were unfamiliar on his tongue. His smooth forehead creased in concentration.

Cassia smiled at the only joy of her life and pulled him close. It was time for him to have a life. Time for both of them. "Family, Alex." She turned to Magdala and smiled, hope for the future filling her heart.

"We are going to Petra."

FIVE

HAGIRU KNELT ALONE IN THE CENTER OF HER PRIVATE incantation chamber.

Here none would dare disturb her.

The cold stones beneath her chilled her limbs, for no fire warmed the tiny chamber, only the feeble flicker of oil lamps. She closed her eyes and reached out through the darkness with her soul, searching. Always searching. Why did the gods always make her beg?

The black-and-gray blocks of the chamber walls undulated with the orange-and-black shadows thrown against them by the circle of tiny oil lamps surrounding her. She swayed on her knees with the rhythm of the flames, and a low hum built in her throat, more animal than musical.

Come to me. Come to me.

She would drink in their power tonight. She would have their knowledge. But always, even when she summoned them with the confidence borne of her position as high priestess of the god Dushara, a corner of her heart knew the truth.

She was at their mercy.

The gods came when the gods would come. So it had always been.

Hagiru's incantation chamber lay like a black jewel in the center of the palace. *The dark heart*, she called this special place. One day all of the Nabataean kingdom, including her capital city of Petra, would be ruled from this place.

This was why she sought the gods tonight. To be reassured. To be stroked and petted and told she still acted within their will.

But something blocked her union this night. She fought through the thickness in the air, grasping for the presence. Still on her knees, with arms outstretched and head thrown back, she invited the powers that ruled her to come once again and fill her to overflowing.

Nothing.

Hagiru dropped her head, then, teeth grinding, stood and went to the edge of the room where a narrow ledge held instruments of worship and incense.

Her fingers closed around a small but lethal dagger. She returned to the center of the circle.

Satisfied with her position inside the yellow flames, she laid the dagger's flat blade across her whitened palm, then slowly closed her hand over it.

One quick cut. She inhaled sharply at the dagger's bite and pulled it from her closed hand. Again she swayed, but this time with the dizziness of pain.

She opened her palm and saw the red gore spread across her skin like oil soaking into parchment. Two quick steps took her to one of the lamps, where she held her hand over its light, letting the blood drip into the flame.

This is what I will do for you. This and much more. Come to me.

The flame popped and sizzled with its anointing, and she turned her humming into chanting, louder and more insistent. Had she not shown them her loyalty?

The flow of blood slowed, and Hagiru hoped it had been enough to please the gods. She put her tongue to the gash like a kitten to milk and smiled.

Still dizzy, she lowered herself to the floor, this time stretching out inside the circle, arms and legs forming an X, putting herself at the mercy of the gods.

And then they were there. With their blessed chaos and enchanting fury, they rushed out of the darkness beyond and scratched and clawed their way into her body. Heat washed from her head to her feet, and then a chill chased after it. She trembled on the floor but kept herself outstretched and exposed. Let them have her, all of her.

Shards of bright colors shattered behind her eyes, red and orange, purple and yellow. Bright stars falling out of the sky, burning her thoughts.

And then the voice she knew best among all the others. Dushara, chief god of Petra, was her special connection.

Hagiru.

The voice was as clear as her own, though she never knew if others would hear it had they been present.

"Speak, Dushara. I am your servant."

There is danger.

A tremor shook her body. "What is this danger?"

The rule of Petra is not secure.

Did he speak of his rule or her own? She swallowed and lifted her chin, driving her head against the stone floor. "I am equal to any challenge. I must only know that my actions here are right. That I follow the right path."

Be watchful. Ready to destroy.

"I seek the will of the gods always."

She waited then, waited for the reassurance that she acted according to their purpose, but when the message came, it did nothing to calm her spirit.

Be warned, Hagiru. Danger comes to Petra.

SIX

———◆———

THE CITY OF PETRA LAY WITHIN A SANDSTONE GORGE, cut into the mighty mountains of Arabia as though the finger of a god had carved a slit through the dark-red stone and hidden the city away. Or perhaps the gods had thundered over the red cliffs until they split apart, and the city had bloomed in the crack like a desert cactus.

But it was not the origins of Petra that troubled Cassia as she and Alex stumbled from the desert and joined the caravans that passed into the narrow gorge leading to the city. It was the future.

Though they had survived the treacherous journey south over the King's Highway, braving both heat and predators, the biggest challenge still lay ahead.

The narrow Siq, the road into the city, was only a stone's throw across, but the sandstone walls on either side towered so far above them, Alexander nearly fell backward trying to see the sky. Cassia guessed the walls to be the height of forty men. The heavy pack he wore on his back threatened to pull him over. His arms were bruised from the encounter with Aretas's killers. He lagged behind, transfixed as always with the camels, but in danger of being trampled by one of the many that lumbered through the pass, laden with merchandise.

Cassia tugged on his arm. "It grows late, Alex. We must make it into the city before nightfall."

In truth, it was not so late. But the soaring cliffs that walled them in did not allow the rays of the setting sun to reach the limestone paving stones of the Siq. Her anxiety to reach the city had more to do with the unknown than the nightfall.

The press of the crowd carried the two weary travelers like tiny pieces of desert grass bobbing on a swollen river. Cassia wondered at the numbers of traders and families heading into the city at this late hour. It must be a great city, indeed, to welcome all these guests into itself.

But would it welcome them?

She circled Alex's shoulders with one arm, keeping him close as they walked and staying near the right side of the Siq, with its red and ochre ribbons of sandstone running through, like the stripes of a woven blanket. She wished he did not have to carry so much, but they had put all they could take on their backs before leaving Damascus, all they had in the world.

"Mama, look at this!" Alex said for the hundredth time. He pointed to a shallow trough cut into the wall of the Siq. "A river in the wall!" He pulled away and dipped his fingers into a terra-cotta-lined channel that rushed with water and ran the length of the Siq ahead of them, into the unseen city.

"Amazing!" They had seen the dam built into a small wadi before entering the Siq, most likely the stream that used to flow through this gorge. Here was evidence of more skilled engineering, where the precious resource of water being collected at the dam was channeled through this long passageway into the city.

Alex put two wet fingers into his mouth. "How much farther, Mama?"

Cassia stepped farther to the right to avoid the snort of a camel's muzzle. Its driver walked beside, a short man covered in the sand of the desert, and seemed not to notice. He switched at the camel's fore-legs with a thin, white reed and did not give Cassia a glance.

She peered ahead but could only see as far as the next bend in the Siq. "I don't know, Alex. It can't be far. All these people are going to Petra."

He swiveled his head behind them. "Will there be room for us too?"

Cassia smiled and rubbed grit from her eye. She was as covered in desert dust as the camel driver. "We are very small, don't you think? We wouldn't take much room."

Alex shrugged.

If only she could give him assurances, but she had none to give. His question had plagued her as well, when they had bedded down in the cold desert nights, as they sought shelter from townspeople along the way, as they consumed the very last of their meager food supply this morning. *Will there be room for us in Petra?*

When they left Damascus she'd been so filled with determina-tion to find Aretas's family, then work hard to create a respectable place for herself and her son in this city. She determined not to tell anyone of what Aretas had become, nor how he died. Rather, she thought, she would save money and find them a home of their own.

Now, ten days later, hope flagged as she realized the gamble she had taken. She knew very little of Aretas's family. What if she could not find them? She and Alex had nothing. No food, and only a few silver *sestarii*. How long could they survive?

The Siq pressed them even closer, funneling them into a narrower pass. Alex slowed again, and she followed his gaze to see what had intrigued him. The sandstone wall across the road had been carved expertly into the facade of a miniature temple. It stood roughly the height of a man and the width of outstretched arms, and its shallow indentations, where a temple's doors and windows would have been, were filled with votive offerings and flickering oil lamps.

The rest of the jostling crowd seemed to think nothing of this elegant wall sculpture, passing by without notice. But a chill passed over Cassia, and she recognized it as part of her special sight. Evil was here, and the blood in her head pounded. She took Alex's hand and quickened their pace. The Siq had held them for nearly an hour. Surely they were close to reaching the city.

And yet more niches and altars, with inscriptions carved above them, followed, revealing not only the great skill of the Nabataean sculptors of Petra but also the religiosity of its people.

Surely people this skilled and this religious could find a place for one young woman and her little boy.

Alexander laughed.

Cassia was so taken with the rare sound she nearly forgot to wonder what he had found humorous.

"I like this one best." He smiled and pointed.

She followed his outstretched finger to the opposite wall of the passageway. A huge camel and driver had been cut into the rock wall. Cassia hugged Alex to herself. "Of course you would like one with an animal better than any other."

The crowd ahead seemed to slow. Was there some disturbance that would prevent them from entering the city? She still could see no farther than the next bend in the rock.

And then they rounded the bend, and she and Alex slowed as well.

For the Siq ended. The narrow split in the rock they had traveled concluded with a beautiful archway carved overhead. And there, through the slit, they got their first glimpse of the pride of Petra—another sandstone pink rock-cut facade, one that dwarfed all they had yet seen in both size and beauty. The central figure carved between columns high above appeared to be a Nabataean goddess. But a mixture of Greek and Egyptian deities also graced its bays and recesses, and the stone columns with their elaborately carved capitals and intricate pediments astonished the onlooker.

Cassia inhaled sharply, pierced by the surprise and fighting a wave of unexpected emotion.

Petra!

She looked down to Alexander, who raised wide eyes and a gap-toothed smile to her. "Are we here now?"

Cassia blinked back tears of exhaustion and relief. "We are here."

The Siq birthed them into an open space before the beautiful carved facade, a large open plot that was perhaps the city's agora, the marketplace destination of all the traders who traveled the Siq. Even at this late hour, the area teemed with merchants and their tables, townspeople, camels with drivers, and rich traders wandering among the merchants, hawking their merchandise and striking deals. Damascus had been a trade city, but nothing like this. Petra's secure location at the crossroads of trade routes running both north-south and east-west brought goods from India and China, Egypt and Syria, and carried them east to the spreading Roman Empire. The great silk, spice, and slave routes all ran through Petra, increasing its wealth.

Cassia held tightly to Alexander's hand as they wandered the tables. The air hung heavy with the scents of spices, of frankincense and myrrh. Tables glittered with Chinese silk and pearls and gemstones. There were exotic animals, perfumes and unguents, rice and grain.

But the market was breaking up. Clearly the night was soon upon them, and shoppers and merchants alike were preparing to head home.

Cassia felt the sudden aloneness, the realization that they had nowhere to go in the darkness. It was time to begin her meager plan, the only idea she had contrived to make their way in Petra.

She bent to Alexander, put her hands on his cheeks to turn his face to hers. "Listen, shekel, stay close to me. Don't wander away when I'm speaking to people."

He nodded, his face sober.

"If we should ever get separated"—she looked around the agora—"ask someone who looks like a mother to take you to the city fountain, to the Nymphaeum."

Alex surveyed their location. There was nothing of the city to be seen here but the one amazing rock sculpture. Impassable rock walls blocked one end of the canyon, and the other end bent away, out of sight. "I don't see the fountain."

"But wherever it is, I will find you there."

His brow furrowed in concern.

She kissed his cheek. "Stay close to me, and we won't be separated."

He clutched her tunic in a small hand. "Promise?"

"I promise."

A young woman passed them, arms filled with bulging sacks, and Cassia stepped to the left to intercept her. "Excuse me." She smiled. "I am new to the city and looking for family."

The girl studied Cassia for a moment and shifted one bag to her hip. "Yes?"

Cassia swallowed. "My late husband's family, actually. His name was Aretas, but he left here some years ago. His mother's name was Gamilath."

The girl snorted. "Gamilath and Aretas. Like every other child born in this city." She pushed past them, but Cassia stayed her with a hand on the girl's arm.

"Please, we must find them. His mother liked to grow things. She had beautiful gardens, he once told me."

The girl's mocking smile chilled Cassia. "Have you been into the city?"

Cassia pointed to the end of the Siq. "We've just arrived from Damascus."

The girl inclined her head over her shoulder, toward the open end of the canyon. "We may live in the rock, but we have more gardens than sand." She shifted her bags again and walked on, shaking her head.

Cassia squeezed Alex's hand and approached another woman, this one older and perhaps closer to Aretas's mother's age. She repeated her question, watching the woman's eyes form narrow slits as she looked Cassia up and down.

"People in this city have enough to take care of their own. They don't need outsiders coming to live off them."

Cassia straightened and pulled her shoulders back. "We are family."

The woman shrugged. "I can't help you." She turned her back and called out to someone across the agora.

"Mama, Petra people aren't nice." Alex's words were too loud.

"There are kind people everywhere, Alex. We must only find them."

"Where do we find them?"

Cassia looked at the emptying market. *Where indeed?*

She approached a merchant who was packing up his perfumes and unguents into satchels and loading them onto a tired-looking mule. He shook his head. "You will have trouble, I'm afraid, if that's all you know. The names of Nabataean royalty are overused in every family." He grinned and scratched his head. "They believe a royal name will bring wealth, I suppose."

Cassia thanked him and turned from his table.

"You'd best get shelter for the night," he called after them. "While it's still safe."

With what money? I must find family.

She pulled Alex from merchant to merchant, stopped towns-people, repeated her request so many times she lost count, always with the same answer or no answer at all. Alex's hand grew heavy in hers, and it became an effort to pull him forward.

And then night fell.

It came suddenly, when the sun dropped behind the mountains, taking Cassia by surprise, for the market was not yet empty. But when she searched for another merchant or stranger to question, she realized the market was a caravan camp, and the crowd that remained were all traders, bedding down for the night under stick-propped woolen blankets or black goat-hair tents, against their camels for warmth and protection. They slept in small rings of fellow travelers, with one sitting watch to protect their merchandise.

She turned a circle in the center of the canyon, now more like a nomadic settlement than an agora, and felt the isolation bear down upon them.

They had no blanket, no stick, no camel. No one to watch over them.

No one who cared.

Cassia's stomach clenched with loneliness and fear. Her eyes connected with a dark-skinned trader who lay stretched on a colorful blanket, propped on one elbow, beside his camel. He gave her a half smile, and she looked away, uncertain of his intent.

"Come, Alex." She led him toward the end of the market. Her sense of danger sparked, and she knew they were followed.

"Where will we go now, Mama?"

"Keep walking, Alex. Keep walking."

She knew no better than Alexander where they would go. The open area that had welcomed them from the narrow gorge led only in one direction, but ahead she could see a dark cliff outlined against the night sky. The valley must turn to the left, and the city lay beyond. They walked on, until the cliff face on their left curved and they turned. It was too dark to see much, though the ground rose slightly beneath their feet. Cassia sensed water on either side of a rise. Ahead, flickers of light here and there indicated homes, perhaps. But how could there be many houses in this narrow valley between high cliffs?

Alexander's pace slowed, and Cassia felt the usual stab of guilt at all the boy had endured. She pulled him toward the side of the road. They needed to find shelter.

At the roadside they stepped onto a stone platform and Cassia studied the darkness, searching for any place to lay their heads. She realized with surprise they had stumbled upon the town's amphitheatre, with stone seats rising above them into the cliff face. They stood on the orchestra platform, as though about to recite or perform.

There must be halls behind the seats. And they would be deserted at this hour.

A scrape of sandal on stone behind them caused Cassia to turn. It would be the first person they'd encountered since leaving the traders, and she hoped for a friendly face.

But a shape flew toward her out of the darkness and rough arms shoved her. She stumbled backward, tried to keep her balance. Her left shoulder cracked against a column at the back of the *scanae*. The blow jolted her head forward and sent stinging needles of fire into her shoulder.

The grubby face of a trader leaned into hers. "What have you got in your pouch there, woman?"

Cassia turned her face away from his foul breath. Her shoulder burned with a white heat. She brought her knee up quickly, but he was too wary. He sidestepped her effort, then ripped the pouch from her neck. She had lost sight of Alex and prayed he hid in the shadows.

Her attacker rifled through the pack, yanked out clothing, and tossed it aside. When his fist emerged with her money pouch, her heart sank.

The trader tossed the pack to the ground and disappeared like black smoke rising into the night sky.

"Alexander!" Cassia kept her voice low but urgent. The boy appeared at once and rushed into her outstretched arms. She bit back a cry of pain. Something was not right with her shoulder.

"Everyone wants to hurt us." His simple statement, as though it were a fact of his life, slashed at her heart.

"We will be fine," she promised, knowing it was foolish. "I need you to gather our belongings, Alex." She pointed to the clothing strewn about the stage. "There is the pack."

He darted around obediently, snatching up all they had left in the world and stuffing it into the pack.

She watched him circle the orchestra, and her head seemed to circle with him, a strange, spinning feeling, as though the stars above were silver leaves in a black eddying whirlpool. And then the blackness rushed down from the sky and scooped her up, and she felt herself falling . . .

And then nothing as the blackness carried her away.

SEVEN

———•———

THE BLACKNESS WAVERED ABOVE CASSIA'S HEAD, NOW dark, now orange and flickering, now ribbons of yellow and black in a reddish sky. She fought the heavy pull of her eyelids, fought the thickness that held her with a weighty hand.

Beside her, behind her, there were murmurs. Tiny fragments of conversation, slivered into words and phrases she could not comprehend.

Alex. Where are you?

The pain in her shoulder intensified. She tried to swallow but her throat felt like the Nabataean desert, and the effort caught and choked her.

She felt the rim of a cup at her lips, held by an unseen hand, and sipped warmed wine, gratitude filling her.

The darkness came again, but when it lifted, she was able to open her eyes.

She lay upon a bed, soft with layers of woven blankets. An oil lamp smaller than her hand burned in a niche in the wall. The room was small, though still mostly in shadows, unreached by the tiny flame.

A man sat beside her. His soft brown eyes studied her, silent but kind, with deep lines like the rays of the sun extending from the corners. Cassia tried to raise herself. Pain, like none she'd ever felt from Aretas's beatings, shot through her shoulder, down into her arm, across her back, and seemed to light her very being on fire.

"Peace." The old man touched her arm with a wrinkled hand. "Your shoulder is out of joint. Do not try to move."

Cassia licked dry lips. "My son."

The old man smiled and inclined his head toward the other side of the room. Two or three figures moved in the shadows.

"He sleeps. Precious boy."

Cassia tried to read his eyes and heart. Was there danger here? She mustered a smile. "Thank you for helping us."

He shook his head. "I've done nothing yet. But we shall see."

"I have no money."

A quiet laugh sounded from the shadows. A woman, Cassia thought. His wife?

The old man patted her arm again. "I have no need of your money."

Cassia's eyes grew heavy again.

"Sleep." He pulled a blanket over her. "You will need strength for what is to come."

She felt herself slipping away, but not before his words chilled her. There had been a time, several years ago, when Aretas had been in a market brawl. The man he had cheated left him with his shoulder out of joint.

Cassia knew what awaited her. Better to sleep.

But sleep was not merciful enough to remain. She awoke to hushed words again, but this time believed there were more than two in the shadows. She took in the room, trying to remain unnoticed.

Something was strange about the walls and roof. Smoother than any mud-brick home in Damascus had been, as though there were no cracks between the bricks. And the roof, no stray thatch poked from the mud. Instead, the walls and roof were subtly striped with color. Reddish orange, with blacks and yellow. It reminded her of something . . .

The rock! Of course. The walls of the gorge that had led them to Petra were striped in this way.

She was not in the front room of a mud-brick home in town. She lay entombed in the rock!

The older man appeared at her side, cup in hand. She reached for the cup with her good arm, but he shook his head and held it for her. The wine was heavily watered, and she was thirsty.

The room did not feel like a rock-cut tomb. It smelled of meat cooked with curry, and the warmth of it, compared to the last ten nights of desert cold, was like an embrace.

Her benefactor set the empty cup on the floor and leaned over her. "I am Malik."

"Cassia." She dipped her head. "And Alexander."

He smiled. "Yes, young Alexander is very proud of his namesake."

A flutter of anger touched Cassia's nerves. It troubled her to think of Alexander talking with these people while she lay senseless. She knew nothing of them, nor what they might want. "How . . . how did we get here?"

"We carried you." The words were spoken simply, as though nothing strange had occurred. He smiled. "Alexander helped."

She studied Malik. He was quite old, though still upright and strong, with a lean frame. His hair had gone to gray and was only present in a fringe around his head, above his ears. His face was deeply lined, but when he smiled his eyes sparkled like those of a younger man. Cassia felt her heart drawn to him, but she could not say why.

"We must take care of your shoulder."

She bit her lip. "Are you a physician?"

He smiled sadly. "No."

She exhaled and closed her eyes. Were Aretas here, she would have insisted he find a physician, even if it meant opening the money pouch he kept only for emergencies. But Aretas was not here. And she had no money. None. Who was she to insist upon help that would cost?

Inhaling strength, she opened her eyes and nodded.

Malik brushed her hair back from her gaze, the gesture so gentle Cassia's throat tightened. She would have fallen to tears, but she needed to be strong. Above all, she must not wake Alex with her cries. He had been frightened enough by the days of danger.

Malik covered her shoulder with his bony hand, never taking his eyes from hers. He reached under her shoulder with his other hand. She bit her lip to keep from crying out, even at this lightest of touches. How was she ever to endure what was to come? She tried to gain strength from Malik's eyes, but to her dismay, he closed them.

Cassia's heart pounded, and the fear tasted like a bitter thing in her mouth. *Do it. Get it done.*

Malik was moving his lips silently. Did he pray to his gods? Cassia was unsure what gods ruled over this part of the Nabataean kingdom. Were they the same as her Damascus gods? Should she pray to Dagan as well? What if other gods were here and she angered them with her misplaced prayer? Her confusion and fear mingled until she thought she might cry out even before the great pain that was to come.

Across the room, she heard the murmured voices again and realized the women, for it seemed most certainly to be women, were also chanting prayers softly.

She waited, eyes closed.

But the great pain did not come. Instead, a deep and penetrating warmth seemed to emanate from Malik's hands above and below her shoulder. It burrowed deep into her body, not a hot tongue of fire like the pain when she had fallen against the stone wall. This was a warm blanket on a cold night. Like a heated cup of wine, going down with softness and filling her with a peace that leeched the fear from her muscles and made her sleepy.

Malik's lips still moved silently. His eyes remained closed. And Cassia realized the warmth was not surrounding the pain, it was replacing it.

And as the pain receded, in its place washed in a deep and profound emotion Cassia could not name. Somewhere between terrible grief and sparkling joy, between black death and bright life, it welled up inside of her and overflowed. Tears streamed from her, flowed down her cheeks and dripped from her chin, and flowed even still, until she shook with a powerful sobbing she could not contain.

"What . . . what is it?" she whispered.

Only then did Malik open his eyes, slowly remove his hands, and smile.

The emotion subsided, the warmth drifted away.

The pain did not return.

"A gift." Malik's voice was like warm oil. "You have been given a gift. You have been healed."

Cassia wiped at her face, first with one hand, then with the other. With the other!

She lifted her arm above her head, rotated her shoulder. *What did he do to me?*

The healing astonished her. The emotion it had drawn forth baffled her. She felt almost sadness as it subsided.

She studied Malik's eyes and could think of nothing more to say than "Thank you."

He patted her cheek and called over his shoulder, "She should eat."

Two women hurried to her bedside, as if they had been waiting for the summons. Each held a plate of steaming food, more than
Cassia could possibly consume. She pulled herself to sitting, and one
of the women handed her a plate of flat bread and seasoned beans,
then pushed cushions behind her back.

She was much older than Cassia, but perhaps not so old as Malik.
It took only a moment of watching them both for Cassia to sense
the woman was not his wife. The other woman sat beside her on the
bed, holding another plate. She was younger still, younger even than
Cassia. Cassia knitted her brow, trying to make sense of this strange
family that was not a family. She could easily read several emotions
passing between them. Both women felt great love and respect for
Malik. But there was also a tension between the two women.

Cassia dug into the beans. They were spicy and warm on her
tongue. She closed her eyes in delight. They had eaten nothing more
than hard bread and dried meat during the long journey here.

She pushed some of the beans aside on her plate. "For Alexander.
He will be hungry when he wakes."

The three laughed together. The older woman shook her head.
"I cannot believe that boy could eat anything more for three days!"

They had fed Alexander while she slept? Cassia thought she should
perhaps feel concern again, but there was nothing left but gratitude.

"Thank you." She studied her plate. She had uttered that phrase
too many times. They must want something in return.

Malik seemed to sense her concern. "It is a special joy of ours. To
feed and to care for the sick and strangers, even for the least of them.
A special joy."

Cassia looked into his eyes, and she believed him.

"Finish your bread." He smiled.

While she ate, the women fussed around her, bringing damp

cloths to wash her face and arms, and the older applying some kind of ointment from a tiny jar onto Cassia's scrapes. Zeta and Talya, she discovered, were mother and daughter, though Talya must have been born late in Zeta's childbearing years. This was their home, and Malik was their friend.

Friend. The word made her think of Magdala back in Damascus, and she felt all the more bereft.

Again, as though he could read her thoughts, Malik spoke. "You are alone here in Petra?"

She shrugged one shoulder. *Still no pain.* "Alexander and I have come to find family. His father was born here."

"He did not travel with you?" Malik's eyes were kind. He already knew the answer, she could see.

"He was killed fourteen days ago."

"What was his name?" Talya asked. "Perhaps we were playmates."

"Aretas."

She smiled. "Yes, I knew an Aretas. Six or seven of them, I would guess."

Cassia sighed and set her empty plate aside.

"His parents?" Malik asked. "Do you know of them?"

"I know his mother's name only. Gamilath."

Malik shook his head. "Another common name, I fear. Have you nothing else?"

Cassia leaned back against her cushions and searched her memory. Aretas had told her so little of his life before they met. Snatches here and there, but nothing that could be pieced together to create a picture.

"He told me something once about his home." She tried to call up the memory from the dark corridors of her mind. "About where it was located. Beside the Temple of al-'Uzza."

Malik's head lifted sharply.

"He told me that from the outer corridor of his home he could look straight into the first courtyard of the temple. He seemed to despise both the temple and its goddess, though I never understood . . ." Malik looked at her so strangely. "What is it?"

"Aretas, son of Gamilath? And his home lay beside the Temple of al-'Uzza?"

She nodded, fear clutching at her heart with cold fingers.

Malik looked to the two women, and Cassia saw eyebrows raised, mouths open. "What is it?"

But Malik did not answer. He stood quickly, snatched the oil lamp from the niche gouged into the stone wall, and strode across the room to where Alexander lay, still asleep.

Cassia swung her legs from the bed, stood, and was at his side before the two women could react. "What are you doing?"

Malik had bent to her son's side and held the lamp close enough for the light to play across his beautiful face. He slept with lips parted, his thick eyelashes sweeping his cheeks like raven feathers.

The two women appeared beside them and studied Alexander as well. Malik turned to Zeta, the older of the two. "How did we not see it?"

She shook her head. "He is the very image of Aretas."

Their words struck Cassia with fresh hope, tinged with alarm. "You knew him." She clutched Malik's arm. "You knew Aretas as a boy."

Malik turned to her. "You must rest still." He guided her back to the blankets.

She did not resist. "Tell me. Tell me who he was."

When they had restored her to her place of ease, the three ringed the bed.

Malik spoke. "As I said, your husband's name, his mother's name, are both used by many parents because they are royal names."

Cassia looked to Alexander. Aretas had indeed insisted they name him after greatness.

"But this is not why *your* Aretas had this name."

Cassia's breath came a bit shorter, and she waited in silence.

"Your Aretas *was* the royal house."

"I . . . I do not understand."

"You know of the Nabataean king, Rabbel, no doubt?"

Cassia nodded, willing him to speak quickly.

"Gamilath was his first wife. She died many years ago. They had only one son, heir to the throne. That son was your Aretas."

That man comes from money. It's written all over him. Magdala's words.

Cassia fell back on the cushions. The revelation was like falling into a cold river on a hot day. First the shock, then a welcome refreshment. *Aretas, royalty!* His family were not bandits like he was, nor struggling in poverty as she. But then, like the coldness of river water, the news sank deep into her. The prince of Nabataea! How could she ever approach them? A tremor shook her and her teeth chattered.

"Rest now." Zeta pulled blankets over her body, all the way to her chin. "You have had a shock. More than one today, as it were. There will be time enough to think of how to breach the palace tomorrow."

She meant to comfort, Cassia knew, but her words brought no consolation. *Breach* the palace? As though she were a hostile, invading army?

She sank down into the bedding, and the three moved away, taking the tiny lamp with them and leaving her in shadows.

She would sleep, yes. But then what?

EIGHT

—◆—

MORNING DAWNED WITH LIGHT POURING IN THROUGH
a gap in the heavy cloths that formed the fourth wall of the home, the
room where Cassia lay.

She pulled herself to sitting, again marveling at the absence of
pain in her shoulder, and surveyed the room.

She had been correct in the night—she did lie in a room cut
into the red stone cliffs. It extended behind her into shadow, and the
side exposed to the open air was hung with blankets. She glanced
at Alexander, saw he still slept, then crept to a gap in the fabric and
nudged it open with one finger.

The sight stole her breath.

The city lay beneath her, as though she were a bird nesting in
a cleft of the rock wall. All of Petra was contained in the narrow,
curving valley, and she saw houses and temples, gardens and foun-
tains, and above all of it: dozens of openings in the cliff wall, many
elaborately carved. The floor dropped away on the other side of the
blankets, a frightening fall no one could survive.

How do they get up here?

A noise behind her drew her back into the safety of the room.

Zeta brought a steaming bowl, and Alexander stretched his thin brown arms and blinked away the night. He fixed his eyes on her and smiled. She held out her arms, then retreated from the flimsy wall when he jumped from his bed and ran to her.

"You are well, Mama?"

"I am well, shekel."

Talya set a bowl of fruit and yoghurt on the table. "Malik left in the night. I am to tell you he will help you in whatever way he can."

Cassia smiled. "I am not sure how anyone can help me. I must gain the favor of the king, when even his own son could not."

Talya shook her head. "I was too young to know what happened when Aretas left Petra. It is not spoken of. But it was so long ago. Perhaps . . ."

Cassia shrugged and pulled Alexander to the table. "Resentment and bitterness can live longer than even memory at times."

They ate of the fruit, and Zeta brought more—platters of dates and honeyed bread, warm and sweet. Malik appeared, pushing through the blanket wall as though he had flown above the city and alighted in their nest. And then others came. Men and women went through the morning, asking questions of Cassia and visiting with each other. Cassia could not determine who any of them were. They seemed to be an extended family, and yet they did not arrive as smaller family groups nor address each other with family names.

They were all curious about Cassia, however. And about Alexander even more so. Cassia heard the phrase "heir to the throne" more than once, and the words both thrilled and terrified. She tried to distract Alex from their talk. He would learn soon enough of the great change that might take place in his life.

And it was far from certain. Aretas had left this place on terms that were not good, though no one spoke of it this morning. What would his father say when she and Alexander appeared in his palace?

Cassia stood finally, drawing the attention and then the silence of the chattering group.

"We must go." She nodded to Zeta and Talya. "Thank you for everything. You have been most gracious. Please give Malik my thanks as well." She took Alexander's hand. "Now, if someone could tell me how to get down from this rock."

The room erupted with laughter.

Within minutes Cassia and Alexander were picking their way down narrow steps carved into the rock face. The staircase, if the niches could be called such, would be nearly invisible from the street, blending as they did with the variegated rock colors.

She wished she could study the city, but the descent required all her concentration, between placing her own feet on the narrow steps and watching Alex's. The boy would have skipped down to the street level if she had let him, his fearlessness at climbing exceeding his ability.

Finally they were safely on the ground, and Cassia took the time to orient herself to the fascinating city of Petra.

The narrow gorge they'd traversed yesterday had led them only to a preview of the city's grandeur. The astonishing facade she'd seen carved into the stone wall when they emerged from the crack in the mountains was now repeated, with variation, along the facing red cliffs that formed the natural city walls. Dark recesses like rectangular eyes dotted the rock walls from above head level all the way up to dizzying heights similar to that which she had descended. Some of these recesses were mere holes cut into the sandstone, a blank face that could be tomb or home.

But others were grand in size and elaborately carved, like the one she saw yesterday, with columns and plinths, carved urns and figures of Isis and Dionysius, pedestal tops above the openings and ornamental friezes sculpted with vines. The combined art of Egypt, Greece, and even Rome had found a home in the walls of Petra. The effect was stunning.

To their left, Cassia could see the half circle of the amphitheatre, sweeping away from the street—the last place she remembered seeing before awakening in Zeta's home.

The street was crowded with the press of townspeople and the combined traffic of camels, mules, and carts. She and Alex were forced to flatten themselves against the rock wall to avoid the traffic.

At a break in the crowd, she pulled on Alexander. "Come!" They dashed across the open street to the other side, where the smaller mud-brick shops and homes left space for walking before the rock wall rose behind them.

Cassia walked slowly in the direction of the palace. Zeta had pointed to it before they had left her home and assured them they would not miss it. Directly beside the Temple of al-'Uzza. Ah yes.

She was enchanted with the city. After the open sandy plains of Damascus, this hidden city, tucked into the cliffs, felt like a shelter from a lifelong storm. As though it embraced her with its rock-strong arms and promised security. She dared to hope that Petra would be home now with family to care for them.

But such dreaming would have to wait until after she had approached the king. Cassia's knees felt a bit weak. Here she was, thinking of a secure future in Petra, when she still must walk into the palace of the Nabataean king and claim rights for her son, the son of the outcast prince.

The city smelled of crowds and spice and dung, typical city smells, but to Cassia somehow it all mingled and pleased. The heat, the color, even the music that wafted from homes and market stalls, wove together into a tapestry of the senses and brought a smile.

They passed people of the town, Nabataeans most certainly, but also some of darker skin than she had ever seen, perhaps from Nubia or Persia. And light skin as well. She knew not where such light skin may have come from. Some dressed as merchants and travelers, but others as though they lived here in Petra, and Cassia wondered at the complexity of this place.

Alex tugged on her hand and pointed. "Look at the camels, Mama!"

Indeed, the field of resting camels to their left was a wonder, too many to count. They had traveled from places too distant to imagine, no doubt, and must rest before returning with new goods from other lands.

Petra had only one main street, really, running between the rock cliffs and bending to the left as they walked. After the bend, the ground leveled off to their right, with the cliff face continuing away from the city, and a man-made wall had been erected here, the only one needed in this naturally protected place. As the road bent south, it followed the streambed of the Wadi Musa, the stream that fed all of Petra, and was diverted into reservoirs and channels she had seen as they entered the city.

They left the section of homes and tombs and market stalls behind as they walked, and the road opened wider ahead, a paved street that led to the upper-class part of town, where the temples and palace and Nymphaeum would be found.

They came to the Nymphaeum first. A crowd had gathered near the city's main fountain area, where most would come to collect the day's water. It must be a slow-flowing water supply to have caused such a wait for the townspeople to fill their jars. But the crowd had the hushed expectancy of people watching an event, so she walked on, head turned to see what everyone seemed to be studying.

"Is it another theatre, Mama?"

"I do not know. Strange place for it, if so." She let go of his hand to let him squeeze through the crowd ahead of her. Her height never allowed her to see much from the back of a group, and she felt no compunction about moving to the front, as no one would have difficulty seeing over her head.

It was not a theatre, but only the Nymphaeum as she thought. Not surprisingly it had been created of the same red stone that comprised all of Petra, though it had been reinforced with granite. The face of the fountain house stood as high as six men and was also elaborately carved with columns and figures of the water nymphs it honored. High above, a statue of Cyrene stood in a carved recess, and water trickled from her tipped stone urn to fall to a wide circular pool in the courtyard of the building. It trickled only, not enough to keep the pool full, certainly.

And then Cassia saw what held the crowd's attention. Something had blocked the flow of the water from Cyrene's urn. Perhaps a chunk of sandstone. It was impossible to tell. But up the face of the Nymphaeum a man climbed, scaling the wall with fingers and toes wedged into tiny holds, as though he were a grasshopper scrambling up an acacia tree.

Halfway up, he paused in his climb, his hand scrabbling for a hold. At that moment his right foot slipped from its perch and sent crumbling sandstone to the ground. The crowd gasped as one. But he found another toehold, turned his head to the crowd, and gave a small salute with his free hand.

Sighs of relief and titters of amusement rippled through the people. Cassia herself felt her lips twitch into the beginning of a smile. He reminded her of a monkey she had seen in Damascus once, trained by its owner to perform tricks and then grin for the audience.

They watched breathlessly as he climbed higher, until he reached a stone ledge that ran the width of the building and took him to the base of Cyrene and her slow-flowing urn. It should only take him a moment to clear the blockage.

But it would appear he had not yet received enough of the crowd's attention. He turned a tight circle on the ledge, until he was facing outward. Glancing at the nymph pouring her water, he struck a pose quite similar to hers and stood like stone himself.

The crowd laughed, and one man yelled, "You are almost as beautiful as the goddess!" at which the people roared. Cassia shook her head but smiled. She had seen this type of man before, hungry for attention with the charm and wit to earn it. Aretas had been such a man, and it was those qualities that drew her to him so many years ago. Did Alex see the similarity? She looked around her to see his reaction.

Alarm jolted her. *Alexander, where are you?*

She pushed through the crowd, all of them still focused on the antics above. "Alexander?" The boy's propensity for wandering off never ceased to frighten her.

Faces turned toward hers, then away in disinterest. She twisted through the glut of people, her stomach churning. Where would he go?

And then she knew. She jerked her head to the face of the Nymphaeum, and her fear was confirmed. Alex had already found enough toe- and handholds to scale to the first ledge, about four cubits below the ledge that held the performer.

Cassia nearly cried out his name but did not want to startle him. His attention was fixed on the ledge above, and his head turned back and forth, searching for a hold. She shoved through the crowd, into the courtyard.

Above Alexander, oblivious to the boy, the climber reached into the blocked urn. His arm disappeared to the elbow, then reappeared with a handful of something. The water flowed after his hand, cascading to the pool below. The water hit the stone floor of the pool and sprayed outward, soaking Cassia.

The water restorer raised a triumphant arm in the same moment the crowd noticed Alexander. At the lack of the cheers the man no doubt expected, he put his hands to his hips—then seemed to realize the people's attention was fixed below him. He leaned forward slightly. The crowd cried out its collective concern.

Cassia watched in horror, unable to retrieve her son. "Alexander, you must come down now."

If he heard her, he showed no sign. She repeated herself, her voice raised against the murmurs of the crowd. But his back was to her, and his fingers traveled the face of the building, searching for deep cracks between the stones. He seemed to find a place, for he suddenly lifted himself above the surface of the ledge, connected only to the wall. The people gasped as one, and Cassia felt she might be sick.

Above Alexander, the performer must have begun to resent the loss of attention. He edged along the lip of stone, then pivoted at the end, bent to grip the ledge with his fingers, and swung his feet away.

Again, the crowd reacted, entertained by the danger. Cassia positioned herself under Alex. If he fell, she hoped to break his fall enough to keep him safe. The spraying water from the fountain pool soaked her through, but she barely noticed. Fear chilled her and set her shivering. "Alexander! Come down at once!"

And then the climber was balanced on Alex's ledge, cubits away from the boy. "Where are you climbing to, son?"

The man's voice, quiet and smooth, was, Cassia guessed, audible to no one but herself and Alexander.

Alex's mouth fell open. He looked above his perch, then back at the climber. "I wanted to climb up to the water lady, like you."

The man edged closer to Alex with slow and deliberate caution. Cassia took a step backward, her fingers twisted in her wet tunic.

"Ah." His voice was grave. "Well, I've been to see the water lady already, and do you want to hear a secret?"

Alexander held still, except for a tiny nod.

The man leaned closer and mock-whispered, "She's really quite ugly up close!"

Alexander giggled. "Mama says it is rude to call people ugly."

He glanced downward, then winked at Alex. "Your mama sounds like a good person. Would you take me to meet her?"

Alexander bit his lip and looked above him again.

"I know much better places to climb." The man edged closer and Cassia's heart stopped. "I could show you sometime. What is your name?" Then he took a step nearer, and his arms braced on either side of Alex's body like a net. If either of them lost their balance, they both would fall.

Alexander looked over his shoulder, his attention roving over the silent crowd, his expression a mixture of shyness and embarrassment. "Alexander."

"Ah, good name for a strong boy like you. I am Julian. Let's go and meet the mother who gave you such a name, shall we?"

Alexander hesitated, then shrugged and took one foot from the rock. Cassia's hand flew to her mouth, but she stayed silent. Alex's sandaled foot scraped the rock in circles as he tried to find a hold.

"There, to the right a tiny bit," the other climber told him. "There, right there."

One step at a time, Alex lowered himself to the ledge.

A smattering of applause bubbled up from the crowd, but the two were not down yet and no one was ready to walk away.

The man turned his body and Alex followed, so the two of them faced outward on the ledge. "Put your hands behind you, like this"— he placed his palms on the rock—"and now we step together. Ready?"

Alex nodded.

"Now, left foot—step. Right foot—step."

Cassia snatched a look at the climber for the first time. He had the light skin of the West and the nose of a Roman. He seemed tall, but he was not skinny. With his arms braced against the wall, Cassia could see the muscles tensed.

The two progressed across the ledge to the end, where another indentation in the wall housed yet another small figure. The man whispered something to Alexander, and the boy grinned and nodded, then climbed into the niche and straddled the shoulders of the nymph Cyrene as though he would ride her down to the courtyard.

The man slipped past Alexander, did a neat turn, and dismounted from the ledge to the courtyard below. His knees flexed as he fell, and he landed in a crouch like a cat jumping from a stone wall. He took one step backward, lined himself up with the niche where Alex sat, then held up his arms.

"Now is the best part, Alexander!" His voice was light, as though the two had come to the Nymphaeum for an afternoon of fun. "You get to jump!"

Cassia inhaled sharply and drew close to the tall man. "It is too far," she whispered.

He did not take his gaze from Alex. His voice low, he said only two words: "Trust me."

Cassia watched, her heart swelling with fear as Alexander emerged from the niche and looked over the edge. The man beside her gave a quick nod and beckoned Alex with his upraised hands.

Alexander grinned once more and jumped.

The crowd's gasp echoed from the walls of the Nymphaeum, then the tension released with a cheer.

With Alexander safely in his arms, the man turned to the crowd, lifted Alex's arm above the boy's head, and yelled, "Alexander the Great!"

Alex was laughing, his gap-toothed smile beaming across the courtyard.

But a deep, inexplicable anger mixed with Cassia's relief and surged from her chest. "Put him *down*!"

The man turned a slow circle to her and smiled. "Ah, this must be your wise and beautiful mother."

"Mama!" Alex wiggled to be set down. "Were you watching? Did you see how high I climbed?"

Alex's rescuer lowered him to the courtyard and set him in front of Cassia. "Your son, my dear lady, restored to you." He raised an arm to the fountain pool and lifted his voice. "And the water restored to all of you!"

The crowd cheered then, as anyone who had seen such showmen before could have predicted.

Cassia grabbed at Alexander's hand and started to push past the man.

He blocked her retreat, drawing up as though a royal prince himself. "No gratitude?"

Cassia straightened in front of him, her head barely reaching his chest, for he was quite tall and clearly highborn in his arrogance. "Gratitude?" she said through clenched teeth. "You expect to be thanked? It is men like you who put little boys in danger. Why do you think he climbed up there?"

The man's lighthearted smile faded a bit, and he seemed to study Cassia. She felt suddenly aware of her dirty tunic, frayed from the many days of travel and now soaked through from the splashing water. His gaze traveled to her feet and back to her face, and Cassia felt a strong pull of attraction and then another surge of anger. She did not need her unique ability to know what he was. She'd already had a man like this.

Never again.

Alexander tugged on the man's hand, drawing his attention away from Cassia. "Julian, when will you show me the better places to climb?" His face was alight with hero worship, and it pained Cassia to see it. "We are going to the palace now"—he grinned—"to see our family, but after that I can climb with you again."

The man's eyebrows raised at Alexander's declaration, and he turned inquisitive dark eyes back to Cassia.

"Come, Alexander." She pulled him toward the now-dispersing crowd. "It is time."

The boy called back over his shoulder to his new friend, "I like the striped rocks best!"

"As do I, Alexander," he answered.

Cassia left the Nymphaeum behind and kept a tight grip on her son's hand. They were quite near the palace now, but she could not announce herself to the king in a wet and dirty tunic. A line of shops bordered the limestone-paved street on the opposite side, and she led Alexander behind the strip and instructed him to keep watch as she changed into the only other article of clothing she had brought in her pouch—the yellow silk. It had suffered in the escape through the streets the day Aretas had been killed, but it was still finer than anything else she owned. She felt a little twinge of glee at donning it without Aretas's permission. A new day had come.

It was time to see the king.

NINE

———◆———

Julian watched the striking woman and her little boy push through the crowd. Watched as people gave way to her, in spite of her petite build and peasant clothes. As she crossed the street, her head covering slipped down to reveal dark and unruly hair with unusual reddish streaks. She was like a bird—tiny, but quick and sharp. Strong, but still fragile. Smart enough not to shriek when her son was in danger. She had spoken to him like an equal.

He was still watching her as the two ducked behind the shops across the street.

Julian, you fool, you know better. And yet he was no longer nobility. Did he think a peasant woman beneath his new status?

"She is special, I believe." The voice at his shoulder surprised him.

Julian turned. A lean old man, his hair nothing more than a white fringe above his ears, studied the shop where the woman had disappeared.

Julian shrugged and put his back to the street. "She is pretty. Nothing more."

Townspeople streamed to the fountain pool now, filling unglazed water pots. Many nodded their smiling thanks to him as they returned to their homes or pressed his arm in gratitude. Crowds once again bustled through the shops selling merchandise that surrounded the Nymphaeum's courtyard.

It had pleased him, the climb to restore the water. Both the goodness of the deed and the attention of the people, the cheers when he brought down the boy.

"There is work for someone with your skills here in Petra."

Julian looked sideways at the old man, whose gaze was still focused across the street, as though he waited for the woman to emerge.

Had he met this man since he arrived in Petra? He should think that he would have remembered the deeply lined face. He forced a casual note into his voice, unwilling to let his interest show. "What kind of work?"

The old man shrugged. "The tomb sculptors are always in need of men who can climb."

Julian looked at the sculptured figures set into the Nymphaeum wall. *You've no idea what I can do.*

"And yet I am given the feeling that you are meant for better things." The man turned his eyes to Julian's face.

At the man's look, a current of something ran through Julian, like the touch of lightning in a desert storm. The buzz of fountainhouse conversation seemed to recede, leaving only the two of them in a hushed and private meeting.

"Better things?" Julian repeated, his mouth suddenly dry.

The old man was silent, but his eyes seemed to speak of their own accord. Every person Julian had met since arriving in Petra a few days prior had simply skimmed over him, including the woman with the boy, Alexander. They all saw only what they expected to see. But this old man, appearing from the crowd, had eyes that saw *through* him. A chill ran the length of his back.

"You are not alone here." The old man was still seeing through him.

Julian swallowed and found his voice. "Yes, yes, I am alone. Just traveling through, really. In search of my fortune." He had meant to sound casual, but the words sounded like grains of sand forced through a straining cloth.

"There are others." His hand grasped Julian's forearm, and at his touch the chill fled, replaced with warmth. "Many of us."

Julian felt his strength evaporate. *How does he know?*

"Will you come and meet with us?"

Julian hesitated, emotion threatening far too close to the surface. It had been so long. Too long. He shook his head. "I . . . I have no time. I must find work." He inhaled, filling his chest, and took a step backward, away from the man's hand. "The tombs, you say? Where would I find those who are hiring?"

The old man smiled slowly, those infuriating and wonderful eyes still burning through Julian's bravado like the sun through a thin morning mist. "We will meet again." He said it as though the promise should give comfort.

Oddly, it did.

And then he was gone, into the crowd of women carrying their water pots. Julian searched the street but saw instead the tiny woman and her son, though he nearly didn't recognize her, wrapped in a fine yellow dress. She and the boy hurried toward the palace without a backward look. Julian took another deep breath and tried to shake off both disturbing encounters, to focus on the task at hand.

If Petra was to be his new home, he needed to find work. And Petra was perfect.

The perfect place for a Roman to hide.

TEN

———◆———

HAGIRU WAS IN HER INCANTATION CHAMBER WITH BETHEA when a slave brought the news.

The chamber had no windows, and the door had been closed when they entered, so the burning ring of oil lamps in the center of the floor failed to light the blackness with their tiny tongues of yellow. The room smelled of incense and tasted of blood.

Just before the slave burst in with his unwelcome message, Hagiru had been watching Bethea's stringy dark hair swing from side to side as the girl swayed over the lamps, trying to chant the prayer in the ancient language Hagiru had taught her.

I should like to take a sharp knife to that hair.

She hated Bethea, hated the whining, bored, pathetic, and useless girl as she hated everyone in this forsaken rock city. Her vision of hacking the hair from Bethea's head faded, replaced by other thoughts of what *was* in her power to do, acts far more frightening than cutting hair. But that was why Bethea was here. To learn from the high priestess of Dushara how to call down power from the gods and use it against one's enemies.

When the door opened, the girl's singsong chant left off abruptly. Hagiru spun to face the slave, her dark robes sweeping in a circle behind her and nearly catching the flame of the lamps.

"What is it?" Her voice sounded sharp in the tiny chamber. The slave's white tunic glowed with an unholy light in the darkness, and she had no patience for being interrupted with trivial palace business when she was in her special place.

But the news was not trivial. No, not trivial at all.

She turned on Bethea after hearing it, and the girl's face paled. Hagiru shoved the slave aside. "Inform me at once when they are approaching. In the throne room."

The slave disappeared.

"Come." She beckoned to Bethea. "We will be rid of this annoyance quickly."

She swept from the incantation chamber, her purple robes trailing behind her like a dark stain. She had hired the best dyers in Petra to fashion her robes and instructed them to dye them black, but this deep purple was as close as they could come. Hagiru contented herself that she combined her darkness with her position as royalty.

As the Nabataean king's second wife, Hagiru had position, indeed. Perhaps once she had dreamed of love, but that was long ago, a faded memory, to be sure. She had replaced the childish fancy of love with the mature acquisition of power. Power from everywhere she could soak it up.

It was power that filled her, that satisfied her, that gave her strength to live out her days in the middle of a desert, surrounded by rocks.

Halfway to the throne room, a young boy appeared in the hall ahead. Hagiru slowed, and Bethea bumped her from behind. Hagiru half turned and slapped the girl across the face, then swung to the boy, arms outstretched.

"Obadas! I have not seen my pet all morning!"

The boy, ten years old and racing toward manhood, slowed and dropped his gaze.

Hagiru pulled Obadas into a tight embrace, muffling his face against her chest. "You have no time for your mother anymore, do you, my sweet?" She smiled and took his face in her hands. "You are all exploration and conquering, eh?"

He shrugged and his glance shifted to Bethea. Hagiru patted his cheek, reclaiming his attention. "I suppose it is what young princes do."

Obadas remained in her grasp, but Hagiru could see he wanted to be elsewhere. She released him, then bent to kiss him quickly. "Go on, then." He ran past her, with a glance to Bethea, then on down the palace hall. Hagiru watched him run, her heart tight. He grew too fast. Almost a man, and her plan had not yet come to fruition.

She resumed her march to the throne room, Bethea trailing like a trained pet.

The throne room was like an inverted reflection of her incantation chamber. Spacious and bright, its lofty ceiling glowed as though it were lit from within, its white marble floors, fluted columns, and alabaster throne in contrast also to all that red rock outside. Colorful fabrics hung on the walls and canopied the raised throne, and the slaves that lined the walls also were kept in bright colors as Rabbel wished. Two of these slaves pushed away from the wall at her entrance and stepped to her side immediately.

Thank the gods Rabbel is not here. The man could be such an annoyance. He was probably still in his bed. Rabbel had not been well of late. Hagiru's lips twitched in a half smile. So much the better. This was an interview she wished to conduct alone.

So Hagiru took to the throne, for she was the queen, after all. When she had settled there, with her head against its high back, she waved Bethea off and allowed her favorite slave to approach from behind and begin his ministrations against her perpetual headaches.

She closed her eyes at his touch, inhaled the perfume of the room, and tried to let the tension flow out of her as he massaged her temples, then raked his fingers back through her long dark hair.

The treatment did not last long enough. Running footsteps echoed into the throne room, and a slave appeared a moment later. He skidded into the room, then dropped to a knee some distance still from the throne.

"Well?" Hagiru lifted her head from the alabaster headrest.

"They approach, my queen. The woman and her boy."

Hagiru nodded to release the messenger, then waved away her attending slave. "Later," she instructed him with a meaningful look. He bowed and backed away.

She turned back to the entrance of the hall, spread her purple robes across the lustrous throne, and smiled. "Bring them."

ELEVEN

THE PALACE WAS INDEED IMPOSSIBLE TO MISS.

The wide paved street that lay parallel to the Wadi Musa continued straight through the city, but the Temple of al-ʿUzza and the grand palace beside it seemed to Cassia to be the heart of the city. She led Alexander to the palace steps, her heart beating unevenly.

The palace had been built on a slight rise above the street, making it appear even more impressive. Two sets of steps, with a platform between them, led up to a high-columned portico. The palace was faced in white limestone, and the late-morning sun seemed to set it afire with a white glow, a pure and holy light that calmed Cassia's spirit and seemed to invite her to ascend the steps and find her family.

She smiled down on Alexander, then laughed at his wide eyes. He grinned his gap-toothed smile at her. "It is very white!"

Cassia laughed again. She used her fingers to comb his hair to the side. Thankfully, his climb had not dirtied his white tunic. She wished he had finer clothes to appear in the palace. "Are you ready?"

He nodded, and she took a deep breath and started the upward journey to royalty.

Halfway up, on the platform between the two sets of steps, Alexander ran ahead to lay a hand on one of two matching stone blocks that had been placed on either side of the platform. The squared blocks were all of one piece but twice Cassia's height, and she marveled at the ability of the Petrans to move them to this spot.

"What are they, Mama?"

"They are djinn blocks, where gods reside."

Alex snatched his hand away and put it behind his back. Cassia reached him and hugged him. "Do not fear, Alexander. The gods are smiling on us today. Come."

They reached the portico, and Cassia steeled herself for her first encounter with the two slaves who stood on either side of the palace entrance. The lofty arch had an ornately carved lintel above it, more beautiful than any she had ever seen, and to pass under it seemed to her like it would be passing into another world.

She swallowed her fear and lifted her chin, trying to sound as though she had a right to be here. "I have come to see King Rabbel. On an important family matter."

Both slaves bowed at the waist, then stepped aside to let Alexander and her pass. She looked back and forth at each of them, surprised beyond measure to be treated thus. But they were letting her pass, so she took Alexander's hand and entered the shadowy front hall of the palace. A shudder passed through her, an evil portent such as she had felt in the Siq.

Another slave met them inside, appearing out of the darkness and startling Cassia. She gripped Alexander's hand.

The slave dipped his head. "I am to take you to the throne room." He extended a hand ahead of them.

He is only a slave. You are the mother of the prince! But the words were hollow even in her own mind. She knew exactly what she was.

Following in the slave's footsteps, she finally voiced her suspicion. "Are we expected?"

He did not turn. "The queen has been informed of your presence."

The queen? So Rabbel had married again after Aretas's mother, Gamilath, had died. The news raised Cassia's anxiety. She had hoped to present Rabbel with his grandson, had imagined a tearful reunion of long-lost family. To be ushered to the second wife seemed less promising.

"I wish to see the king." Her voice sounded hoarse.

The slave said nothing, and they could do nothing but follow. Cassia barely took notice of the palace halls and frantically tried to formulate what she would say to the queen.

They reached the throne room all too soon, passed through its entryway and into the gleaming chamber with its grand fluted columns, shining white. Alexander slowed and Cassia slowed with him, taking in the luxury and wealth of the room. She felt embarrassed of even the yellow silk, and the overwhelming surge of inferiority nearly swept her from her feet.

The slave was behind them now, pushing them forward to the throne, across white marble stones, their square outlines framed in dark mortar. Cassia's throat felt like hot sand and her eyes burned. She forced her gaze from the floor to the throne.

She had still hoped to find Rabbel in the throne room, but there was no doubt it was the queen who sat there. Every bit of the woman spoke royalty, from her purple robes to her haughty eyes. She had hair the color of raven's wings, beginning from a delicate point in the center of her forehead and waving away from her face and past her shoulders. She had eyes as dark as her hair and thin bloodred lips. She was easily the most beautiful woman Cassia had ever seen, a beauty that stole one's breath and made Cassia want to fall to a knee in front of her.

And in fact, she did. Pulling Alex down with her, Cassia bent a knee and lowered her head to the queen, then waited to be summoned to stand. When the instruction came and she lifted her head, Cassia found the queen smiling—but it was a smile that chilled.

Alexander stood as well, and Cassia heard a gasp from the side of the room. She turned to the sound and saw a younger woman, about the same age as she, with dark hair that hung in straight strands about her face. The woman's gaze was fixed on Alexander, and her lips were slightly parted as though she had received a shock.

The queen, too, had shifted her attention to Alexander, and her look made Cassia queasy.

"I am Hagiru, queen of Nabataea."

Cassia dipped her head once more. "My name is Cassia." She hardened her voice until the tremor was gone. "And this is my son, Alexander." She breathed for a moment. "We have come to see the king."

Hagiru reclined backward on the throne and watched them through lowered eyelids. "The king is unavailable. You may speak with me."

Cassia met the queen's stare. Speaking to Rabbel would be far better, but what choice did she have? She was in no position to make demands. "I have brought the king's grandson." She rested her hand on Alexander's shoulder. "This is the son of his son, Aretas."

The queen's expression did not change, which could mean only one thing: she had foreknowledge of the claim. How had the news traveled so fast? Was it the people she met in Zeta's home? Had one of them run ahead with a choice bit of gossip?

"Impossible." For all the queen's haughtiness, it was clear she did not believe her own words. "Aretas is dead."

Cassia lowered her gaze. "That is true. But he has been dead these fifteen days only. Before that we were living in Damascus."

"And we are to believe that *you* were his wife?" The disdain dripped from her voice.

Cassia hesitated, closed her eyes briefly. "Yes. And Alexander—"

"Impossible!" The queen waved the young woman forward from where she stood near the wall. "This is Bethea. She is Aretas's wife."

Cassia's knees wobbled for the first time since entering, and she felt Alexander's eyes turn upward to her. At only six years old, he was still old enough to understand. She had kept the truth from him all his life. But today was a new beginning, and beginnings were sometimes painful. She lifted her chin.

"It is true. I was not his wife. Aretas—acquired me—some years ago. But that does not change the fact that Alexander is his son."

The queen waved her hand as though Cassia were an annoying insect plaguing her. "We have no reason to believe you. Already you admit that you are a liar. Take your misbegotten son and leave."

But Cassia's feet remained rooted to the marble floor. She was not leaving yet. "I am not lying—"

The sudden shuffle of slaves to her right silenced her. A man entered, largely built, with a frame that had at one time been muscular, no doubt, but had since turned to extra weight. He walked slowly, with the gait of royalty, but Cassia also sensed physical weakness. It took her only a fraction of a moment to see Aretas in the man's features.

The Nabataean king, Rabbel.

Cassia's heart thudded in relief, and with the anticipation of this next encounter.

In front of her, Hagiru vacated the throne, clearly reluctant to do so, but necessitated by protocol. Two slaves brought another, smaller chair and set it beside the carved throne, but she did not sit. Instead, she stepped down from the platform, passing Rabbel on his way up, and acknowledged him with a nod. "You do not look well today, my king." Her lips pursed. "Perhaps you would be wise to stay in your bedchamber."

Cassia used her ability to read the three principal characters in the drama before her. From Rabbel she sensed apathy toward the queen. From Hagiru, disdain for her husband and the girl. And the girl, Aretas's wife . . . a seething jealousy.

Rabbel shook his head, reached his throne, then turned and sat heavily. His gaze traveled across the room, as though he assessed the state of his kingdom by the activity in the chamber. His attention came to rest on Cassia, and his eyebrows lifted slightly with an interest men often showed in her body. She tried to smile. He shifted his attention to Alexander.

Cassia did not expect such a reaction. The king's face drained of color, then flushed red. His jaw fell open, and he gripped the arms of the throne as though he feared he would be knocked from it.

"Who . . . who is this?" His glance flicked between Cassia and Alexander.

"Some slave girl." Hagiru stepped in front of Alexander to block him from the king's view. "Trying to swindle the throne—"

"My name is Cassia. And this is your grandson, Alexander." Cold sweat broke over her neck, but she did not drop her gaze from the king. This was her moment and she would do what it took, for Alex's sake.

The king looked to Alexander again and he breathed heavily.

Alexander, oblivious to the drama, peeked from behind the queen to get a better look at the man on the throne.

"She has no proof—" Hagiru was saying, but Rabbel raised a hand and the queen went silent.

"The proof stands before me." His voice was heartbreakingly soft. "It is like my own Aretas, come back at last." His words caught with emotion, and Cassia felt a rush of joy and pride.

"Come here, son." Rabbel extended his arms.

Alexander looked to Cassia, and she nodded, smiling. He hid his face against her hip. Cassia patted his back. "Go."

Hesitantly, Alexander climbed the few steps to the platform and walked to the throne. When he was still a few steps away, Rabbel leaned forward, gathered him up in his arms, and crushed the boy to his chest.

Tears spilled from Cassia's eyes and tracked down her cheeks. An immediate sense of belonging here in Rabbel's palace washed over her, despite the queen's angry presence.

Hagiru made a little sound, low in her throat, and when Cassia turned to her, the hatred in her eyes was palpable.

Alexander sat on Rabbel's lap. Hagiru circled around Cassia, sizing her up like a piece of market meat. "I hope you have not forgotten what trouble Aretas caused here, Rabbel—"

"My son?" The king's attention was on Cassia. "He is here as well?"

Cassia wiped her tears with the back of her hand and lowered her eyes. "I am sorry, my king. Aretas died fifteen days ago, in Damascus. He told me of his family here in Petra, and I came, hoping to find a home for my son."

Hagiru snorted. "Yes, I am certain you did."

Cassia lifted her gaze to the queen. "Aretas did not tell me his father was the king." Her voice took on strength. "I came hoping only for a good family, an honest place to make a home." She looked back to Rabbel and nearly regretted her words, seeing the pain that Aretas's denial of his family caused his father.

"So"—Hagiru still paced around Cassia—"we have the concubine of the rebellious son and their child. We should throw them both out, Rabbel."

But the queen was beaten already. Rabbel had not taken his arm from around Alexander and barely heard his wife's speech, so taken was he with his grandson.

Hagiru must have sensed it too. Her features took on a harder edge and she faced Cassia. Her dark eyes burned and Cassia felt a coldness burrow through her body, as though the queen were chilling her from the inside out with only a look. Evil flared in the gaze that Cassia did not fully understand.

Another boy ran in at that moment, a few years older than Alexander, and bounded toward the throne. He stopped, surprise painting his features when he saw Alexander on Rabbel's knee.

Hagiru went to the boy at once and put her arm around his shoulders. He twisted from her grasp.

"It appears this is your nephew, Obadas. Your brother Aretas's son."

Cassia tried to assimilate this new appearance. Clearly this boy was far younger than Aretas, too young to be his brother. And Malik had said the king's first wife, Gamilath, died many years ago. The boy had to be . . . *Hagiru's* son.

And then the pieces fell into place.

TWELVE

———◆———

THE TRUTH OF THE SITUATION HIT CASSIA LIKE A BLOW.
With no heir present from the first queen and the first son, Aretas,
Obadas was heir to Rabbel's throne. But Alexander . . .

Alexander was the eldest son of the eldest son. A direct line, and
one that bypassed Hagiru's son.

And Hagiru.

The realization sent another chill through her. She and Hagiru
were rivals of a sort, both mothers of royal princes. Alexander's claim
was greater, and in one way it put Cassia in a position above Hagiru.
The thought weakened her knees and made her sweat. The queen was
clearly not a woman to relinquish power.

Hagiru was speaking, and Cassia tried to follow the exchange in
spite of her turbulent thoughts.

"The Romans are on our doorstep, Rabbel. Waiting to swallow
all of Nabataea and make it one of their provinces. It is not a time to
appear divided. The boy will make us seem weak, uncertain about the
future of our kingdom."

Rabbel shook his head. "You would have me cast out the boy,

as though he were nothing? You know I have long desired to have Aretas back in Petra where he belonged." His voice wavered again, and Cassia felt a wash of pity for the man who had just learned his son would never return home.

Hagiru's lips tightened. She looked sideways at Cassia, at her own son, whose folded arms bespoke jealousy already, then at Bethea, standing mute at the side of the room. The queen inhaled, threw her shoulders back, and seemed to make a decision.

"Then we must make it right." She shot a sideways glance of loathing toward Cassia. "Bethea never bore Aretas a son, but she was his true wife. Bethea should have the boy. This . . . this slave woman is clearly unfit to raise the prince." She waved a hand over Cassia. "Look at her. And look at the boy." She pointed to Alexander. "Look at the bruises on his arm. No doubt she has beaten him. Beaten the royal prince!" Her voice lifted to an indignant shriek.

"No!" Cassia stepped forward. "He was hurt by those who killed Aretas! I would never—"

"Silence!" The queen had ascended the platform now to stand beside Rabbel as though the two were a united force against her. "You would speak to the king as though his equal? Already you grasp at a position that is not yours!" She half turned to Rabbel. "Think what she would do if we allowed her to stay, husband. She would have the whole palace bowing and scraping before a slave girl by the Festival of Grain!"

Cassia opened her mouth to speak, then thought better of it. She looked to Rabbel for her defense, but the king seemed confused.

Understanding—and a stabbing fear—went through her. For all the pomp of his entrance and Hagiru's apparent deference, the king was like wet clay in his wife's hands.

Rabbel put a hand to his stomach.

Hagiru bent to him, her voice much softer. "We will sort this out, my king." She touched his shoulder lightly. "You should rest. The excitement of finding your grandson—it is enough for one day." She patted his shoulder, then pulled Alexander from him. "I will come to you soon, dear."

Rabbel looked to Alexander.

"I will bring the boy to you later. After you have rested."

Rabbel nodded then and stood. Cassia's heart seized. "My king—" She searched for the words. "I know I have no claim here. I have no wish for anything for myself. Only allow us to remain for my son's sake. And for your own." A note of desperation had found its way into her voice. Her heartbeat seemed to catch and hold, suspended.

Rabbel sighed and looked to Hagiru. "Take care of the woman." He made his way down the few steps. Hagiru bowed to him as he passed, and the room fell silent as he exited, attended by several slaves.

When he was gone, Cassia turned back to Hagiru and found the queen already on the throne. Alexander tried to descend the platform, but Hagiru reached from her seat and grabbed his arm. His eyes widened.

Cassia felt a pressure in her chest.

Hagiru called Bethea forward and the woman approached the throne, but her attention stayed on Cassia, her expression a mixture of disdain and curiosity.

"Do something with the boy," Hagiru said to her.

Cassia took a half step forward. "I expect nothing for myself. I will work here in the palace, in whatever way you choose, and I can look after my son."

Hagiru laughed, a mirthless sound more like a growl. "Ah, but you have fulfilled your purpose already. You have given Aretas a son. We have no further use for you here."

"Alexander is the king's grandson—"

"Yes." Hagiru's voice was a hiss. "And it appears he will be claimed as such. What has that to do with you?"

The pressure on her chest increased. Cassia shook her head, refusing to acknowledge what was becoming clear. Alexander would belong here in the palace. He would have the family and the security she had always desired for him.

But what of her?

Cassia indicated the slaves lined at the edge of the hall. "Let me be a slave here in the palace. Nothing more. Only let me remain—"

Hagiru stood, towering over Cassia from her perch on the throne platform, a dark shadow in the white room. She spoke as if giving a formal pronouncement, and the words were like a death sentence.

"The boy will be raised a Nabataean, without foreign influence." She took another step toward Cassia. Alexander pulled away from Bethea and came to stand beside Hagiru, looking up at her with frightened eyes. Hagiru positioned herself behind him and clutched his shoulders possessively. She spoke to Cassia. "You will give up all claims to the boy." Alexander winced beneath her grip. "From this day forward, you will be dead to him."

Cassia's legs trembled beneath her, and she reached out to steady herself, but found nothing.

"You will leave Petra." Hagiru's voice plunged into her like a piercing knife. "Today. There is nothing for you here."

The trembling overtook Cassia's whole body, and her blood chilled. "No. No! I will not leave my son!" She held out a hand, and Alexander broke away from the queen and fled to her. She gathered him to herself and lifted her head. "You cannot separate a mother from her son."

Hagiru laughed again and inclined her head to the nearby slave who had attended her earlier. "Take the boy."

Cassia pushed Alexander behind her body. Hot tears sprung to her eyes, and she blinked furiously. "Come, Alexander." She turned them both to leave the palace.

At the back of the throne room, three male slaves stepped into the arch that led to the front halls.

Cassia turned a slow circle in the center of the room, still clutching Alexander. There was no other way out.

Hagiru's slave reached her and wrapped a hand around Alexander's arm.

"Mama?" His terrified voice ripped open her soul and called her tears forward, not to be denied. He wrapped his arms around her waist.

The slave pulled him away, but Cassia followed, reaching for him. "You cannot do this!" She called out the words to the entire room, surrounded as she was by the hostile glances of royalty and slave alike.

Another slave appeared at her side and snatched her hand away from her son.

Cassia's vision blurred and her stomach roiled. She lunged for Alexander. The second slave pinned her arms behind her and held her fast.

"Alexander!" She could do nothing but shout his name, and her body seemed as though it would shake into a thousand tiny fragments.

He was retreating from her now, his light eyes still wide with terror. His mouth opened in a small O, and his bottom lip trembled. "Mama? Where are you going?"

"I am not leaving!"

But the gap between mother and son widened.

Cassia twisted and kicked and even pulled free for a moment, but the slave ran at her and swept her from her feet.

"Alexander. Alexander!"

She hit the palace floor but barely felt the pain. Even the kick he landed in her midsection did not slow her. She scrambled across the marble toward Alex's feet and reached a hand out to him.

Too far.

Another kick. Pulled to standing. She felt the yellow silk rip in the slave's hands. She leaned away from the tearing fabric, thinking to get free. An arm around her waist lifted her off her feet.

She kicked backward, connected with shins. The slave cursed in her ear.

The room was a bloodred haze now, blurred by fear and anger and terror. She thrashed in his arms. Her hair tangled around her face.

She screamed, but her voice had gone hoarse. How many times had she screamed already? Above her scream she heard the queen's laughter.

And he was gone.

She searched the room and could not find his sweet face. They had taken him away. Taken her son away. *Alexander!*

Still thrashing, she felt the room spin. The slave dragged her backward.

And then they were in the halls, then the portico outside the great palace, and then stone steps rushed up to meet her and she clenched her eyes and brought her arms up to protect her face. She fell and bounced. Her knees and arms met each step with an angry jolt, until she reached the platform between the steps and rolled to a stop at the base of the huge djinn block.

She was still for only a moment before she scrambled to her knees and retched.

When her stomach had exhausted itself, she fell against the djinn block, godforsaken, bruised and bloody, and alone.

Alone.

THIRTEEN

———◆———

THE SUN DESCENDED AND STILL CASSIA LEANED AGAINST
the djinn block, her eyes on the palace entrance as though Alexander
would skip down its steps and into her arms.

Where else could she go?

She shivered in the shadow of the stone as blood and sweat dried
on her skin. She grew fearful as the shadows lengthened. Fearful of
the night, and of the palace slaves who might come and find her on
the steps and beat her again.

So she crawled forward, loose pebbles scraping her knees, until
she felt she could stand, then stumbled down the second set of steps
into the street and retraced her path through the city until she reached
the Nymphaeum.

Only a few women drew water, late as it was, and they mostly
ignored her. She did not blame them. Her torn and bloodied dress,
her bruised arms and swollen lip—they shouted to anyone who looked
that she was an outcast.

At the edge of the fountain pool, she cupped her hands and filled
them with water, then tried to wash the blood from her arms. The deep
scratches burned. She did not even know how they had gotten there.

When she had washed her arms and face, she sat on the stone edge of the pool and faced the street.

Alexander is gone.

It seemed to be the only thought she could form. And there seemed to be nothing left for her.

It is what I deserve. She had always thought Alexander was a gift from the gods, one they had mistakenly bestowed upon her, a weak and worthless slave girl who did not merit such a gift.

And now Alexander would be loved and protected by royalty and brought up to claim the kingship of Nabataea. The thought did not surprise her. It seemed fitting for the boy that he was. She should only be surprised she had been allowed to have him at all, even for a short time.

And now, now I am no longer needed.

She felt hollowed out, as though all that had made her human had been removed.

Alexander would be better off in the palace. It was her only solace.

And she? Where would she be?

You will be dead to him, Hagiru had said. Yes, perhaps it would be best if Cassia were dead.

A shadow passed over her. Death had come to take her even then. But it was the shadow of a man, not a specter, and she looked up to find the man who had restored the water earlier that day leaning over her, his brow furrowed.

"What has happened to you?" He tried to lift her head. "Who did this?"

Cassia said nothing. She did not have the strength.

He reached for her arm, and she jumped away from his touch.

"All is well." He spoke softly, as one might to a wounded animal. "I will not hurt you."

She dropped her eyes, as it was too difficult to hold her head up.

"Let me take you to your home. Tell me where you live."

Cassia sighed. "Alexander is my home. But he is gone."

"Your boy?" She sensed he searched the fountain-house court-yard. "Where is he?"

Again, she could not summon strength enough to answer.

"Where is Alexander?" The man's voice pressed her now, more urgent, concerned.

Julian. That is his name. "They took him." The words escaped on another sigh and seemed to suck away her life. She swayed where she sat, and a moment later felt herself swept into the man's arms and cradled against his chest. She leaned into his solid shoulder and sighed, grateful beyond words to be carried from this place.

"I must take you somewhere. Tell me where you have friends to care for you."

Cassia closed her eyes. "I am alone."

He walked toward the street and her head bumped his shoulder. "You must know someone in Petra."

"Malik. I know only the old man Malik."

She was vaguely aware that he moved through the streets, asking anyone who passed to direct him to Malik, an old man.

Eventually he seemed to get an answer, then walked with more purpose. Soon they climbed, and she dared not open her eyes to see how narrow the ledge, nor how high their destination.

The sound of music drifted to her, and within minutes she felt they had passed into a rock-hewn chamber like the place she had spent the night. The music was louder here, though the voices were subdued and melancholy and sang of fortresses and towers, which seemed quite strange to Cassia.

She opened her eyes. They stood at the open end of what appeared to be a large tomb cut into the rock. A fire burned at the ledge, and the burial slots were only dark eyes in the back of the chamber. The central part of the chamber was filled with people reclining on low couches around the three-sided stone table, with their eyes turned toward the two new arrivals.

"I am looking for Malik," her rescuer said.

Cassia lifted her head and recognized Zeta and Talya, and the two women got to their feet quickly, followed by Malik, and hurried forward.

"You!" Julian said. "You are Malik?"

Malik paused only a moment, the corner of his mouth lifting in a quick smile. "Did I not tell you we would meet again?" But then his attention was on Cassia. "What has happened?"

She squirmed to be set down, but Julian held her still, until the two women led them forward and several people vacated the couch to make room. Julian laid her gently on the cushion and stood.

"She hasn't said much." He shook his head. "But something has happened to her boy. She says someone has taken him."

Malik knelt and brought his lined face close to hers. The white fringe of hair around his bald head glowed in the firelight. "Who took Alexander, Cassia?"

She had thought herself drained of all tears, but they welled again. "The queen. That terrible Hagiru. She took my boy! And had me thrown from the palace."

Malik ran a hand over her head. "I feared as much. Rest now. Eat and rest. And then we will talk."

Malik stood and turned to the water restorer. "So you have been brought to us already, eh? What is your name?"

The man seemed to have weakened, and Cassia felt a flicker of shame. He should not have tired himself on her behalf.

"Julian. My name is Julian."

His voice was thick with emotion, which Cassia did not understand.

"Welcome, Julian," Malik said. "You are right where you belong."

Julian sank to the couch beside her, almost as though his legs had given way. Malik smiled and patted the younger man's shoulder.

The sun dipped low enough then to spill its rays into the tomb, lighting the chamber and the faces of its inhabitants. There were perhaps thirty of them, Cassia guessed, and each one had turned a curious and friendly face on the two guests. She was conscious then of her filthy clothes, her beaten body, even the odor of sweat and blood she carried.

But over the next few hours, she found all of her needs attended, and as her body was cared for, her heart clung to a bit of peace as well, though she did not understand its source. She tried to read the hearts of the group, but her fatigue left her baffled. The women bathed her cuts, fed her well, even took her to a small, connected chamber and replaced the ripped yellow silk with a clean white tunic and red belt. She returned to sit beside Julian, who watched her with the protectiveness of an older brother.

There was more singing, with words she did not recognize, and after the meal was shared, there was a passing of wine and bread, which seemed to have special meaning to the strange group that was not a family but certainly behaved as one. She felt the warmth and joy and comfort of the place. A severe contrast with the cold throne room.

Malik led the group, and they responded to him with love and respect, as Zeta and Talya had in their home.

The meal was removed, strange prayers were offered up to an unnamed god, and then the people dispersed into the darkness, each offering a blessing upon her as they left. Soon she shared the tomb chamber with only Malik, Julian, and Talya, who still tended the fire near the ledge.

Malik sat upon the edge of her cushion, and Julian had not left her side since they arrived. "Are you ready to speak of what has happened?"

She twined trembling hands against her chest, a nervous habit, then forced them to her lap. With a deep breath, she related the terrible truth, from Damascus to the Nabataean palace.

"But he is better off now," she finished, the words catching in her throat. "He will be taken care of."

Julian pushed off the couch and paced through the cave-like room, his feet scuffling. "That is foolishness, Cassia! Alexander belongs with his mother!"

Malik smiled.

"But who am I to claim him? I was not even Aretas's wife." She hung her head. "I do not have any power here."

Julian stopped his pacing to stand in front of her. "You are the mother of the future king! That is who you are! And do not tell me you have no power. I saw it in you, even at the Nymphaeum when I brought your son down from the ledge. You may be small, but you are strong!"

Cassia studied the man. He had the bearing and speech of nobility. Both his appearance and his passion of expression marked him a Roman. Why had he come to Petra? *I do not want yet again to be drawn to his kind of strength.*

An irrational desire to weep against his shoulder washed over her, and she shook her head. "How will I fight against the royal house?"

Malik touched her arm. "Julian is right, Cassia." He frowned, and the lines deepened on either side of his mouth. "There is an evil in that palace. Forces you know nothing of. They are at work to keep the people in bondage. You must not leave Alexander in the hands of the queen." His gaze bore into her, and she felt again that strange sense of strength passing into her.

Wanting to escape those eyes, she struggled to her feet and walked to the open ledge.

They were high above the city again, and bright moonlight shone on the cliffs, on long flights of steps, on rooftop gardens and terraces and caves, so strangely intermingled in this place. Their ledge looked toward the palace. Toward Alexander.

Julian was right. She had brought them across the desert, and she would not lose her son here. Aretas had not defeated her, and neither would his family.

She felt the blood flow into her legs, her arms, her hands, and she raised a hand toward the palace, framing the building between her thumb and forefinger as though she could crush it there.

She dropped her hand and turned back to the two men, who watched her from within the chamber. As appealing as Julian was, with his dark wavy hair and generous Roman lips, she would not give herself to a man again, nor ask him to do what she could do alone.

"I will get my son back." The words echoed back to her and seemed stronger than she had spoken them. *"I will get him back."*

Beside her, Talya stood and held out a small parcel. The yellow silk.

Cassia took it from her, turned it over in her hands, and thought of all the times Aretas had forced her to wear it, to be a playing piece in his deadly games.

Never again.

With a look at Malik and Julian, and a chin lifted in defiance, Cassia dropped the yellow silk into the fire and let it burn.

FOURTEEN

——◆——

CASSIA HAD BEEN SENT OFF WITH TALYA TO TAKE SHELTER with her and her mother. Julian followed Malik to his home—despite his misgivings.

The elderly Nabataean ambled through the dark streets, into the crowded section of housing where the mud-brick homes were built close together to maximize the shade. Julian walked beside him, grateful for his hospitality. But did it come at the cost of a conversation he was not willing to begin?

But Malik was silent, and they reached the entrance of his home without words. The house turned a blank face to the street, as all houses did, but once through the doorway, it was Julian who spoke, not bothering to hide his surprise.

"Malik, you old goat, you are a nobleman!"

Malik chuckled and led Julian through a wide passageway, into his central courtyard, its corners lit with brazier fires to welcome the master home. "Petra is not Rome. We are not so consumed with nobility in Arabia."

"Even so"—Julian waved a hand over the expansive courtyard

garden, with its bubbling central fountain and greenery, glossy with moonlight and firelight—"I believe you have money growing from your ears."

Malik shrugged. "I will show you to a room. We will talk of true riches in the morning."

The house had been expanded by using central pillars and supporting walls that could sustain upper stories. Bright frescoes lined every wall, combining the best art of both East and West.

Julian slept well in the luxurious bed, with its carved wooden headboard and plush bedding. He awoke early and found Malik already sitting in the garden, a steaming bowl of wine in his gnarled hands. The old man smiled and held up the bowl.

"Come, sit with me."

Julian's assessment of the previous night had been accurate. The villa was as grand as his parents' villa in Rome, with a garden lined by colonnaded walkways for shade and filled with exotic plants. Oleander in reds, pinks, and whites hugged the painted walls, and their realistic scenes of waterside and woodland fooled the eye, enhancing the coolness and size of the garden.

Julian dropped to the stone bench beside Malik and folded his arms across his chest. They sat beneath a trellis draped with grapevines. "Yesterday you spoke of work I might find." Julian smiled and lowered his head. "I suppose if I want to keep eating, I must do a bit of work, eh?"

A servant appeared with another bowl of wine and placed it in Julian's hands. He sipped it quickly and burned his tongue.

Malik looked sideways at him. "I would not guess you are much accustomed to labor."

Julian bristled. "I can work as hard as the next man!"

"Yes." Malik laughed softly, shifted on the bench, and grew serious. "Tell me of Rome, Julian."

He rolled his shoulders to release tension. Malik's abrupt manner and apparent knowledge of all that concerned him were unnerving.

Malik did not wait for an answer. "I hear it grows dangerous for our people."

Julian looked away, focused on the tub that sent grapevines over their heads. "Rome is a beautiful city, and all who live there are blessed by the gods."

Malik growled in apparent frustration with Julian's answer. "How long will you continue to deny that you are a follower of the Way?"

Julian dropped his shoulders and turned to the old man, searching his eyes. It was clear his attempt at deception was futile with Malik. "You see things, don't you, old man?"

Malik half smiled. "More than I wish to see at times." He sobered. "So tell me of Rome."

Julian shrugged and sipped more of his wine. "Not the best place for a follower these days."

Malik nodded. "I have had letters. From other elders, in Syria and Alexandria. The Roman provinces feel the reach of the emperor in ways we have yet escaped here in Arabia. They are holding strong but say that Trajan is beginning to find ways to dispose of believers."

Julian could not bring himself to look at Malik. His hold on a casual tone was very thin, and he feared the old man would break it with his soul-searching eyes.

"The blood of martyrs begins to flow again, as it did in the old days under Nero." He took a deep breath to try to release the pressure on his heart. He was unsuccessful.

"You have lost someone."

Julian set his bowl aside, stood, and plucked a leaf from the grapevine, then ripped it apart. "It does nothing to speak of it."

"Hmm."

"For now I am a resident of your fine city. Far from the reach, as you say, of Emperor Trajan. And I must find work if I am here to stay."

"I know this guilt you feel, Julian. I know it well." Malik's voice strayed away, causing Julian to turn back to the man. His head was bowed. "For some of us, the days of Nero are not so far removed."

Julian sat beside him again, finding no words.

Malik patted his leg and straightened. "But God has brought you to us, and we shall see what He has planned for you."

"I came here to remain unknown." Julian looked away. "I seek nothing more."

Malik smiled. "We shall see. Men such as you do not often remain unknown. Besides, the Romans are at the door, and the Nabataeans may soon go the way of the rest of the world, into the hands of the Empire. The people desire to be annexed without bloodshed, but I fear our royal family has other plans. Perhaps you have been brought to us now, to help us find our way into what is next."

Julian crossed his arms again. "I was not *brought* here, old man. I came of my own accord."

"Hmm. Tell me what you thought of our people here."

The question surprised him, but he was happy to give his opinion. "They are devoted to each other, that is clear. And you have taught them well in the truth. But they are complacent. They are not ready for what is to come. You must show them how to be strong."

Malik smiled and looked away, as though amused. "He sees *and* speaks, Jesus," he said under his breath. He waved to a nearby servant, who hurried over to retrieve their bowls. "Come." He brushed his hands together. "I will find you some work."

Finally.

The remarkable engineering of the city had not been lost on Julian. The massive facades carved out of the solid iron-laden sandstone, the hydraulic engineering required to channel the spring rains that fell on the mountains into the huge tanks and cisterns. Certainly there was much work to be found here, even for a nobleman who had pursued only leisure and hobbies in his Rome.

Malik and Julian strolled out of the house, from the cool greenery of the garden to the red heat of the city. Across the *Cardo Maximus*, the main thoroughfare, they drifted alongside the marketplace that ran the length of the street. Merchants walked in the shade of the morning, organizing their caravans and striking deals. Shop owners lifted the flaps of their shops, revealing stalls of hanging meat and Petra's elegant red earthenware, of leather goods and cloth, metal utensils, and fruits and vegetables.

Malik led him to a shop filled with breads and cakes and hailed the slight shop owner with a kiss on each cheek. "Alawin, here is a new friend, Julian."

Alawin, whose hair would make women jealous, sought out Julian's eyes. He held them for a moment, then nodded and broke into a wide smile. "Welcome, brother." He extended his arms. Julian gripped the man's arms and nodded. With a flash of insight akin to Malik's, Julian felt the man was also a follower of the Way.

Alawin gave them each a tan cake drizzled with sweet golden honey. He leaned close to Malik. "I am sorry I have not been able to come in the evenings. Samiyah has been unwell."

Malik frowned. "We will pray for Samiyah's health, then, and hope to see you soon."

Alawin bobbed his head, and a lock of thick hair fell into his eyes. "Thank you, Elder." He gripped Malik's arm. "I thank you and Samiyah thanks you."

Julian did not miss the look of respect Alawin lavished on Malik. Oddly, he felt a jolt of something like envy.

"Give Samiyah my love, Alawin." Malik finished his cake and licked the honey from his fingers. "We must find Julian some work."

Julian thanked Alawin for the cake and smiled when the man refused Malik's money.

The two men walked to the end of the *Cardo Maximus*, toward the eastern end of the city where the fabulous tombs were carved astonishingly high into the cliffs.

Malik looked up. "You will climb to work?"

"Absolutely."

"They are always in need of masons to chip away the stone."

Julian hesitated, still resisting any divulgence of the details of his former life. "I . . . I am able to do a little sculpting as well."

Malik halted and turned on him. "Give me your hands."

Julian held them, still sticky with the honey cake, out to the man.

Malik took Julian's hands in his own and examined them. Then closed his eyes.

Julian swallowed. Again, he felt the discomforting thought that the Elder of Petra was calling him forth to a task he didn't want to undertake.

Malik opened his eyes and released Julian's hands.

"The hands of a sculptor." He tilted his head and studied Julian. His voice deepened and his eyes grew fiery. "But God has given me to know these hands will do more than carve stone. They will carve a place for Jesus' church in Arabia."

Julian broke the hold of Malik's eyes, wiped his fingers on his tunic, and resumed walking. He had felt that fire once, the flame he saw in Malik's eyes. It had caused nothing but harm. He would not feel it again.

Malik hurried after him. "Your heart is tightly guarded. But God will do a work." He laughed. "And perhaps it will begin with the little Syrian woman and her son."

Julian gave the old man a sideways glance. Had his interest in Cassia been so obvious? "She is too bright for that, I believe. I fear she sees right through me."

"And what does she see?"

Julian kicked at a stone in the street. "A man who has failed at every important thing in his life."

Malik said nothing and Julian chose not to look at him. He eyed the tombs ahead. "You know someone here who will give me work?"

Malik drew alongside him, held his arm until Julian turned to him. "There is work for you here, Julian. Indeed, more than you want to acknowledge. But first you must accept the call." Those eyes were afire again. "It is time to forget the past. It is time to open your heart."

FIFTEEN

ALEXANDER IS GONE.

Cassia had spent the night in the home of Zeta and Talya once again and awoke to the crushing desolation of Alexander's absence and the memory of her vow the night before. She crept from the bedding Talya had laid near the front blanket-wall of the home, pushed aside the heavy tan fabric, and sat cross-legged at the ledge, surveying the city still in the shadow of the cliff that housed her. The rising sun's early beams lighted the countless swirls and shades formed in the rock face across from her ledge.

How was she ever to retrieve her son? How could one small woman, with no money and no army, come against the royal house?

Far below, a donkey wandered the desolate street as though it belonged to no one. Cassia watched its plodding steps and felt the confidence of the prior night slip away.

Whatever her plan, she could not impose on Zeta and Talya any longer. She needed to find work and a place to live, however temporary, until she could find a way to get Alexander back.

She smoothed the white tunic Talya had given her last night. The yellow silk was gone. The pouch she had brought all the way from Damascus with their few possessions had disappeared in yesterday's struggle at the palace. She had absolutely nothing, and even the clothes she wore were not her own.

If she did not find work soon, she would be reduced to begging. The thought barely troubled her when compared to the loss of Alexander, but to spend all her time begging for enough to survive would not help her get him back.

The two women were soon awake, and Cassia busied herself with helping them begin the day, hoping to repay them in some small way for their generosity.

They ground meal and baked bread through the morning, until a voice called out Zeta's name from outside the rock wall.

"Come," Zeta returned, and the three paused in their work to wait for the visitor to enter.

The blanket parted and the tall, lean frame of the Roman, Julian, appeared.

Beside Cassia, Talya visibly straightened, and Zeta clucked her tongue. Cassia couldn't help smiling at the two women's reactions.

Julian's attention, however, was on her, and she flushed under his steady gaze. He stood at the edge of the home, his hand on the rock wall. "How are you this morning?"

Cassia inhaled and nodded. "On my feet, though a bit bruised."

Zeta waved him into the home. "Come away from the ledge before you fall to your death, boy."

Julian smiled. He was a few years older than Cassia, and she smiled, too, hearing Zeta call him "boy."

He took a few steps toward her. "I am glad to hear your injuries are not serious. But I was asking more about your heart."

Cassia turned away, back to the bread, her thoughts jumbled at the unexpected question. "I am trying not to feel much right now."

There was a silent pause, in which Cassia felt the attention of all three on her in pity, but she did not look up from the kneading.

"What will you do?" Julian finally asked.

She shook her head. "Today I will find work and a place to live. Necessary before I can do anything for Alexander."

She reached for the bowl of flour across the table, and Julian pushed it toward her. "That is what I came to tell you. I have found some work for us both, if you are interested."

Cassia studied him from the side. "Why?"

He shrugged. "We are both new to Petra. I needed to find work myself and thought of you when I was asking around."

It surprised Cassia to hear that Julian was new to the city. His performance at the Nymphaeum yesterday had convinced her he was a favored son of the city, in spite of his obvious Roman birth. "What kind of work?"

"I will show you."

Zeta and Talya shooed them out, instructing Cassia to return later and give them news of the day. Within minutes she and Julian had descended to the city street, walked north a few minutes until they reached a section of the cliff face that held a series of enormous tomb facades carved into the rock. The face of the largest had been sculpted into three stories, with its lowest being a series of arches built in front of the cliff. The shell-pink wavy ribbons undulated through the topmost section, but it appeared only half finished, with rock ledges cut to accommodate the sculptors.

Julian pointed upward. "There it is."

Cassia followed his gaze. "What?"

"Our new employment."

Cassia huffed. "I am no mason!"

Julian looked down on her and laughed.

"That is funny?"

He craned his neck backward to scan the top of the tomb. "It amuses me that your objection concerns your masonry skills and not the unseemly height of the project."

Cassia shrugged one shoulder. "I have never feared heights."

"I am beginning to think you fear nothing."

Cassia could feel his gaze on her but hardened herself and did not turn. "You have mistaken me for someone else."

Julian did not respond but a moment later said, "I found work for myself as a stonecutter up there." He pointed. "But for you, I offered them the services of a woman to collect and bring down rock chips and to fetch the water necessary for the sculpting."

Hard work. And dirty. "Thank you, Julian."

"I'll try not to drop rocks on your head." He smiled.

⚜

The morning passed quickly, in a haze of red dust and burning calf muscles. Cassia worked below Julian, collecting the pieces of rock that fell from his chisel as he gouged a new niche into the sandstone. She then filled clay pots with the rocks and lowered them by rope to others who worked below her.

From her perch above the city, she again marveled at the engineering that had carved a city out of this rocky gorge. In the distance beyond the single city wall, she could see farmers fighting against the stony soil, their yolked plow animals dragging the wooden blade.

Halfway through the morning, she was instructed to switch places with a woman below and assume the task of getting water from the Nymphaeum down the street.

It was here she became truly thankful for the work Julian had found her, for the fountain house was the central location for women to gather and gossip, and it was here she heard of happenings in the palace. This morning the talk was all about the new prince who had appeared from nowhere. The disappearance of Aretas was only alluded to, and Cassia gained no new knowledge there, but she grasped at every scrap of information regarding Alex while trying to remain casual. It would not do for the queen to hear she remained so close to the palace.

She left the Nymphaeum with a heavy heart. How could one powerless woman defeat the mighty queen? And how could she take Alexander from his birthright?

Back at the massive tomb project with her pot of water, she watched Julian's progress above her and the way he shouted down to the woman who had replaced her. Even from the street level, Cassia could see the girl's laughter, could hear Julian's teasing voice falling on her. Even the other masons working on the rock face seemed amused by him. It appeared as though the workforce had begun to center its attention around him. She watched the athletic grace with which he leaned out from his platform to hack away at the rock and compared him to Aretas's muscle-bound physique.

"The water won't return without you." The harsh voice at her elbow startled her. She turned and raised her eyes to the mason gang's leader.

A flush creeped into her neck and face. "I . . . I am sorry."

The mason looked above them to where Julian pretended to toss down a large rock piece on the head of his female helper below. "If he weren't so good, I'd get rid of him. Too distracting."

Cassia grabbed an empty terra-cotta pot and hurried toward the Nymphaeum again, away from Julian's charms.

The mason was right. And of all women, she should know better.

⚜

The days passed in quick succession. Julian's assigned niche deepened and matched the growing hollow place being carved out of Cassia as she made no progress in retrieving Alexander. It was all she could do to keep up with the rigorous work of the day, then do her part in the home of Zeta, who had insisted upon housing her. She fell into bed each night and slept like one dead, angry that she had no plan but satisfied at least that she was earning money. Some of it she gave to Zeta to pay for her keep, but most of it went into a tiny box Talya gave her, secreted under her bedding. How long would it be before enough accumulated to fund their escape from Petra?

Julian came each day to take her to the tomb project, saying it was not safe for her to walk there alone. She tried to understand how she had warranted his strange respect. She had never been treated thus by Aretas, and even Julian seemed not to have the same opinion of any of the other young women at the workplace. With them he was all flirtatious humor and teasing. With Cassia he was like a somber and sometimes irritable older brother. She had his respect, perhaps, but she fought the desire to gain anything more. Besides, he was far more interested in his work, obsessed almost, now that it had been discovered he could sculpt, and the work gang watched his artistry turn the tomb facade into beauty.

She often tried to draw him out, to discover why he was in Petra and to hear of his life in Rome. She learned little. He had a brother, close in age but not in spirit. Though he would not say why they were estranged.

In the evenings Zeta and Talya would often disappear, leaving her alone in their home. They joined their group of friends, but they did not invite her, and she found them somewhat secretive.

But it was the cool waters of the Nymphaeum that drew her each day, with its loitering townswomen and palace slaves, and its welcome gossip.

One morning, when she had been working at the tombs nearly a week, two women in the long white dress of the palace, with their hair braided with pearl strands, filled their unglazed pots slowly as they talked. Cassia slipped alongside them and listened.

"He's a sweet boy, but how long will he remain so?"

The woman's friend clucked her tongue. "There is more than his character at stake, I fear."

Cassia bent her pot to the fountain to fill it, letting the water rush over her hands.

"Obadas is a bully, to be sure, but you think the boy has evil intent?"

Her friend shrugged and leaned close. "He is his mother's son."

The other steadied her filled pot on her head. "Perhaps there is more to the taunting than simple jealousy. It pains me to see the boy unloved and unhappy."

"We shall see how long it lasts. I fear worse for him."

And then they were gone, leaving Cassia to puzzle out their conversation as she wandered back to the work site, the jar on her hip. It did not take long, and her pace increased to match the pounding of her blood.

Her feet churned up the dusty ground on the road to the site, and when she reached the tombs, Julian stood on the street and raised his hands as a shield.

"You are like one of the Furies, flying over the sea to exact vengeance. Did someone insult you at the fountain?"

Cassia lowered her pot to the ground with a *thunk* that made Julian wince, but she did not care if the thing broke into a thousand pieces. "They are hurting Alexander!"

Julian took her arm and pulled her close. "Think, Cassia. You must lower your voice."

She tried to breathe slowly, speak softly. "I heard them at the fountain. The queen's son is cruel to Alexander, and the servant women think something worse will happen."

Julian surveyed the crowded work area around them, then bent his head to her. "Worse?"

"I do not know!" Her voice climbed again and she fought to control it. "But I must go and help him!" She whirled away from Julian and headed toward the palace in a near run.

He was beside her in a moment, his long stride easily keeping up with her pace. "I know you want to help Alexander. This is not the way."

She huffed out her annoyance. "I cannot simply keep clearing away rocks and fetching water! I have waited too long already."

"And what will you do? Charge in, unarmed, and demand your son?" His voice sounded angry now, and Cassia slowed a bit.

"I must—"

"Yes, you must get Alexander back. But this foolishness will get you killed and will do nothing to help him!"

Her steps faltered then. Emotion caught up with her, swelled over her like a wave, threatening to send her to her knees in the dust. "What can I do, Julian? I have nothing . . . I am nothing."

Julian pulled her to face him. "Look at me, Cassia."

She turned her tear-streaked face upward, wanting him to tell her otherwise.

"I do not know who it was that convinced you of this, but you are not *nothing*. Look at what you have done in these few weeks." He still held her arms and anger flickered in his eyes. "You have survived Aretas's death, brought your son across the desert to a new city, weathered the attack of that trader, stood before royalty and endured their abuse, and then won the hearts of everyone you have met." He shook her slightly, as though to drive his words home. "You are the strongest woman I have ever known!"

She searched his face for a moment, drinking in the strength. "Then what am I to do for my son?"

Julian pulled her to his chest in a rough embrace. She felt him look upward at his work, as though making a decision.

"We will find a way, Cassia. I promise you, we will find a way."

SIXTEEN

THE SUN SLIPPED LOW ENOUGH OVER THE DESERT TO send its warmth into the large rock-cut tomb where the church met. Malik arrived early and alone, content to start the fire and wait for the others to arrive.

They trickled in as they finished their work for the day, bringing parts of the meal and greeting Malik with honor and affection.

The *triclinium*'s three stone tables, laid as a square with one open end toward the rock ledge, had only been used for their shared meals. Never a funerary banquet, for which the tables had been built. The large tomb belonged to one of their own, but none of the slots in the back had yet been used to house remains for the customary year before the bones were gathered into a stone ossuary and placed in a smaller niche. Until it was needed for family burials, it served as a meeting place for the Petran church.

Malik watched the tables fill with food, both rich cakes and poor breads, and the chamber with those he loved best. His heart expanded with the joy of it. This was his flock, his family. As the Elder of Petra for these many years, he had watched the community increase in number and in love for each other, and the growth of his church pleased him far more than the material wealth he had also accumulated over those same years.

Eventually, he took the central place on the middle couch. Not because he considered himself the guest of honor, but because he would teach tonight, and this was the best place to be heard and seen by all. The other places on the couches quickly filled with the eldest of their group, and the younger ones sat cross-legged with their plates on the floor or leaned against the walls. A child or two even sat behind him in the holes carved for burials.

When the crowded chamber had filled to capacity, Malik lifted a hand over the group and they silenced at once.

"Father in heaven, Maker of all that is, we are Your poor children, and all that we have is given by You. We lay our hearts before You, ask You to move among us and speak to us this night. We give You thanks for the meal You have given us to share, but even more for giving us each other. And above all, we thank You for Jesus the Redeemer, and we pray for His soon return and His kingdom to be established."

A murmured "amen" came from the group, and when Malik opened his eyes and lifted his head, a new figure was among them, standing at the end of the table to his left.

"Julian!" Malik's heart swelled to see the young man, to know he had sought them out. The Holy One had already given Malik a love for this boy, even in the short time he had known him.

All heads turned to the new arrival, and Julian seemed to shrink back. Malik waved him forward.

"Children, Julian was with us a few nights ago, but he was not yet ready to identify with us. Perhaps he is ready this night?" Malik waited, giving the boy his chance. He watched Julian's chest expand, his shoulders flex, watched him survey the room, his expression a mixture of fear and longing. The chamber stilled and waited for his response. Malik breathed a silent prayer.

Finally Julian nodded as though in agreement with each heart present. "Yes." He broke into a shy smile. "Grace to you and peace from God our Father, and the Lord Jesus Christ. It is good to be among those who also claim the blood of the Jewish Messiah as their atonement."

Malik watched his flock respond, pride filling his heart once again. Men jumped to their feet and gripped Julian's arms, women smiled and brought him food. Malik knew they would be cautious still. It would be some time before Julian would be fully accepted into the body, but he would be welcome until then.

The meal commenced, and the believers did what they did best—listened to each other's hearts, shared the struggle to remain true to the teachings, prayed over each other in love. Several served, not because they were servants, but because it was their joy and their gift to do so. Zeta herself brought Malik his bowl of wine, watered and warmed in just the way he enjoyed. He smiled up at her, then savored the simple meal of flat bread and brown beans, with creamy white yoghurt and figs afterward, and enjoyed his community. Near the front of the room, Julian held court with a group of boys and young men, entertaining them with some story that had them all laughing.

Before the meal ended, however, Julian broke away from his audience and approached Malik. Malik shifted on his couch to make room for the boy to set down a knee beside him and speak in his ear.

"May I speak to the community, Elder?" The boy's tone seemed strangely reverent.

Malik raised an eyebrow. "You wish to teach?"

"No, no, not teach! I . . . I want to request their help on behalf of Alexander, Cassia's son."

"You mean the son of Prince Aretas."

Julian's hand formed a fist at his side. "He belongs with his mother."

Malik swept his hand over the flock. "And what can they do?"

"I have a plan. But I need assistance."

Malik smiled. The young always had plans. They had not yet learned that life does not always yield the fruit one seeks to harvest. He dipped his head. "You may speak to them."

He had thought to introduce Julian again, to call the attention of the people, but with the impetuosity of youth, Julian jumped to his feet and clapped his hands to quiet them.

Within minutes he reminded them of Cassia, whom they had served here several nights earlier, and who even now was being housed by Zeta and her daughter, Talya. He explained the revelation Cassia had received on arriving in Petra, and then with the skill of a stage dramatist, he related the snatching of Alexander until tears were in the eyes of more than a few.

"I believe we must help her," Julian finished. "The boy is being treated roughly in the palace, and no one is there to love him. I fear for him. He should be with his mother. I have a plan."

He had their attention, Malik had to admit. But still, it was with the skill of a performer. Malik did not doubt the young man's sincerity or his passion, only his maturity. But the Spirit spoke into his heart, telling him to hold his tongue.

Julian's plan to rescue Alexander called for as many as were willing to pursue employment in the palace, in whatever role they could find. He believed if enough of them were positioned inside the royal house, an event could be staged that would pull the attention of the king and queen to one place, while those inside could secretly slip the boy away and whisk him from the palace to his mother.

"And then what?" one young man asked. "The entire Nabataean army will descend upon her."

"She will leave Petra. I will see to it. There are places she can go, where she would not be found."

Malik did not speak when Julian had finished. He would allow his flock to make this decision, to respond in whatever way the Holy One led them. Julian appeared patient as well. He asked whoever was willing to join him to speak to him after the meeting, and he yielded the floor to Malik.

Malik rose to teach them then. Nahor brought him one of their precious copies of the apostle's letter to the church in Thessalonica, and then a part of a letter Paul had written to Malik himself, several years after Malik had left him in Rome.

They wanted to hear more of Malik's years in Rome, as they always did. Those had been both the best and the worst years, as the older apostle had trained Malik in truth while the persecution grew fiercer with each passing month. Finally Paul had sent Malik back to Petra, to lead the church he had begun there himself when he sojourned in Arabia years earlier. Three months later, Paul was dead. Martyred at the hand of Nero.

But Malik did not speak of this tonight.

When he finished his teaching, he pulled yet another papyrus from his belt, a letter he had received today and saved to read to the community.

He held it aloft. "News from the province of Syria. From Ignatius, Elder of Antioch."

Faces lit with joy at the name. Ignatius wrote encouraging letters, filling them with hope at the rapid growth of the Way in Syria, despite the opposition.

"'To the church at Petra,'" Malik read. "'Grace and peace to you in the name of our Lord Jesus Christ. I write this letter with my own hand, with the knowledge it is likely my last.'" Malik stumbled over the words and paused. A collective gasp went up from the chamber.

"'The days of peaceful existence for the followers of Jesus are ending, my friends. The occasional disturbances have become more frequent, and the arena again cries out for the blood of Christians. I have not been silent as our emperor allows this evil. While he has not yet sent out his soldiers to round up believers, he has taken the policy that any who gain his attention are to be put to death.'"

Malik scanned forward a few lines, and when he spoke again, his voice thickened. "'Trajan has commanded that I come to Rome, to await trial for apostasy as I have denied his divinity and refused to bow to the gods of Rome. I go willingly, knowing that our God is using the deaths of His beloved to grow His church.'"

The letter went on, full of encouragement for the flock in Petra, and Malik read it, but his heart was near to bursting with grief. It was too soon, too soon to lose his friend and to see his leadership passed to another. Malik prayed there was one there in Antioch worthy to accept the mantle of authority.

It is your time as well, Malik.

The Voice burned through him, a fire in his veins. His heart pounded in response. He finished the letter, set it aside, then rose and went to the rock ledge to look out on the city. The others left him to his thoughts, no doubt believing his grief kept him isolated. But it was not the grief alone. It was the Voice. One he had come to know well.

"They have need of me still, Lord," he whispered into the night. He thought about the faces around the table, at the edges of the room. Which of them was ready to lead? "Not yet." He shook his head in the darkness. "No one is prepared."

Then you must help him.

A chill shook Malik's thin frame, and the knowing came upon him, falling like dew on his head, turning him back to his flock, who already watched him carefully.

"The word of the Lord," he began, and felt the tears flow as they often did when the Holy One gave him a prophecy to speak out to the people. He knew not what it would be yet, but he suspected. And even as the words poured forth, he felt a resistance to them, a fear for the future of his church.

"Ignatius will soon go to his fathers, and my time is coming as well." His tears fell unchecked, matched by the emotion of others in the room. "But God is faithful and will not leave His people bereft. Even now there is one among you who will be raised to lead."

They waited, he knew. Waited for him to speak a name. But though the name was given to him, it was not for him to speak it yet, the Spirit said.

The knowing, the word of prophecy, was finished. The room buzzed, but Malik turned back to the ledge, back to the star-flecked sky, and shivered.

He is so young, Lord. So foolish and lacking in maturity. Surely not. Surely not.

But the Lord had spoken. And so Malik bowed his head, though filled with fear.

Yes, Malik. Julian will lead My church.

SEVENTEEN

MEN AND THEIR PLANS.

Cassia brushed a pile of pebbles together, scooped them with her hands, and dropped them into a chipped pot. She perched on the narrow ledge where Julian worked, three stories above the street level. In the past few days, Julian had been assigned a particular area to hack away, and when it was discovered Cassia had no fear of the great height, she was given the task of cleaning up his debris.

"Good progress today." Julian wiped the sweat from his forehead with the back of his arm.

Cassia grunted. Her mind was full of Julian's plan to engage Malik's friends to find jobs in the palace and help get Alexander out.

It all reminded her of Aretas's elaborate plots. And more than that, it left nothing for her to do. *Am I to go on clearing rocks, taking no action to save my son?*

The notion galled her. She had relied on men to rescue and take care of her for too many years. But that time had ended, and she would be strong on her own behalf. Who were these friends of Malik's that they would help her?

"Your admirer is staring again." Julian interrupted her reverie. She looked up at him, confused.

"There." Julian jutted his chin toward a ledge farther down where Og, a younger mason, chipped at the rock wall but with his eyes trained upward.

Cassia snorted and returned to her cleanup.

"You are not flattered?" Julian's voice was teasing. "He is very handsome. At least that's what I hear."

"Flattered, perhaps. Interested, no." She dropped a few rock chips and chased them before they fell from the ledge.

"Not what you are looking for?"

After a strong exhale, Cassia stared Julian down. He was clearly baiting her. Fine. She would tell him what she thought. "I am not looking at all, Julian. I have found men in general to be disastrous for me."

Julian whistled through his teeth and kept working. "All of us, swept aside like so many rock chips?"

"You don't know me, Julian. I am finished with men."

He stopped long enough to stare down at her. She shook her head and hoped he understood the message: *Do not ask.*

The midday call came up from the ground, and Cassia picked her way down the rough-cut steps for the brief meal and respite from the sun. Julian followed, but she ignored him. He was in a bantering mood today, and it made her feel unbalanced.

The workers ducked into the lower level of the tomb, under one of the massive arches that had already been carved, and found places on the dirty floor. Three servants circulated, handing bowls of bread and chunked meat in a thick gravy. Cassia downed the food hungrily, sitting with the other women she had befriended over the days of work. Julian sat nearby.

The servants brought beer, made from strongly leavened bread crumbled into water and warmed over a slow fire. Bits of bread still lingered in the cup. Cassia passed her bowl back to the servant unfinished in the customary way. It was the only food they would receive.

The talk at the meal was all of the day's religious ceremonies. Cassia asked Adva, a new friend, about the significance.

"You'd think they would give us a holiday," Adva muttered between bites of thick bread. "But only the royals are important enough to take time away from all their hard, hard work."

Cassia gave her a smile of agreement, as she felt the same hostility for the royal family, albeit for different reasons. "What does the royal family do on the day of the full moon?" She finished her meal and accepted the jug of lukewarm water being passed from hand to hand.

Her friend shrugged. "It's the queen more than anyone." She pointed across the open space outside the tomb to the precipice of the massive rocky cliff. "She is carried to the High Place to make sacrifices, and then there is a feast in the palace tonight."

Cassia squinted at the top of the cliff, but the plateau was so far above, she could see no activity. The thought of that windswept exposure made her shudder.

"It must take half the day for the queen to get up there and back."

Adva brushed crumbs from her coarse white tunic and stood. "Never bothered to try it."

Cassia turned to search out Julian, wanting his opinion. He had been close enough to hear and now raised his eyebrows at her. "I know that look. What are you planning?"

She jumped to her feet. "The queen is occupied throughout the day. Gone from the palace!"

"The king is still there. And enough slaves and servants to stop an army, no doubt."

Cassia rubbed her hands against her thighs and looked out toward the palace. "If I can get in there to see the king, I know he will listen to me. It is only that woman—" She left her thought unfinished and hurried out of the tomb without waiting for Julian's response.

"Stay a moment!"

She was already in the street when he caught up, and she saw Malik walking toward them. The afternoon sun had driven most indoors, and the street was quiet.

"What has happened?" the old man asked.

"Nothing yet." Cassia clapped her hands together. "That is the problem. But I am going to change that."

Julian informed Malik of her plan while she shielded her eyes from the sun and studied the palace in the distance. She was anxious to be off. *I don't need the permission of these two.*

Malik's attention was all on Julian, however. "Go with her."

Cassia kicked at the dirt with her heel. "I do not need—"

But Malik still spoke only to Julian. "The forces there, they are strong. The queen's role as high priestess affords her much power, and it is centered there in the palace. A dark place indeed." He gripped Julian's arm. "Pray against it, my boy. Encircle her with prayer and protection."

Cassia understood none of it. "I am going." She left the two behind her. Julian was at her side a moment later. She spoke without turning. "Do not tell me I am not strong enough to face the king."

"There are forces that are stronger than even you, Cassia."

In truth, she was glad, very glad, for Julian's presence. Though she was not interested in giving her heart to another man, she had decided Julian could be a good friend. She admired his strength and could learn from it.

Her anger and desperation built as she stalked down the street. She had not seen Alexander in more than a week, and the separation was like a spreading infection.

They passed the housing district on their right, with its flat-topped roofs empty of women performing their household duties for the afternoon. On the left, the market street's taverns and shops had lowered their flaps.

They reached the palace steps and Cassia did not slow in her ascent, not even as she remembered being thrown down them the last time she was there. They crossed the portico, into the front passage-way. Only then did Cassia consider that perhaps she would not get far enough to reach the king. She glanced back to Julian, but his eyes were unfocused and his lips moved silently. Did he pray to his gods as Malik had instructed? The thought unnerved her. But perhaps his prayers were working, for they continued unaccosted.

Their good fortune did not hold. At the edge of the palace's lush garden courtyard, several male slaves appeared, their bare chests rippling with muscles and biceps that held their arms nearly aloft. Cassia slowed. "I am the mother of the prince, Alexander. I wish to see the king."

Beyond the slaves, the courtyard was an oasis in the desert, a large square of greenery, tumbling over white marble benches and paving stones. In the center, a huge fountain sculpture of a goddess sent water crashing to the pool beneath it.

The slaves said nothing, but Cassia had already spotted the king, redolent in the center of the courtyard, on a chaise beside the fountain. Two women stood on either side of him, fanning him with large woven fronds, and a child-slave skimmed flies from the squared pool.

"King Rabbel!"

He opened one eye and turned his head toward her.

"It is Cassia, Alexander's mother. I must speak with you!"

He pulled himself to a sitting position and studied her a moment, then waved her over. She approached, sensing the slaves held Julian at the entrance to the courtyard.

Then I shall do this alone.

She drew close to the fountain, and its circular wall of inlaid red-and-black tiles seemed like a series of hostile eyes, watching each step she took.

"I thought you had left Petra." The king pursed his lips and looked her up and down.

"I could not leave my son, King. Surely you understand that."

Rabbel smiled and leaned back in his chair. "I do not pretend to understand mothers, let alone foreign ones."

Cassia tightened her muscles to control her fury, fearing she might attack Rabbel. "King, a boy needs his mother. I am asking you to allow us to remain together."

"You want to live in the palace, do you?" Again, his tone was amused.

"I care not where I live, as long as it is with my son!" She turned cold eyes on him. "I will live anywhere you say, Rabbel. And I will bring Alexander to you as often as you wish. Only let me remain with my son!"

Rabbel pulled a grape from the nearby plate and placed it in his mouth. "He has been given to Bethea. She can mother him." He shrugged. "Limp little thing that she is, it would do her good."

She straightened. "And when your son, Aretas, was parted from you, did you content yourself with the thought there would be others to take your place in his life?"

The king's face darkened, and warmth rose through her neck and face. She dropped to the marble floor beside his feet and placed her hands and forehead on his ankles. "I will do whatever you ask of me." She knew well what she offered, for she had seen his look of interest. Could Julian hear from the courtyard's edge? He would know what kind of woman she was.

Rabbel waved away the two attendant slaves, leaving them alone.

She grew cold and pulled her hands from his body. Looking up from her knees, she met his eyes and saw he considered her request. He would let her stay in the palace, perhaps, if she made herself available. The thought both sickened and strengthened her.

There was no cost too high to protect Alexander.

But the king's attention shifted from her, toward the entrance to the courtyard, and without turning Cassia sensed a dark and heavy presence, as though a cold wind had tunneled into the palace and wrapped them all in icy tendrils.

"Isn't this a lovely sight." The voice, low and threatening, moved across the courtyard.

Cassia stood and turned to face the queen. The woman's pale skin stood in contrast with the black hair that framed her face. Her thin red lips were a tight slash.

Behind her, Cassia caught a strange glance of Julian, again with his eyes closed, and his hands raised to waist high and palms outward, as though he would push away the dark threat.

The queen swept toward them, her dark robes billowing. "Did I not instruct you to leave the city?" She turned to her husband. "Rabbel, this woman is a danger to the future of your kingdom. And she has disobeyed a royal command. She should be executed at once." Hagiru snapped a finger and two slaves moved toward Cassia.

Rabbel held up a hand. "Peace, wife. She means no harm."

Hagiru halted in her angry march, close enough for Cassia to see her flaring nostrils and clenched teeth. Her slaves stopped behind her. "She does not understand that Alexander belongs to Petra. She would have him scrabble in the dirt with her, a filthy peasant."

Cassia lifted her chin to speak, but Rabbel cut her off. "She is a mother who misses her son." He stood to move behind Cassia. "Have some pity."

Hagiru studied Rabbel for a moment. "Very well." She gave a tight shrug of one shoulder. "We shall not execute her. But she must leave the city!"

Cassia waited for Rabbel's disagreement, but instead she felt the force of Hagiru's control reach past her and grab at the king's will-power. It shook her, this nearly tangible hold the queen seemed to have on Rabbel.

He sighed. "Perhaps that would be best."

Cassia's heart crashed to the ground.

Hagiru's triumphant eyes shifted to Cassia. She flicked her head and her two slaves approached.

Cassia twisted from them. "I can go myself."

She tried to push past the cold figure of Hagiru, but the queen shifted to stand in her way, then leaned forward to whisper into her ear. "Careful. Not everything I do is known by the king."

Cassia sidestepped the woman and walked to where Julian had remained through the encounter.

"Come." She grabbed his still-raised arm. "Your prayers have done nothing here."

EIGHTEEN

JULIAN ALLOWED CASSIA TO PULL HIM FROM THE COURTYARD, but he retreated without turning his back on the queen. Cassia did not see the pure hatred that poured into him from Hagiru. He and the queen locked gazes for only a moment, but it was long enough to realize she saw him as an adversary.

Cassia was wrong. His prayers *had* been effective here, far more than she could understand.

The dark presence that had rushed into the palace on the heels of the queen seemed to wash over him like a foul clot of mud. His spirit became at once alert to a clawing desperation to destroy, destroy, *destroy*.

He had begun to pray, knowing no other weapon with which to fight the presence.

Father, shield me from the flaming arrows of the evil one.

The evil did not retreat, but he felt it checked, as though it waited for him to weaken.

Escaping the courtyard changed nothing. The palace was full of the darkness.

He turned at last in the front hall, ready to whisk Cassia down to the sunbaked street. She was gone.

Fear sparked along his veins.

Senses unnaturally heightened, he heard the scrape of sandal on stone at the end of the hall. He caught sight of a flutter of white fabric before it vanished around a corner.

He called a hushed command after her. "Cassia, stop!"

Clearly she was oblivious to the danger, a threat more deadly than simply an angry queen. Julian felt a surge of protective fear. *Where are you, Cassia?* He ran for the end of the hall.

She had made it clear she did not want him, but he would not leave her to the destructive power that surrounded this place.

Around the corner, he skidded to a stop. They were on the west side of the palace, where a large courtyard was bordered by a range of stables on one side and the shade of trellised vines hung over the other. The Temple of al-'Uzza towered alongside, and Cassia knelt in the center of a small, sandy enclosure with a waist-high stone wall.

She knelt beside Alexander.

A woman stood nearby. Long dark hair and an uncertain demeanor. She chewed her lip as though deciding whether or not to raise an alarm.

Julian felt the suffocating pressure grow again, a surging call to stand and protect mother and son in this place for a few moments. It was not simply his affection for Cassia. It was like a holy calling. He held back, raised his palms to the two, and lifted silent prayer.

Behind his prayer, his thoughts tumbled like water over rocks. *What is happening to me?*

Again he felt his senses grow impossibly acute. He could hear the talk of palace slaves somewhere inside, feel the quality of light shift as the sun moved, smell the burnt remains of a sacrifice.

He did not take his eyes from Cassia. She slipped her head covering down behind her head and embraced the boy, burying her face in his neck. Alexander patted her back, like one older than his years.

They spoke in whispers, and Cassia smiled, a wide, toothy smile. He had never seen her happy.

All the while, arms upraised, he continued to pray, to plead with the Father to keep all enemies away, to protect Cassia, to watch over Alexander. And he could feel the darkness. He had the strange sensation that he hovered over the two, arms outstretched like mighty wings, taking the brunt of the onslaught of evil, protecting them somehow, in some way far beyond his own ability.

He began to tire—and the presence was there, beating against him, waiting, waiting for its chance.

The woman with Alexander stared at him through eyes like pitch, and he sensed she was held in place against her will.

"Cassia," he finally whispered, drawing her attention. "It is time."

She frowned and shook her head. Alexander looked over to him and brightened. The boy waved a greeting, and Julian could read his name on the boy's lips.

Julian slipped into the sandy enclosure, close enough to speak to Cassia, still trying to deflect the evil. "We must leave, Cassia."

She glanced up at the woman, who seemed to be Alexander's caretaker. Was this the wife of Aretas Cassia had told him about? She seemed to have suddenly awakened. Had he been the one to keep her from acting? She tugged at her hair. "I will scream if you try to take him."

Julian felt himself slipping. He put his hands on Cassia's shoulders, where she still knelt in the sand before the beautiful boy. "Come." He bent to whisper in her ear. "We will return. Remember the plan. It is dangerous to stay."

She shook off his hands. "I only want to be with my son."

He was tired. So tired. But he could not let go yet. She was in danger. "Cassia! We are leaving *now*."

Her ramrod backbone collapsed, and she gathered Alexander into her arms once again.

"Be strong, my son." She pressed him against her. "Do not let them hurt you." She rocked back on her heels and placed her hands on his cheeks. "How can I make you understand?" Her tears were flowing now, but Julian's concern for their safety grew.

She looked up at him. "I don't want to frighten him." Then in a whisper to Alexander, "If they are hurting you, you must run. Even if you don't know where I am. Do you understand?"

The boy's eyes were round and luminous. He nodded, lips pressed together.

Cassia looked to the woman, still held at a distance. "Take care of him."

The dark presence increased around them. Julian had weakened, and now it was too late. He was too exhausted to spread strong wings over them again. He reached under Cassia's arm and pulled her to standing, then toward himself. She leaned down for a last kiss on Alexander's cheek, then let Julian take her from the enclosure.

He did not release her until they were on the street, but then he broke away. He labored for breath, felt a bitter nausea reaching up into his throat.

Cassia walked as one dead, seeing nothing of his exhaustion. Had she even felt the evil?

They walked in silence for some minutes, but then Cassia made a tiny sound, the whimper of a bird caught in a trap, and she seemed to crumple before his gaze. He caught her and wrapped his arms around her shoulders. She buried her face in his chest and wept.

The palace encounter had so shaken him that he felt he might weep as well. The force of oppression that had been so tangible, the sense of power flowing through him—power to understand, to protect, to fight—and now this small woman in his arms, a woman who had burned through his resistance in only a few short weeks.

"There is something terrible in that palace, Julian." Her voice was muffled against his chest. "I felt it pounding through me like . . . like a river of evil."

He stroked her hair. "There is much you need to understand, Cassia. A battle is being waged here in Petra, and I fear your Alexander is at the heart of it."

She raised her face to him, still in his arms. "You and Malik, you seem to understand. Do you know how to fight this battle?"

Julian looked back toward the palace. Did he? He had never experienced anything like the confrontation he had just encountered. And though he had nothing to show for his effort in the palace, no sculpture created, no audience impressed, he sensed his work there had been more important than anything he had ever accomplished.

He had come to Petra to remain hidden and to remain apart.

He laid his hand on Cassia's cheek. He had failed.

NINETEEN

CASSIA HAD THOUGHT SHE COULD NOT CONTINUE TO WAKE
and sleep, work and eat, after once more leaving Alexander in the
palace. But somehow the sun rose and set each day as it always had,
and she rose with it, spent her days at the tombs and her evenings with
Zeta and Talya. They had a small plot of land near the wheat fields
on the northern side of the city where they grew herbs. Cassia willingly shared some of her secrets, and the two women swore the plants
doubled in growth each time Cassia touched them.

But her heart was in none of it, not the tomb work nor the herbs,
not even the evenings when Malik and Julian came to visit with
the women. Sometimes Julian asked Cassia to tell him more about
Alexander, and the stories she told made her feel connected to her son
still, as if she had given him a thousand kisses and tucked him into
bed in the next room.

Often Julian and Malik talked with Zeta and Talya about their
One God. The talk was odd to her, as Malik and the women were
Nabataean and Julian was Roman, and they seemed to want to
include her, a Syrian. "God of all," Malik would tell her. She did not

want to contradict him, but their god had done nothing for her. Still, she sensed a darkness in the palace and wished she understood more of this battle.

Julian's plan to remove Alexander took shape by degrees. Several of Malik's friends, his *church* he called it, had found work in the palace. Cassia did not understand why they would do this for her, and she was grateful, but the plan moved too slowly. Her son was not safe.

So one evening, when the women had left to join the gathering of the church and Cassia had stayed behind, she slipped down from the rock-wall home and crossed the city to the south, back toward the end of the gorge that had brought her into Petra.

She had not been this way since the night she'd arrived and the trader had followed her to the amphitheatre. But the wide street led only to the gorge, past the theatre, and she found it easily.

Her next task would not be accomplished so simply.

The amphitheatre, like so much of Petra, had been cut almost entirely out of the rock cliff. Its half circle of seats divided into six wedge-shaped sections, the *cunei*. The orchestra had been cut from an outcropping of bedrock and extended across the entire stage.

Cassia entered at the second level of the three-story facade that faced the seating area and quickly found the barrel-vaulted corridors that would take her down a level to the orchestra.

The darkened passageway slanted downward, then led to steps. She emerged at the side of the stage, her footsteps echoing back from the seating. The three-story *scanae* at her back was clad with marble and painted plaster, but the seats were red Petra sandstone, and the setting sun lit them like fire. She searched the side walls of the theatre for a passageway below.

She found a narrow slit in the rock and entered it, ducking under the lintel into the darkness. The passage smelled of damp stone, perhaps a spring that flowed under the theatre.

Cassia called out a greeting, hoping for a response. Ahead, a dim light beckoned her to enter deeper into the bowels of the theatre.

A face appeared at the end of the passage, an older man if the long white-gray hair was an indication.

She pressed on and the man stared, as though he had never seen a woman below.

"I am looking for the gladiator training," Cassia called.

He shook his head. "None for sale."

She reached the end and stopped before the old man. He wore a rough tunic with the sleeves cut off, revealing a network of ancient scars on his forearms. His hair hung below his shoulders, unwashed for some time.

"I do not wish to purchase anyone. I wish to find his trainer."

His eyebrows shot up and he clicked his yellowed teeth together twice. "Follow me."

He led her deeper underground, through narrow passages lit only by an infrequent torch and smelling of unwashed men. Cassia was rethinking her decision, as it felt as though she descended to the underworld with this man. Finally they reached some sort of central chamber with cells surrounding it.

Their arrival was met with a shuffling scramble of sandals and the hoots of a dozen men in the cells.

"Stand down, fighters," the old man called. "She is not here for any of you jackals."

The lewd calls continued, and Cassia lowered her chin but studied the men from the corner of her eye. Foreign, most of them. No doubt captured somewhere and marched here to be trained for the entertainment of the city. Had any of them been fighters before their capture?

"Now." The old man turned to her. "You are selling a slave, I take it? How old? How strong?"

Cassia shook her head. "I have nothing to sell."

He clacked his teeth together again. *Strange habit.* "Nothing to buy, nothing to sell. You interest me very little, then, woman."

"I wish to be trained."

The chamber erupted in laughter.

The old trainer held up a hand, his wide smile still showing those teeth. "You wish to be a gladiator."

Cassia lifted her head. "No. Only to fight like one."

The old man grew serious and studied her. "He beats you, then?"

Cassia frowned.

"Your husband."

She hesitated. Would he be more likely to train her if he thought it was merely for defense against a nasty husband? She searched his eyes a moment, reading into his soul, and found her answer. "I am tired of being his victim."

The man clacked his teeth and nodded. "These men today, they think they can do as they wish with their wives . . ." His voice trailed off as he turned away from her, still muttering. She had read him correctly. Something in his past had given him a loathing for abusive men. Odd, given his line of work.

He turned back to her, worn strips of leather in his hands, and held two of them to her. "Let's see what you can do."

Cassia took the leather and eyed the gladiators, each of them standing at the front of their cells in rapt attention. "Here?"

He followed her gaze. "Hmm. I suppose not. Come."

He led her back through the dim underground passage and out into the fading light of the amphitheatre. She followed his lead in wrapping the leather strips around her hands as they walked. "No one comes when there is no event. We will be alone."

And then, before she had a chance to prepare, he flew at her, his right arm aloft.

Cassia reacted out of instinct, with the defensive dodge that Aretas had taught her, and the old man's arm swung down through empty air. She whirled, leather-wrapped fists raised.

He chuckled. "Perhaps I should hire you for the arena after all. Think what crowds would come." He pointed to the vacant seating area. "You'd have all eight thousand seats filled each night."

Cassia half smiled and dropped her fists a few degrees. "You have seen the extent of my skill, I am afraid. And one can only evade for so long. I wish to learn the *offense*."

He smiled, and she saw that she had won him over already. "Then I shall teach you."

"I want to come every few days. I will pay."

He held up a hand. "We shall talk of money later. For now, let us have our first lesson."

Cassia inhaled and stepped forward.

"What is your name, little woman?"

"Cassia."

He bowed. "And I am Yehosef."

Cassia dropped her head. "I am honored to be under your learned instruction, Yehosef."

He grinned at the flattery. "So, you are ready, Cassia?"

"I am ready."

Within minutes they were engaged in a mock battle, though it felt nearly real. Yehosef's long white-gray hair flew out from his head in damp strands. Cassia blocked bony forearms with her own and tripped over swinging feet. But as the shadows grew long over the stage and the scrape of their feet and grunts of pain filled the theatre, Cassia felt a sense of power flow through her and it was good.

There had been nothing but inaction since she had come to Petra. Fruitless, frustrating stillness. But this, to fight like this, it felt like strength. Her arms ached and her vision blurred with sweat and effort, but still she fought on. The thought of Alexander's abuse in the palace and the impossibility of his rescue fueled her anger and strengthened her arms.

Yehosef spun and struck her shoulder and she went down. She turned in time, but her head and her cheek smacked the cold paving stone. She tasted blood inside her mouth but jumped to standing and whirled to face him, fists raised.

Yehosef clapped his leather-bound hands. "Like a panther she is, with the energy to match!"

Cassia remained still, chest heaving.

"I have never seen the like in a woman. But that is all for our first night." The old man bowed. "You will come again soon."

She unwrapped her hands, then reached under her tunic for her money pouch. Again, Yehosef held up a hand. "Later. When I have seen your skill increase."

Cassia bit her lip, then ventured another request. "I want to learn to use a sword as well."

Yehosef's brow furrowed. "Your husband—"

"He puts me in dangerous situations." Her experience with Aretas would serve some good after all. It gave her story the ring of truth. "He . . . he sometimes brings danger upon our family. If we are attacked, I want to be prepared."

He still frowned but nodded slowly. "Next time, the sword."

She smiled. "Thank you, Yehosef."

He stepped closer and looked down into her eyes. "Be wary, Cassia. You are a fighter, it is true. But you are not yet ready to fight. Do not be overconfident."

She nodded and handed him the leather strips. "I will see you soon."

She left him on the stage and ascended through the corridor up to the street level again, her legs aching with the upward climb.

She had only gained the middle level of the *scanae* when a man jumped from the shadows to block her path. She cried out.

He was huge and dressed as a slave, with a shaved head and two gold posts through his ears, symbols of his service. Cassia had the sense she'd seen him before. The palace?

He reached out for her and she tried to block his arms, but this was no training exercise, and he was nearly twice her size. He wrapped beefy arms around her middle and lifted her from the ground.

She screamed and kicked at him.

A moment later he released her and dropped her to the pavement on her hands and knees. Then fell beside her.

She flipped her body and stayed in a crouch.

Yehosef stood over the prone attacker, grinning. "Your husband?"

She shook her head. "How did you do that?"

He shrugged. "We shall leave that for another lesson." His face darkened. "Training with swords, now this." He jabbed a thumb toward the man on the pavement, who groaned and stirred. "Perhaps you should tell me more of your troubles."

Cassia stood. "I don't know who he is." It was true, in part.

Yehosef scowled. "Then we shall ask him."

He bent to the man and pressed his fingers into the place where his neck and shoulders met. The man howled and curled into Yehosef's hand.

I must learn how to do that.

"Who are you?" the old gladiator asked.

"A slave, nothing more." He tried to wriggle from Yehosef's grasp, but he held him still, then kicked at the slave's finely woven tunic. "Not like any slave I have seen." He drove his thumb and forefinger deeper, and Cassia winced.

"In . . . in the p-palace." The slave moaned and closed his eyes.

Yehosef's glance shot to Cassia. How much did she dare tell him?

"You are not surprised," Yehosef said to her. "That much I can see." To the palace slave he said, "Were you sent to kill her?"

He nodded, then sucked in breath. Yehosef released him with a shove. "Tell them you were successful. It will be better for all."

"Until she comes again to the palace." The slave rubbed his neck and pushed up to his knees. "And then what of me?"

Yehosef shrugged. "Then return today and tell them you failed."

The slave's eyes went dark, and Cassia feared he would lunge at her again, but Yehosef advanced on him, and the man held up his hands.

"Go!" Yehosef raised a hand. "Before I regret my mercy!"

The slave scrabbled to his feet and backed away, then turned and ran.

She waited for Yehosef to face her. When he did, she read suspicion in his expression. "It is not healthy for a man to raise the ire of the royal family."

"I am sorry, Yehosef." She hesitated, then decided to take the risk and tell him everything.

When she finished, he rubbed at the stubble on his chin. "And now the queen wants you dead."

Cassia exhaled. "I should have expected it, once she learned I had not left Petra."

"Indeed."

She feared she had lost her opportunity to prepare for the fight to retrieve Alexander. Yehosef no doubt relied upon the good favor of the royal house.

He looked up the street, toward the city, where her attacker had disappeared. "If that brute decides the truth will better serve him, then neither of us is safe."

"It was unfair of me—"

His gaze returned to hers. "So you had better come back soon."

TWENTY

THE YOUNG WOMAN BEFORE THE CITY COUNCIL LOWERED her eyes at the accusations that flew against her from the semicircle of white marble seats in the Great Hall. Torches ranged the room, smoking as the meeting wore on into the evening.

Malik waited for his chance to speak, outraged that the only reason the council was unsympathetic to her plight was she was Jewish. She had tried to lay claim to her late husband's property, but his family was attempting to reclaim it because she was foreign.

He served on the city council for this reason—to be involved in the ongoing relations between the Nabataeans of Petra and the many others who called the city home, including Jews.

Twice he stood and voiced his opposition. Both times he was shouted down. He sat and pounded a fist against his palm.

The room buzzed with conversations both public and private as council members griped to those sitting next to them. The half circle of stone seats trapped the conversation and swirled it into confusion.

Others on the council believed him to be a Jew-lover. Well, what of it? He had embraced the Jewish Messiah, it was true. And he held a deep desire to see them realize their Messiah waited for them with outstretched arms. He had studied the Law and the Prophets, and his mentor, Paul of Tarsus, had been Jewish.

"She is not one of us," someone yelled. "Why should we give our property away?"

Once again Malik stood and shouted, "Because it is right and just!"

The girl glanced up at him, gratitude in her eyes.

But the council majority would not be swayed, and the meeting ended with the woman thrust from them, her property officially seized.

Malik left immediately, not caring to engage his fellow council members in conversation. The darkness of the city left him blind after the bright torches of the Great Hall, but he walked on by memory, crossed the *Cardo Maximus*, passed the Nymphaeum's noisy fountain, and entered the housing district at its beginning, wanting to stay off the main street where he might be approached. The street narrowed to a mere alley, but Malik had lived here for a lifetime and knew well the cobbled ruts. Here and there lamplight flickered from open doorways.

All the way he fumed, replaying the meeting in his mind, making his arguments to the empty night air as though he were given another chance to speak.

Though the Jews brought with them valuable trading connections because of their access to the Great Sea and they held positions of wealth and influence in the city, there seemed to be some inborn animosity that all of Arabia had for the Jews. It was hard to understand, as they had not been a military power for many years, swallowed by Rome more than thirty years earlier. That the Jewish people had no love for the Christians, he knew. But by God's grace the believers had been grafted into Israel, whether or not the Jews approved.

Malik scuffled through the dark alleyway behind a line of mud-brick houses. The alley was rancid with the stench of waste and garbage, and the darkness was nearly total. He ran a hand along the stone wall on his right and fixed his eyes on two yellow torches in the distance, staring at him like two evil yellow eyes.

Why did he even bother? He should step down from the council. It did no good to call out his opinions there, a lone voice among hostility. Discouragement rolled over him, and he dropped his head and shuffled forward, heedless of his surroundings.

Perhaps none of what he did mattered. Rome was beginning to roust believers from their churches and make examples of them. How long until they came after him? Ignatius went boldly to martyrdom. Would he do the same? The melancholy melted into fear, slowing his steps.

He should be talking to Jesus about this, not himself. He resisted the Spirit's pull on his heart and continued his reverie, winding through the dark streets toward his home.

His thoughts tumbled and seemed joined by other voices that accused.

And then the other voices grew louder than his own.

Malik quickened his steps. The voices followed, shouting to him.

You cannot lead people! You cannot even be heard in a council meeting!

He tripped over a loose stone in the alley, caught himself, and hurried on. His heart felt squeezed, as though the voices had hands and coiled into his very being.

Let go, useless old man. Give up this fruitless effort to be a revolutionary. You cannot fight Rome!

The voices clawed at his mind, and Malik rubbed his blurred eyes, trying to rid himself of the foul presence.

But when the inner cacophony had nearly blinded him and he

felt the urge to hurl himself from the High Place, Malik finally quit his panicked run through the alleys and drew himself upright, hands held before him as though for protection.

"Enough!"

The voices fought him, a roar of fury in his head.

"I know you, prince of Petra! You may have this city, but you do not have me!"

The pitch lowered, like a threatening, angry growl.

"In the name of Jesus Christ, Son of God, I command you to leave!"

The voices were a buzz now, like an annoying insect in his courtyard garden.

"Jesus, I come under Your protection. I ask You to remove this evil from my presence."

There came a rushing sound, like air being sucked from lungs.

In the stillness that followed, Malik leaned on the nearest brick wall, his head against his forearm and his eyes closed. He asked for forgiveness for the thoughts he had allowed, for the anger that had made him weak and vulnerable to the voices that were ever watchful for their opportunity.

A warmth filled him. He was forgiven.

Behind him, the scuffle of someone moving through the darkness pulled him from the wall.

A figure appeared out of the night, only cubits from him. A man, with a small dagger held outward from his waist.

Malik nearly laughed. He had known since Julian reported his encounter at the palace that the queen would retaliate. She knew the only power in Petra that ever held her in check resided with his church.

But her killer had chosen an inopportune time. Malik had called on the mighty Name, and the power that filled him now was greater than any Roman shield.

The man rushed him. Malik held his weathered hands before him. The attacker was flung backward, as though he had run into a wall.

Fury crossed the man's features and Malik knew he drew strength from the evil one. But it was not enough. He ran at Malik again and was again rebuffed. This time the knife clattered to the street. Clearly he would not be successful, and rather than try a third time, he turned on his heels and fled.

Malik once again sagged against the cold wall, breathing a prayer of thanks.

The battle will go on, even without you.

It was the Voice he loved this time, though the words were convicting rather than comforting.

"Malik!" The call came from the end of the dark alley.

"Julian!" Malik found his breathing heavy. "What are you doing here?"

The boy's eyes scanned the alley. "I . . . I do not know. I was waiting for you to return, and I felt . . . I felt something."

Malik stood and faced him, pulling the boy's attention to himself. "Tell me."

Julian swallowed and tried to shrug as though it were nothing. "It was like a voice. Not aloud. In my head." He watched Malik, perhaps waiting for ridicule, but Malik only nodded, willing him to finish.

"I heard, *Malik is in danger.* And when I ran from the house, I knew to come this way." Again he shrugged. "But you are in no danger. And I, perhaps, am going mad."

Malik smiled and joined the boy as they walked through the night toward his home. He did not speak, for his thoughts were all between him and his Lord tonight.

The Father had not sent Julian to rescue him. This he knew. But He had sent the boy for a reason.

The battle will go on without you.

Yes, Lord. It is time.

He closed his eyes in a heartfelt prayer of surrender, and the warm tears that followed were tears of both relief and the unknown.

It is time to pass the torch to the next generation. Time to trust You with the future.

TWENTY-ONE

·◆·

CASSIA FEARED GOING BACK TO WORK AT THE TOMB after her encounter at the palace. Hagiru's slave had somehow tracked her to the amphitheatre. Was there anywhere in Petra where she was safe?

But she must work, to pay for her keep at Zeta's house and her training with Yehosef. And when Alexander was back in her care, they would need money to escape.

So she walked to the tomb each morning to put in another day of climbing and collecting rock chips and hoped the crowd of masons and sculptors that swarmed over the tomb made her invisible.

Julian insisted on accompanying her to the tomb in the early mornings and back to the house at the end of the dry, dusty workday. She had told him nothing of what happened at the theatre, but their experience in the palace was enough to create concern. Secretly, she cherished his unease for her. It had been a long time since anyone had cared for her safety. Though she reminded herself often that the only man in her life was still missing his front teeth.

In the evenings Zeta and Talya would often disappear to meet with the church. Zeta was mysterious about it, and it troubled Cassia.

But those evenings alone were her chance to escape to the amphitheatre, round up Yehosef from his dark chambers underneath, and have him teach her more of what he knew. She kept this from the women, and especially from Julian, sensing he would not approve. He was a man who liked things done his way, and he had a plan.

Indeed, as the days passed she had to admit that his plan progressed. Almost daily she heard reports of those friends who had found work in the palace, their names unknown to her.

At the end of one such day, she returned from the work site, climbed to the rock home, and waved a small good-bye to Julian in the street below. She ducked beneath the blanket-wall of the home, into the sheltered front room.

Talya gave a squeal of delight at her entrance, clapped her hands together, and jumped from where she had been sitting on the floor, mending palace robes.

Cassia laughed. "I hope you are not wanting me to finish that." She pointed to the strip of cloth cast to the floor. "I am no good with a needle."

Talya shook her head and bounded forward to wrap Cassia in an embrace. "I am to help take care of him!"

Cassia pulled back from the girl's enthusiasm. "Take care—"

"Of Alexander!"

Cassia's legs suddenly felt weak, and she grabbed at Talya's arms. "You have seen him?"

Talya grinned and bobbed her dark head. "More than seen him, Cassia. I have spent the afternoon with him, and will do so again tomorrow!"

Zeta appeared, all smiles, and led Cassia to a low chair. Her heart felt near to exploding. "Tell me." Her hands trembled. "Tell me everything."

Talya sat at Cassia's feet, her head against Cassia's knee, and spoke of the day, of walking the palace corridors with Alexander, of watching him play with two carved camels with ruby eyes. And Cassia begged for the smallest details, from what he ate to whether he ever laughed. When she had extracted every particular from Talya, she leaned her head back against the chair and closed her eyes and wept. To hear of him was not the same as seeing him, but it was a blessing all the same.

Talya slipped away and returned a moment later. "I told him I was a friend of his mother."

Cassia opened her eyes and lifted her head. Talya extended her hand, with something clasped in it.

"We made this together today." She dropped a beaded bracelet into Cassia's hand. "For you. And Alexander said to tell you he loves you very much, and he misses you."

Cassia took the bracelet of black-and-white stones, glanced at Zeta, whose eyes were bright with unshed tears, and whispered, "Thank you."

Young as she was, Talya seemed to sense Cassia needed to be alone, and she went back to her silent weaving at the back of the room. Zeta, too, busied herself at the table.

Cassia had come to love these women, this home with its color-striped rock walls and even brighter fabrics. The way Zeta hummed while she worked. Each time Cassia entered the cave-like dwelling, she felt at home.

But they were too good to her, Zeta and Talya. And even their unknown, unseen friends. Who were they? Why would they help her? What did they want from her? She had nothing to give.

What would happen when they realized this? Would they resent her? See she was not worth helping? And what would happen to Alexander then? For all her training with Yehosef, she needed them.

What could she do in return to earn the help they still seemed willing to give? The questions dampened her joy at the news of Alex and left her fearful.

Several nights later, when Zeta and Talya had gone to meet their friends and she had spent the evening training with Yehosef, Cassia hurried back to their home, sweaty and grimy from her encounters with the gladiator. She hoped to reach the ledge in time to clean up before the women returned.

But Talya met her in the street below, her expression desperate. Cassia's heartbeat raced.

"What is it?" She gripped Talya's arms. "What has happened to Alexander?"

"Not Alexander." Talya's breath came as though she had run to meet Cassia. "Julian."

"Take me."

Talya led Cassia toward the heart of the city, where the wealthier villas lined up against each other. Her words dashed over one another as they rushed through the street. "He was followed to our meeting. Guards from the palace, we think. They came in and . . . and started shouting and shoving people." Her voice shook and she swiped at her eyes. "We were all terrified. But then they singled out Julian and dragged him from the room, out to the street."

Cassia's heart went cold. "How severely is he hurt?"

"I do not know. Some of the others took him to Malik's home. I came to find you. I . . . I knew you would want to know."

Cassia nodded. "Thank you, Talya."

They wove through alleys and streets in the crowded housing district until Talya stopped at the entrance to a home, called out, and was greeted by a servant. He waved her in as though he knew her well, and Cassia followed, her eyes wide.

She had never dreamed Malik was a rich man. Respected, even revered, as a wise man, certainly. But his unassuming humility, his quiet service to everyone, spoke nothing of the wealth she saw here. "This is Malik's home?"

"Yes. How is Julian, Shamir?" Talya asked the servant.

"Beaten badly, but nothing appears to be broken, and there is not much blood." The servant spoke as though a friend of Talya's, and Cassia pushed the strange thought aside to dwell on later.

Julian will survive. She repeated the thought in her mind and heart, holding on to its comfort.

Shamir led them through the spacious courtyard, lit with torches and tended by several slaves who dusted and sprayed the vines.

When she and Talya reached the back room, Julian was pushing away the damp cloth a lovely young woman was trying to use on his bruised face.

His gaze went to the doorway and he smiled weakly at Cassia. "Not my finest hour."

Cassia exhaled, realizing she'd been barely breathing since Talya found her in the street. "You don't look so pretty either." She crossed the room to the bed.

The woman with the rag yielded her place, and Cassia read a wisp of resentment from her. She responded with her own flare of unreasonable jealousy. *Julian has me. He doesn't need more friends.* She sat on the edge of the bed and took his hand.

"Why?" She felt her anger building. "Why did they do this to you?"

Malik's voice answered from a shadowy corner of the room. "We must begin to expect this. The queen is becoming less tolerant of our presence. And after Julian's actions in the palace, it is not surprising he should be a target."

Cassia studied the old man, then looked back to Julian's bruised face. "Why you? You have done nothing!" Would the queen go after everyone important in her life?

Julian looked down, studied her hand on his, then covered it with his own, cradling her cold fingers in his warm grasp. When his eyes found hers and lingered on her face, something passed between them that shallowed Cassia's breathing. She tried to pull her hand away, but he would not allow it.

From the corner Malik said, "Because she senses what I have also been told. That Julian will be a mighty man for God in Petra."

Julian still held her hand, as though she were the one needing reassurance.

"But this happened because you were with me in the palace?" She broke free of Julian's hold on her, refusing to think about the way it had made her heart blaze. "It is my fault, all of this."

Malik appeared beside them and put his hand on her shoulder. "As brothers and sisters we have made a choice to stand with you, and to stand against the evil that pervades our city. This makes us a target, it is true. But it is our choice and not the fault of anyone."

Cassia wiggled away from his hand on her shoulder and stood. Her hands went to her hips and she felt her blood rising. "It is enough. All of this talk of your *friend*"—at this she looked at Talya—"your *brothers and sisters*." She turned to Malik. "I do not understand who you are or why you stand against anything or would help me."

Malik smiled, clearly amused at her outburst, and that infuriated her. "I want to know!"

He reached for her hand and took it between his own wrinkled ones. "Then you shall. You shall indeed." He turned to the others. "We must find a new place to meet, now that we have been noticed there. Tomorrow we will meet as usual and determine where we should go. Spread the word to the rest of the brothers and sisters."

There were nods around the room, and Cassia realized she would get nothing further from them until the next night.

And when the next day's work was done and she had insisted on walking home alone, Zeta met her in the street with a covered basket of hot bread. "Tonight you will be our guest. Come."

Zeta and Talya led her back to the empty tomb where Julian had first taken her, this time filled with many more people than she had first encountered. They pushed their way into the colorful, rock-hewn chamber, through the myriad faces—young and old, rich and poor, even slave and free, to Cassia's amazement. No matter the status, gender, or age, the faces shared one thing. There was a peaceful yet intense joy upon each. Cassia searched their eyes, tried to read some of them, looking for the reason. But it was a mystery to her. She could feel it strongly, but she could not understand it.

The chamber was not well lit, perhaps because all around the room they talked of "discovery" and "persecution." Only a few small lamps tucked into niches flickered through the chamber, leaving most in shadows, with their white tunics standing out below darker head coverings.

The crowd was not a shoving, pressing crowd. It was an embracing one, with people drawn into kisses of greeting and robust hugs. Cassia could not help but smile as several people wrapped their arms around her as well.

Already I love it here, whoever these people are!

She spotted Julian at the back of the chamber, near the burial slots, and he waved her over. She threaded through the press of people until she was at his side, then reached up with her fingertips to touch his bruised cheekbone with gentle fingers. It seemed to have purpled even more since she had last seen him.

He grasped her fingers and smiled. "It is nothing. Come, let's sit."

He led her to a corner near the front of the chamber, close to the central place where Malik stood, speaking softly to another older man. Cassia sensed immediately that Malik was the leader of the group, and it did not surprise her. But what did they gather to do? Did they plot the overthrow of the royal house? At the idea, her heart thudded against her chest.

But then there was singing. A low but joyous flow of words she did not recognize that began with Malik and spread through the chamber like a warm oil being poured out. She had heard nothing like it in all her life.

These songs, this room of people loving each other intensely—it was no military uprising. It was some kind of group dedicated to the gods. But it had nothing in common with the cold chants of Zerika, the temple priest back in Damascus. She closed her eyes as the music carried her on silky wings, and she began to sway with it. Inside her, a long-held tension began to unwind and relax. She could hear Malik's voice, deep and lovely, above the others. Beside her, Julian was part of it all.

And then Malik's voice melted from singing to speaking, a prayer over all of them. He prayed for the evil in Petra to be restrained and for the queen to be released from it to see the truth. All of these prayers he offered up in the name of someone named Jesus. *Jesus?*

They are Christians!

Cassia ran her gaze over the crowd once more, searching for any of the signs she would expect, things she had been told in Syria of the Christians. Atheists, all of them, it was said, because they would not worship the gods. They opposed those in power and withheld their money from many of the industries that supported the government, so most suspected they had some hidden plans of revolt.

Her mind spun. None of it seemed true. She looked to Julian, in prayer with the rest of them.

Julian too?

Malik was extending his hand toward her now and speaking her name.

"We have brought her to us this night because it is in her defense that we have begun to seek access to the palace, and she needs to know us." He bowed slightly in her direction. "Cassia, we have shown you trust by bringing you into our circle."

She dipped her head in response, still unsure of what all of this meant.

Malik seemed to sense her confusion, for he spoke only to her, though loud enough for the group to hear. "We are those of Petra who have become children of the One True God through faith in His Son, Jesus Christ, faith in His sacrifice that was the final payment for our sin. Many of the people of God, the Israelites, did not recognize their Messiah when He walked among them nearly one hundred years ago, but He was a Messiah for all nations, and God has graciously invited us into the family."

Malik seemed to want some response, so Cassia nodded. He turned to address the entire group. "But things are changing for the church in Petra, my friends. We have experienced many years of peace, but I fear such times are coming to an end."

Because of me? Cassia chewed her lip, waiting for the looks of condemnation. None came.

"We must not forget who we are." Malik smiled over the group. "Even if there is harsh persecution to come. Love each other well, and care for the hearts of your brothers and sisters. Fight for each other, fight against evil. Perhaps we have been complacent here in our safety. But we must not forget that we are in the midst of a perverse culture, and we must stand firm yet remain loving. Remember it is by our love they shall know we are His disciples. Love one another, and love them"—he extended a hand outward to the city—"pray for them and love them until they ask you why."

Cassia watched the joyful faces upturned to Malik. Only yesterday the ones he now asked them to love had been here with them and had beaten Julian. It made no sense to her. Beatings did not produce love. This she knew from experience.

"Tonight must be the last night that we meet here." Many of the faces lowered. "It is time to move on. Who can suggest a better place for our flock?"

Voices called out and various homes were offered, but each was turned down as too small. Indeed, they had clearly outgrown even their present location.

Cassia cleared her throat. "What about the tomb still being constructed? Where Julian and I work each day?"

Silence met her suggestion, and she feared she had been presumptuous but pressed on. "The inside is vast, with many chambers. You would be unheard. And no one goes near it once the sun is down."

Malik's lined face broke into a grin. "You will be one of us before long, my dear Cassia." He clapped his hands together and faced the group. "What do you say?"

There was general agreement around the chamber, and Cassia felt the warm glow of having been helpful, however slight her help. Julian leaned into her shoulder briefly and smiled.

Malik read to the group for a while, a letter from a friend of his, a Jewish Paul, whom Cassia gathered was no longer living. But the words seemed alive still, and Cassia drank them in, like water for a parched heart.

"'What if God did this to make the riches of his glory known to those destined for destruction, now the objects of his mercy, whom he prepared in advance for glory? We are those whom he called, not only from the Jews but also from the nations. As he says in Hosea, "I will call them *my people* who are not my people, and she who is not my Beloved, I will call Beloved."'"

The words went on, but Cassia only heard that one word, *beloved*, echoing through her heart. To be loved by such a God . . . She blinked away the sudden swell of emotion.

When Malik finished, she glanced at Julian and found him struggling with his own emotions. She tilted her head and studied him.

"That was a letter to my church in Rome," he whispered, "written not long before I was born. I heard it many times while growing up. It makes me long for home."

Cassia nodded as if the explanation satisfied, but in truth it only raised more questions.

After the reading of the letter, Malik spoke awhile, encouraging them again, then extended his hands. "We must pray in earnest, my family."

Around the room, hands were joined until they were each connected, and Cassia, too, was a part of their circle. Julian clasped her fingers in his own, and she shyly gave her hand to the girl beside her.

Many prayed to their One God then. She listened in wonder as they spoke to Him as though to a loving father. When they prayed for the Jews living among them and elsewhere and then, more shockingly, for Hagiru, Cassia studied their faces, searching for betrayal, for loyalty to the queen. But no, they prayed against the evil she sought to control but in truth controlled her, prayed for her to be released from its mighty hold.

But it was the hand of Julian on hers that most drew her attention. The gentle pressure, the way their hands seemed to fit together as though molded as one. And when the prayer was over and Julian met her eyes, she found herself a bit breathless. The girl beside her released Cassia's hand. Julian did not.

All too soon the meeting ended, out of fear of another attack, and they arranged to meet again in their new location two nights hence. Cassia hoped to be invited again, but she did not dare ask. Not yet.

Malik came to her as the group dispersed. "You have questions still, daughter?"

She frowned, not desiring to offend. "I have heard tales of the Christians." She glanced at those climbing down from the chamber. "But this—these people—"

Malik patted her arm. "Not as you expected?"

"You drink blood and eat flesh, it is said." She flushed. "You have no gods, no priests, no temples. You do not sacrifice. For all this, it is believed you are enemies of society, haters of mankind."

"And is this what you believe?" Malik's gaze on her was soft, full of love.

She spread her arms to the chamber. "How can I?"

Julian spoke beside her. "There is so much truth to share with you, Cassia. When you are ready."

She nodded, unsure if she would ever be ready.

On the road back to Zeta's home, she and Julian walked alone, leaving the rest of the church still talking with Malik.

Cassia moved slowly, still feeling the effects of the warm and joyous people, walking as though asleep and dreaming. Firelight at the edges of rock-wall homes winked at them as they walked, and somewhere in the distance an old woman chanted prayers to the goddess al-'Uzza, a deity very different from Julian's. The singsong chant rode on the breeze, and Cassia shivered.

Julian wrapped an arm around her shoulders. He did not speak, and Cassia was not yet ready to ask her questions, so they walked in silence past quiet homes with their hidden gardens spilling out the scent of white jasmine and warm fruit. She relaxed under his embrace.

If Alexander were waiting for her at home, she would have declared this the perfect night.

"I have a gift for you." Julian reached for a pouch tied to his waist. He stopped in the street to pull something from it, no bigger than his palm. Pale moonlight caught on the tiny white sculpture, revealing intricate details.

"A white tiger!" She took it from him and turned it in his hands. "How beautiful."

"I made it for Alexander. For you to give to him when he is returned to you."

Cassia stroked the tiger. Julian had known of Alexander's great love for animals from the stories he had drawn from her. She blinked back tears and smiled up at him. "Thank you, Julian. He will love it."

Ahead, a stocky figure walked toward them out of the shadows. Cassia had the passing thought that perhaps she should feel fear, but her heart was too full.

Until she saw his face.

Yehosef, the old gladiator she'd paid to train her, showed relief at the sight of her, but Cassia's stomach churned.

"Ah, I am glad to see you safe, my Cassia." He extended his muscled arms. "When you did not come—"

"I am sorry. I was . . . detained."

He glanced at Julian and winked. "Yes, I see. But I was worried."

She smiled. "You are a good man, Yehosef. I thank you for your concern."

He bowed. "Then I shall see you soon?"

Cassia swallowed, aware of Julian's growing coldness. "Yes, soon. Thank you."

Yehosef disappeared into the night, and Julian crossed his arms over his chest. "Who is your friend?" His voice was stony.

She tucked a stray end of hair beneath her head covering. "An old man I visit, nothing more."

"He is a gladiator."

Cassia glanced up at him, surprised by his insight. "An old man like that?"

"He once was, at least. Now I would guess he trains others gladiators."

She dropped her head. "Yes, yes, I think he does."

"And he is training you." Again, that cold voice, like the icy stars had poured themselves into him. His insight amazed her. Did he know her so well?

"Julian, please understand—"

He held up a hand and shook his head, his lips tight. "I do not want to hear it."

"It's not that I don't trust your plan to retrieve Alexander." She reached out and grabbed at his tunic, but he jerked away.

"It's not about trust. I don't care if you learn to fight well. Perhaps you should. But the arena!" He swiped his hands together in a gesture of contempt. "I will have nothing to do with the arena!"

With that, he spun and stalked away, leaving her alone to watch him disappear into the darkness. Cassia feared she had alienated the one person whose friendship she most valued.

TWENTY-TWO

HAGIRU NEEDED THE POWER TONIGHT.

She hurried from the palace, feeling as though the desert jackals snapped at her heels. Something was not right. Some contrary power worked against her from somewhere, she knew not where. Though she suspected.

She moved through darkness alone, needing no slaves for the short walk, past the baths complex to the Temple of al-'Uzza. A narrow road led from the street level up to the terrace of the temple and was lined with richly decorated porticoes that housed all manner of sculpted figures peering out as she passed.

The religious life of Petra drew on the traditions of many surrounding regions, from northern Arabia, from Edom, Syria, Egypt. And all of it strongly influenced by the Greeks. Her patron Dushara was called Zeus by the Greeks, and al-'Uzza, whose temple she approached, was the Greek's Aphrodite and the Roman's Venus, goddess of fertility and abundance.

Yes, there were many gods, known by many names, and tonight the voices whispered and snarled, a shivering confusion she must sift through to find the voice she knew best, the one that calmed her fears and filled her with the power.

The cavernous temple swallowed her into its shadowy depths and pulled her forward into the *cella* to the altar, where a fire had been laid though not yet lit. This room, with its deep niches and sculpted columns, had been painted with all manner of frescoes—tendrils of vines curled around columns and human busts merged with other-worldly animals. The zodiac painted upon the floor held truths too deep to contemplate tonight.

Hagiru stood before the horned altar, caressing the smooth black-and-white marble with eyes closed and head tipped backward, listening, listening, and trying to calm her anxious thoughts.

She heard the scrape of the priest's feet and opened her eyes.

The little man bowed and backed away. "I will prepare the sacrifice."

Hagiru felt her arms tingle with warmth. "I want to watch." She followed the priest to the stone slab in the antechamber, a slightly raised rectangle stained with the blood of a thousand animals.

Two well-muscled slaves led a knock-kneed calf out of the shad-ows, tugging on the grimy rope that bound it. The frightened creature's hooves clicked in a dance of terror on the stone floor, but the slaves pulled until the calf stood on the slab. With a deftness borne of prac-tice, they swept the calf onto its side and bared its tawny neck to the priest's knife. The priest paused only a moment over the artery, then brought his knife across, smooth and swift.

Hagiru's body went cold, then very warm.

Fire-red blood spurted from the cut and the calf shuddered and went still. The priest caught the blood in a bronze basin, and the bowl filled with the sticky warmth.

Hagiru ran her tongue over her lips and sighed, waiting for the calm she sought but did not yet feel.

Only minutes later, she stood as near the fiery altar as she dared, lifting silent adoration to Dushara and begging him to speak.

Tonight she needed more than power. She needed wisdom.

That girl, the peasant mother of Aretas's whelp, had not only remained in Petra, she had aligned herself with the enemy. Hagiru had pretended in the courtyard with the girl and her champion that she had not noticed the authority that flowed from him, protecting the girl from her dark power. But she noticed. And she had been frightened. Dushara had a firm hold on Petra, but there were some, like the newcomer with Cassia, who served another god, one who also wielded power. And Hagiru was jealous for Petra's god, that he not share the city with another.

The flames crackled and popped, and the calf's flesh sizzled in the heat. She stared into the fire, seeing there the faces of the peasant woman, of her protector, even of the old man Malik, who led people in defiance of Dushara. She watched as their faces smoked and blackened, the burning flesh curling upon itself and sizzling like the fatty flesh of the calf.

And with those thoughts, the cacophony of voices quieted and one voice spoke clearly among the host. A whisper at first, but she latched onto it and turned her heart to it, welcoming the voice and its power into her very soul.

The edges of her vision blurred and shifted, as though the walls crawled with spiders, and she smiled, for this was how it nearly always began.

Hagiru studied the yellow flames, the calf's red blood poured on the white altar stones, the bronze bowl tipped on its side. She stepped near enough to run two fingers along the bloody stones, then waved them through the flames themselves, but felt no pain.

"Dushara," she whispered into the darkness. "Fill me with your power. Teach me what to do."

And then he was there. Beside her, behind her, within her, his low voice like the cold tongue of the underworld, his words reassuring and instructive.

Hagiru closed her eyes and surrendered to the knowledge. She saw Dushara's enemies ranging before her mind's eye. The followers of the Way, the Jews who lived among them. Malik. Cassia.

"Yes." She nodded. "I understand."

She feared Dushara's withdrawal and clutched at the filling, pleading for wisdom on the problem that plagued her most.

"The boy. What must I do about the boy?"

For in truth, it was power Hagiru craved, and the boy was a severe threat to that power. Rabbel was dying, that much was certain. And when he did, Obadas would be king. Too young to rule, she would be appointed regent over him in the age-old custom, and she would have complete power over the kingdom of Nabataea.

But the boy, he held a more legitimate claim to the throne.

And if he were made king . . . Hagiru shuddered. *The peasant woman could be made his regent.*

She had been fiercely loyal to Dushara, body and soul, since he had granted her strongest desire years ago, and he had taught her well that power is everything. Once she had believed in love. But love was nothing.

"Tell me what I should do," she begged again.

When the answer blew over her like a hot breeze that incited the altar flames, she lifted her hands and let it carry her to a place of peace.

Sometime later, after she had washed the sticky blood from her hands, she entered the palace courtyard, still brightly lit with flaming torches, where Alexander played near the central fountain pool.

Bethea lounged nearby, barely watching the boy, her heavy-lidded eyes nearly closed.

Hagiru approached the boy in silence, and he did not notice her, so taken was he with a small lizard that darted around the courtyard's square limestones. His little laugh scraped across her senses like rough sand.

She reached a hand toward his gaunt neck. *So small. So easily broken.*

Bethea shifted in her chair behind her, and Hagiru dropped her hand.

Across the courtyard, Obadas tramped out of the back hall. His attention was on something in his hands, and Hagiru chose to slip away, to the shadowy colonnade where the torchlight did not reach.

Whatever Obadas held, he lost interest in it when he saw Alexander and tossed it into the fountain. Alexander greeted Obadas with that small, high voice Hagiru had come to loathe.

Her son circled the fountain where Alexander played. From this distance, with their matching white tunics and red belts and their similar dark skin, they could be mistaken for brothers.

"Shouldn't you be in your bed, baby?" Obadas's heavy lips curled into a smile.

Alexander glanced at Bethea, whose eyes had now closed, and shrugged. "It is not so late."

Obadas stepped behind Alexander and smacked the back of his head. "Too late for babies to be awake."

Hagiru stifled a laugh. Clever boy.

Alexander ignored Obadas, but even from the colonnade Hagiru could see the downturn of his lips. He seemed unsurprised by the smack, and Hagiru assumed he was accustomed to the treatment. So much the better. Obadas shared her distaste for the usurper.

"What have you got there?" Obadas followed Alexander's attention to the stones at his feet.

"It's a tiny lizard!" Alexander spoke as though Obadas's taunts were already forgotten and he was ready to share his pet.

Obadas shuffled over, looked down at the ground, and shrugged. Then he lifted a heavy foot and stomped it down onto the stones.

"No!" Alexander's cry came too late.

Obadas lifted his sandal, then scraped it over the stones, laughing. "Look. It has green blood!"

Alexander turned away, his back to Hagiru, which frustrated her as she wished to see his grief.

"Obadas!"

Rabbel's voice across the courtyard startled Hagiru.

Obadas jumped as well. "Yes, Father?"

Rabbel strode toward the two, his white robes fluttering behind him. "Leave the boy alone."

He reached the fountain, said something Hagiru could not hear, and Obadas trotted away, as though dismissed. His scowl reached across to where Hagiru stood, still concealed.

Bethea, too, was cast off with a flick of Rabbel's head. Hagiru did not miss the look of annoyance from the girl. It was not the first of such displays recently. Rabbel sat on the edge of the fountain pool and leaned his head toward the brat.

"What has Obadas done now?" Rabbel's words came barely loud enough for her to hear.

Alexander pointed to the stones and whined about the lizard.

Rabbel pulled the boy into an embrace. "We will get you a dozen lizards. And put them all in a cage where you can play with them all day. How will that be?"

Alexander nodded and pulled away. "That would be good. But this one will still stay killed."

Rabbel sighed. "Yes, I am afraid there is nothing we can do about that. Obadas was very cruel."

Hagiru's body felt heavy with hatred. His own son tossed aside, and this obnoxious half-breed welcomed into the king's affection!

She strode from the colonnade and inclined her head in greeting for her husband.

Rabbel looked up from the boy, then whispered something to him and patted his back. The boy glanced at her, then ran from the courtyard without a backward look.

Rabbel stood and Hagiru swept up close to him, close enough to let him feel her power.

They were not often completely alone as they were now, and the feeling was a strange one for Hagiru. She forgot her purpose for a moment.

Rabbel stepped even closer to her, their robes twining together. He studied her eyes, then leaned into her, his breath warm on her neck.

Hagiru's heartbeat suspended for a moment at the unexpected closeness. She felt herself lean toward him.

Then Rabbel sniffed. "You smell like sacrifice." His words revealed the reason for his approach. He took a step away.

Hagiru swallowed and straightened her shoulders, disgusted with herself. "Yes." Her voice was low and cold. "The gods have been speaking to me tonight."

Rabbel's glance was both interested and fearful. "And what do they say?"

She turned away, playing out the power of the moment. "They have much to say about the future of the kingdom."

Rabbel grabbed at her arm and spun her toward him. "Tell me. Will the Romans attack?"

In the flickering torchlight his face seemed to lose fifteen years, and he was once again the young and brash king with whom her father had made a favorable alliance that included one naive and hopeful daughter. A long time ago. Hagiru forced herself to abandon that thread of thought.

"The Romans have taken most of the world. It will not be easy to save Nabataea."

Rabbel's gaze strayed toward the front of the palace. "And if my people were to decide, they would hand over my kingdom for the sake of peace."

"They are weak. The gods will favor strength."

"And have the gods given you knowledge?"

She shrugged one shoulder and walked past him to the fountain, where she sat on the edge and ran a hand through the cool water. Rabbel trusted her connection to the gods, and it gave her welcome power over him. "They have not told me how we should defend the kingdom. Only how we can gain their favor and their protection."

He sat beside her, and she did not miss the grimace of pain as he did so. "Whatever the gods desire, this we will give them."

Hagiru turned her face away to hide the smile of triumph.

"The god of Petra has no wish to be displaced by the gods of Rome. Already the Jews have brought their god here, and these Christians refuse to worship at all."

"I have always felt that tolerance—"

"Weakness!" Hagiru turned the force of her anger on Rabbel and felt him bend in her hands, like clay in the hands of a potter. The difference between the king's pliability and old Malik's resoluteness ran across her thoughts, like a rodent scurrying out of a corner. She chose to focus on Rabbel's malleability.

He dropped his head. "What can I do to please the gods?"

She let the question hang unanswered for a moment. Everything depended on what came next. She must not fail. "Dushara requires a sacrifice."

He brightened and lifted his head. "I shall send a hundred bulls—"

"It is not the blood of bulls Dushara desires."

His brow furrowed. "Calves?"

Hagiru sighed as though the truth brought her pain and lowered her head in sadness. "Dushara wishes to see that you are truly devoted to him, above all others. That you would sacrifice something of great value to gain his favor."

Rabbel scratched his head. "Surely not the harvest. The people would not survive—"

She shook her head, then patted his thigh in feigned sympathy. "Dushara wants the boy."

Rabbel tilted his head and looked at her, as though struck dumb. Finally his lips opened. "Obadas?"

Hagiru's blood ran cold. "No!" She forced the hysteria from her voice. "No. Dushara feels the newly found son of Aretas has claimed more of your affection than the gods. He wishes you to prove your loyalty."

Rabbel's shoulders tightened and the line between his eyebrows deepened. "How?"

"At the Festival of Grain. Sacrifice the boy."

Rabbel stood and turned away. "No."

Hagiru waited, knowing the first answer was far from the last. After all, he was the clay and she the potter, and she felt the power in her now, the power to create anything she desired. "I hear the Roman camp in the desert grows larger every day."

She watched her husband's back and felt she could read every emotion that coursed through him. Anger. Horror. Then fear.

Yes, yes, that is good.

The fear melted into surrender. Then grief. When he spoke, the words were hollow. "I cannot do it, Hagiru. I cannot."

She lifted her chin and let the power flow out of her, let it burn a hole through his resistance. The voice she loved whispered to her and she nodded.

Oh, but you will, husband. You will.

TWENTY-THREE

In spite of the strained silence in which Julian and Cassia had worked all morning, Julian was feeling pleased with his progress on the tomb sculpting.

He had been assigned this upper tier, seventy-five cubits above the street, while other, less-skilled workmen would carve from the street level upward. Today he would finish the last touches on the giant urn carved into the central niche at the top of the massive structure. The vine and bud ornamentation was both intricate on close inspection and lovely from the street level. More than one of the masons near the bottom had commented on its beauty, and the master builder seemed impressed.

"Where'd you learn to sculpt like that?" He had eyed Julian with some suspicion.

Julian simply shrugged. "Always been a hobby of mine."

The master builder grunted, the only sign he found Julian's explanation lacking.

But today he would finish the crowning glory of this tomb and begin to work on the rock-carved platform one level down. He congratulated himself not only for the beauty of the work but also for the pace he had established.

There was little need for Cassia at this stage of the carving, since he used the finest of detail tools to carve the elegant vine and floral motif around the giant urn and did not need her to carry rock chips. She worked on the platform below, beginning his work for him of chipping out crevices in the places he had marked. Later he would pound wooden pegs into these chinks, then water-swell the wood. Amazingly, with so little encouragement, the red rock would split along his prescribed lines, enough for his slim chisel to work itself into the crack and widen the split.

Julian glanced down to Cassia. The musical ching of hammer on chisel could not mask the cold silence between them since he had discovered her secret from the old gladiator in the street. His jaw clenched and he went back to work, striking the small chisel off center and pounding his thumb instead.

"Cursed rock!" He planted the thumb in his mouth, then quickly spit rock dust.

Soon enough the work was finished, and after again admiring it for several moments, Julian climbed down to the next platform.

Cassia glanced over her shoulder at him, then went back to work. *We will not speak, then.*

She had already sunk several short pegs into the stone without him to the right depth.

"Who showed you how to do that?" He caught his tone of admiration too late.

Cassia shrugged and let her gaze rest on him. "No one. I watch you carefully."

Julian avoided her eyes and studied the pegs. She had made her feelings clear. *But does she have any idea how hard she makes it?* "We should start with the water."

Cassia bent to a filled pitcher, lifted it to her narrow hip, and waited.

"This one first." Julian touched the left-most peg she had planted. "Pour as slowly as you can."

She brought the pitcher near the rock but then caught his hand as he lowered it. She turned it over, dry and dusty as it was, and rubbed at a callus with her thumb. Julian watched her head bent over his hand and said nothing.

She poured water over his hand, washing the stone dust from it, then indicated he should give her the other. Her reddish, dark hair swung forward over her shoulder as she washed.

When she used her tunic to wipe them dry, all resolve drained from him. "I do not wish to be angry with you."

She did not look up from his hands. "Then do not be."

He pulled away. "You cannot understand." He turned to the rock wall, but she slipped into the tiny space between.

"Then help me understand. What is it about the arena—"

Julian shook his head, cutting off her question. "Too much to explain."

"Yehosef is a good man. Have you ever even *known* a gladiator?"

He laughed at the irony of the question and picked up the hammer and chisel she had discarded. "Yes, I knew someone who once fought in the arena."

"Tell me."

He began pounding at another marked spot. "It was another who should not have been there, and it caused only pain and grief."

"Was he killed?"

"She."

"A woman?" Cassia's tone shifted from curiosity to dread.

Julian continued working. "My mother."

"Your— She was killed in the arena?" Cassia's hands fluttered to her heart. He had noticed that happened when she was greatly troubled.

"No." He hammered on. "My mother is alive and well and living in Rome with my father. And very few people know the arena was where they first met, so if you should ever meet her, say nothing of that." The explanation lifted a bit of the heaviness he had felt since discovering where Cassia spent her evenings.

"And because your mother suffered as a gladiator, you are angry with me for training there."

"Yes." *Ching, ching.* It sounded less than logical from her lips.

"Julian, would you put down that hammer and look at me!"

He sighed and leaned against the rock. Cassia's arms were crossed.

"I am not a gladiator. Not forced to fight, and not in any danger. At least not from the arena. And it would be well for me to learn to protect myself and my son."

"I do not like it."

She dropped her arms and reached for the pitcher. "It is not for you to decide."

"I am not trying to decide! Only to speak reason, which you seem intent to ignore."

"I appreciate your concern, but I do not need it."

Julian exhaled, took the pitcher from her hands, and sloshed water against the rock wall. "No, you don't need anyone, do you?"

She was silent behind him, and it was just as well. Her refusal to open up stemmed from deep hurt, he knew, but it grew frustrating. And she seemed willing to let everyone care for her except him. That truth stung, and he preferred to keep it buried.

Sometime later Cassia spoke again. "Malik says you lost someone important to you in Rome."

Julian didn't pause with the hammer and chisel.

"Will you tell me?"

His jaw tightened at the memory. He let the silence grow, then finally answered. "Her name was Vita."

"Someone you loved?"

"Not well enough."

She appeared beside him with a wooden peg and offered it with sympathetic eyes. He sighed and took the piece of wood. "We were to be married. Though I am not sure why. Her heart belonged completely to Jesus and there was no room for me in it. And I—" He pounded the peg into the wall. "I admired her devotion."

"But you did not love her?"

"She was a sister in the Lord—"

"Julian, did you love her?"

He heard the tension in her voice and stopped working to study her face. "Not like a husband. No. But perhaps it is asking too much to find someone with whom you can share both a passion for Jesus and for each other." The words were bold, as close to a declaration of his heart as he had yet come.

Cassia bent to search out another peg at their feet. "What happened to her?"

"She was killed in the arena."

Cassia dropped the peg and clutched his arm. "Oh, Julian!"

He swallowed, trying to hold the memory at bay. "When the persecutions were beginning, she went willingly. Practically volunteered." He fought to keep the bitterness from his voice. It was unfair of him. "She honored God with her dying breath." *And I ran like a scared child.*

Cassia pulled him to face her, holding both his arms. "There was nothing you could have done. And you honor her memory with your praise." She tightened her hold on him. "You are a good man, Julian Portius Marcellus."

He inhaled deeply and closed his eyes. The name she used was not even his true name, but he longed to accept the affirmation. There had been more failures in Rome than just the day of Vita's death. He was not the son his father desired, never wanted to follow his political footsteps. He had not even honored his family with military service as his brother had. *Restless,* his mother had called him. His father's word was *aimless.* Carving this rock was all the success he had known.

⚜

They worked in near silence for the remainder of the day, and when the shadows grew long, Julian climbed down in relief.

They worked several more weary days, and Julian knew Cassia still went to the theatre to meet the old man. He chose to keep silent. Regardless of her antagonism, he continued to pursue his own plan to rescue Alexander, and they were nearly ready.

And when they worked side by side, Julian began to reveal, in a gentle and cautious way, the Christ and the new life that could be found in Him. Cassia asked relentless questions about the life and death of Jesus, about the followers of the Way, and about the forgiveness and redemption they had found.

On the first day of the week, when the sun had made its daily passage over the site, blending the colors until they fell into shadows, Julian walked Cassia home and left her in the street below Zeta's home. "Tomorrow, then?"

Cassia chewed her lip. "Tonight you are meeting with the . . . the believers?" The word did not fall easily from her lips.

"Yes."

"May I come?"

Julian looked down the street toward the amphitheatre. "You do not have other plans to attend?"

She lifted her chin to him. "Certainly you have heard of tonight's performance?"

He scowled. "Another pantomime?" Julian saw no value in the mimes who entertained the masses with their juggling and dancing farce.

Cassia grinned. "There is more to the theatre than the mimes. Lectures, readings of verse, and rhetoric. Besides, perhaps you should see what makes the theatre so popular. They are saying there will be a panther from Egypt there tonight."

"Ha! I have better things to do." He narrowed his eyes. "Do you truly wish to meet with us?"

"Yes. If you think they would not mind."

Julian refrained from shaking the self-deprecation from her. "You have won the hearts of every one of them. They would welcome you."

She grew serious and looked away. "I need to be able to care for my son alone. It would not do to rely on your friends."

"Come tonight, Cassia."

They waited for Zeta and Talya to descend but only Zeta came down. "Talya's mending from the palace occupies her tonight. She came home only for a few minutes, then returned." Julian walked with the women back to the tomb where they spent their days, but this time they went into the cavernous depths of the bottom floor.

To Julian it seemed their numbers had decreased. Was it simply the enlarged size of their new tomb chamber? But a quick count confirmed they were fewer. His gaze met Malik's at the back of the room, and the older man gave him a small nod, as though he read Julian's thoughts and shared his concern.

Julian seated Cassia and Zeta, then joined Malik.

"There is fear." Malik eyed the group. "And fear always winnows, always purifies."

"These are the faithful, then."

Malik smiled sideways. "Indeed. And let us not forget those who labor in the palace at your direction."

"Not my direction. I only asked for those who would be willing."

Malik's smile disappeared, and Julian felt a chill from him. "Not your direction, then. They act only as their own wishes direct."

Confused by the older man's displeasure, Julian found a seat on the cold floor near Cassia and waited for the meeting to begin.

They sang with more abandon tonight, perhaps because they were set so deep from the street, perhaps because only those remained whose confidence in Jesus' love for them brought them out in spite of the danger.

Malik spoke with passion as well. "We must each grasp hold of that freedom for which the Christ suffered." His face glowed and lifted to the roof above them. "His love for us is a sure foundation. It delivers us from our desperate need for the approval of others and frees us to love each other without the need of a response. Only when we are able to love like this, as Jesus loves, will we be prepared for the fight, for the persecution that is coming."

Julian prayed silently that Cassia would hear and understand. Her gaze never left Malik, as though she drank eagerly of all he spoke.

"We will soon be called to do more than simply identify ourselves as believers, brothers and sisters."

The mood in the room had sobered, and Malik looked around at the people, his eyes compassionate. "But do not fear. Jesus told His apostles He would build His church, and no other power would prevail against it. There has been an unbroken line of truth before you, from the apostles to Paul to even myself, trained by Paul. And it will continue."

Julian felt Malik's attention on him. He shifted his position, wrapped his arms around his bent legs, and studied the floor.

"Julian, perhaps you should speak to the gathering about how your plan is progressing."

It was an obvious ploy. To speak of leadership to the group and then ask him to stand and direct them. Julian shrugged. "There is nothing to speak of right now. I do not wish to interrupt the meeting." He felt a chill once more, this time from both Malik and Cassia beside him.

Malik's shoulders bent forward, and he grimaced as though in pain. He spoke to the group, bringing their attention back to himself, but his words were clearly for Julian. "Those who will not accept their call should be most careful of the refining to come."

A chastened hush fell over the group, broken by the sound of someone stumbling into the back of the tomb.

Talya appeared, holding a small oil lamp. Her eyes seemed sunken, hollow. Julian knew at once that something had changed.

TWENTY-FOUR

—◆—

"WHAT IS IT, TALYA?" ZETA WENT TO HER DAUGHTER AT the tomb entrance. "The Lord protects us still. Do not fear."

But the girl's gaze traveled to Cassia, and it was not fear she read there. It was grief. Deep and painful. Cassia felt a sudden metallic taste in her mouth. "What has happened?"

The girl's hand shook and Zeta took the oil lamp from her. Julian came to Cassia's side, one arm around her waist for support.

"There is talk in the palace." Talya's voice trembled.

Cassia swayed on her feet. *Talk. Only talk.* "Tell me."

"The Festival of Grain approaches." Talya chewed at her fingernails. "They are saying the high priestess and queen will offer a sacrifice to appease the gods, to protect us from Rome." Her eyes flickered to Julian apologetically, as though he were all of Rome.

Cassia did not speak. The words would have been too dreadful to even make it past her lips.

But Talya said them anyway.

"They are saying Alexander will be sacrificed." Her telling of it ended with a sob, and Zeta held her as she dissolved into tears.

Cassia watched the girl fall apart but could not take in the news. She felt as though she had turned to stone. Would she break into pieces?

She found herself seated again and did not remember moving there.

Julian and Malik talked quietly in the corner. Zeta and Talya still wept together beside the entrance.

Cassia stood. No longer could she comfort herself with the thought that although Alexander had enemies in the palace, he also had friends, and perhaps he would grow up stronger for it. No, everything had changed. Her delusion was stripped away and she saw the truth of Hagiru's desperation. No one could keep her son safe. She formed the words that kept repeating in her heart, forced them out, forced herself to face it.

"They are going to kill my son."

Her friends looked at her with both compassion and concern. Had Malik not spoken of persecution? And then, as though the old man's words had been a prophecy whispered to him by his One God, a series of shouts and the stomp of heavy feet came from outside the tomb.

At the sound of intrusion, the believers scrambled as one to huddle together at the back of the chamber. Julian pushed Cassia behind him, and she was grateful her small stature made her nearly hidden.

The opening to the outside swarmed with armed soldiers. *No palace guards this time.* The soldiers were swathed in robes as all Arabians, so unlike Rome's leather and chain mail, but they were armed with long swords strapped across their chests and short daggers tucked into their belts.

Again, Julian and Malik traded glances, and Cassia sensed the elder waited for Julian to act.

"We have gathered peaceably," Julian called to the soldiers. "We want no trouble here."

One of them, his head turbaned in black, stepped forward. "You are ordered to submit! For detainment by the royal house."

Cassia's hand found its way into his, and he squeezed her fingers but did not look at her.

She did a quick survey of their fellowship. There were some strong men among them. But an equal number of women, children, and elderly. To resist would prove fatal for them all. They looked to Julian.

"We will not fight you," he called to the soldiers. "But we insist the charges against us be explained by a representative of the king."

The swiftness with which the soldiers had them bound by rope into a single line was devastating. Julian maneuvered to place Cassia in front of him, but when the first harsh yank of the rope came, she was nearly pulled off her feet.

"Steady, Cassia," he whispered. But her thoughts were not on herself. *Alexander.*

She cared little what happened to her, but she could do nothing if she was imprisoned or worse. She had let herself grow weak. Cassia cursed her own foolish need to belong, that constant frailty that had brought her to these people, and now into bondage.

The streets were dark, though crowded, as the soldiers dragged them in their single roped line. The amphitheatre performance always drew a large audience, and the street was still clogged with giddy townspeople on their way to the night's entertainment.

Cassia tried to look over her shoulder to Julian, but the twisting of her body threw off her balance and she tripped over her sandals. The rope dug into her wrists and burned. She barely noticed.

It was Alexander who occupied her thoughts. Alexander, left alone in the palace, without anyone to fight for his rescue.

Julian whispered words of reassurance to her, to anyone who could hear. She ignored him.

Nearly oblivious to their direction, it came as a surprise when she realized how close they had come to the amphitheatre. The half circle cut into the red cliff blazed as bright as day with dozens of torches, and the smell of burning bitumen stung her nostrils.

Their motley string of bound prisoners drew the stares and occasional kicks of townspeople. Cassia watched Nahor's head in front of her. Was his son, Niv, somewhere in their line? Nahor plodded forward, head down. She could not read his emotions.

Ahead, the amphitheatre roared to life with the laughter of thousands. The *pantomimus* must have begun his act.

Was this where they were to be taken? For what purpose?

They were pulled past a line of smoking cook fires, where opportunistic merchants heated shanks of seasoned boar meat and barley cakes for those without the foresight to bring their own evening's food.

Behind her, Julian was speaking too low for her to hear his words.

Cassia's legs and arms felt a heaviness borne of grief and terror more than fatigue. She forced her feet to follow Nahor's and fought the urge to collapse onto the street and pull the whole line of believers down with her.

Julian's words grew louder, phrases strung together with a passion she had never heard in his voice.

"Walk with us, Jesus. Show us how to suffer for Your sake, give us strength to stand when fear would strike us down, let Your peace flow into frightened hearts."

His words sent chills through Cassia and left her weak.

And then his words were of her.

"Show Yourself to Cassia, Jesus. Give her time to understand Your love. We are ready. She is not. Oh, Jesus, give her more time." His voice broke and Cassia's heart with it.

He believes we go to our death.

Was it true? Had she lost the opportunity to save her boy?

She saw Alexander there in the palace, under the power of Hagiru. Tortured and hated. Alone. Waiting for death on an altar.

The thought squeezed her chest with such force, she felt she might suffocate. The torches and people in the street blurred in her vision and spun and twisted into angry, hateful shapes that would reach out and strangle her. She heard herself cry out as though from a great distance.

"Strength, Cassia." Julian's voice was confident and soothing. "We are nearly there."

Indeed, within moments they were hauled to the dim backstage corridors of the amphitheatre. She caught only a glimpse of the thousands of spectators massed in the stone seats, a rainbow of color in the night, before the rope was yanked and they were hurried down into the corridors she had come to know well.

She half expected to see Yehosef, but tonight was a pantomime night, and the gladiators were not scheduled to fight. So it did not surprise her to be led to the cellar level, to the very cells where she had seen the fighters housed. The irony was a bitter one, and she pushed the thought from her.

They were split into two groups and shoved into dirty cells, with the iron gates locked behind them. Their ropes were unbound, and those in Cassia's cell at once huddled in a tight circle. She stood near the gate, looking out and fighting that suffocating feeling.

She felt a warm hand on her back, knew it to be Julian, and stiffened. She had let him get too close already. All of them. It had led to this. She remembered her promise to herself back in Damascus. She would stand alone and provide a home for her son. Never again let a man control her.

And now look at you.

"Cassia, come back here."

Julian pulled her into their circle, and she saw no point in resisting. Malik was with them, along with Zeta and Nahor and his son, Niv. Cassia took a small bit of comfort from the realization that all of Julian's people planted in the palace had escaped capture tonight. Perhaps Alexander still knew friends.

But without her, without Julian to lead them, what hope did Alexander have?

"Why are we here?"

The group looked at her with some pity, as though she should know the answer but none of them wanted to tell her.

"What?"

Julian threaded his fingers through hers and held her hand at his side. "Some kind of entertainment, Cassia."

"What would be entertaining about us?"

He swallowed. "Remember, there was talk of a panther being brought—"

As if it were a performer responding on cue, from somewhere deeper in the underground halls, a terrifying growl echoed through the cells and chilled her blood. Her eyes widened and took in the expressions of each of the group. Their faces confirmed her fear yet did not reflect it. She remembered Julian's prayer as they walked. *Peace flowing into frightened hearts.* She had none of this peace.

The crowd above did not soon tire of their pantomime, however, and before many minutes had passed, the huddled group in the cell had found places in the straw-covered dirt and leaned against the brick walls to wait. They listened in silence to the laughter that crashed and surged, like thunder before a storm.

Cassia collapsed into a darkened corner, wishing the two walls could close around her.

Nearby, Julian stood with his back to her and spoke with Malik. The confident tone of the street had been replaced with anger.

"Not like this!" He pounded a fist against the cell wall.

Malik put a hand on Julian's shoulder, but Julian shrugged it off. "I thought I could save those I loved from . . . from this"—he jabbed a finger toward the theatre—"when I left Rome. I thought if I ran, if I hid, those I loved would be safe." He glanced down and behind, toward the place where Cassia listened. "But I have only brought it with me, and those I love are still in danger."

Malik sighed. "If you came here to hide from the Lord's call on your life, Julian, then you have been foolish. But the Father has much to teach each of us, beginning with caring only for His acceptance and approval, and not that of man."

"Well, it would seem the time for my teaching has run out." Julian's voice grew bitter.

Malik's gaze found Cassia's, and she looked away, embarrassed to be listening. "I do not know if this is when He calls us home or not, Julian, but there is one who is not ready."

Julian was on the floor beside her a moment later. "Cassia, I have things I must say." His voice was changed yet again, back to the soothing tones of the street. She looked him over, reading the war being waged in his heart. Fear and courage, acceptance and denial. Love and anger. She could see, with the knowing eyes of her heart, that Julian was being called forth to a new place, and he did not go willingly. She had watched him over these weeks of friendship, seen him in study and in prayer, and she knew he sought to please his One God and learn of Him. But there was some part of Julian still resisting.

"Julian," she began, though she knew not what she would say.

He touched her lips with his fingers, then shifted until they each sat cross-legged and facing each other, with knees touching and hands intertwined between them.

"Cassia, I do not know what will happen here. But you must be prepared. If this is the night in which we pass into eternity, you must reach out to Jesus, with faith in His blood, for yourself."

She rubbed the back of her neck. Strange talk at such a time. "What difference does it make what god I call on—"

"*All* the difference, Cassia! There is only One True God. He came to us as a man, to pay the price of our sin, once for all. No more sacrifice to please a god whom we can never please." Julian's fingers tightened around her own, with a fierceness that felt to Cassia almost like fear. "You must trust in His sacrifice on your behalf as the only way to be accepted by the One God, the only way to have eternal life in His presence."

She had listened to so many stories of this Jesus, He had grown familiar to her in some strange way. Malik had told her of his friend Paul's vision of Jesus on his way to her own town of Damascus, and she had nearly wished for such a vision herself, to help her believe. But still she had doubts.

Julian leaned forward until their foreheads touched. "Cassia, you must open your heart to this great love."

The cell seemed to fade away, leaving only the two of them. This closeness, this intimacy with Julian, it was like a banked fire that could warm her for years. She felt herself drawn to tell him what he wanted to hear, if only to make him happy.

Never again.

The words snapped her backward and she blinked.

Would she never learn? Would she go to her death still trying to please men, to gain their love?

She yanked her hands from Julian's and shook her head. He must have felt the change in what was between them and pulled at her hands to regain it. "Cassia, you must know how much I care—"

"No." She held up her hands. "I do not want your affection. I do not need it. If we live past this night, I will be strong, and I will do it alone."

She saw the hurt in his eyes and steeled herself against it.

Malik appeared at Julian's back, and she looked up into the old man's eyes, compassionate and warm on her. "Julian. Let me speak with Cassia."

Julian gave up his place reluctantly, went to the gate of the cell with obvious frustration, and leaned his head against the lashed wood of the outer cell wall. She heard the growl of that frightful beast once again, and then Malik was beside her, his back against the wall alongside hers.

"I suspect I do not have much time, Cassia, so I am going to speak boldly."

Cassia smiled sadly. When did Malik not speak thus?

"This is what the Spirit tells me of you." His voice hollowed out, as though the words came from a place somewhere deep within. "You were abandoned as a child. Your parents did not love you as they should, did not cling to you the way a parent must, and you were lost to them."

Her breathing shallowed and she looked at Malik's profile in the dim light. *How can he know these things?* Those days were long behind her, of parents who found her ability to see through their motives and greed to be odd and had moved on to richer takings without her.

But Malik had not finished.

"It is a fearful and grievous thing to be unloved, and you have sought to never allow yourself to be that child again. You have instead used your gift to see the hearts of people to mold yourself, to please a succession of men, of whom Aretas was the last. You let them control you, abuse you, trample the unique heart given to you by God. And you did all this believing they would love you in return."

The emotion closed off her throat and she plucked at her dress with tense fingers, wishing Malik would stop but unable to ask. Aretas had paid a trifling amount for her at sixteen, and though he never treated her as a slave, he never loved her as she wished.

"You allowed this because you believed that being strong for yourself and your son would leave you unloved again, yes?"

Cassia swiped at an unbidden tear and nodded once. "Yes," she whispered.

"But now you have believed another lie." Malik's hand found hers, as Julian's had. But it was with the kind warmth of the father she had never known. "You believe that you cannot love and be loved and still be a woman of strength. This is not truth."

She looked into Malik's eyes, the pounding of her heart a desperate plea for him to continue.

"You *can* have both, my child. Love and strength. But only when the love of Jesus has taken your sin and filled your heart."

"How?" The word barely escaped her tight throat. "How can I have both?"

"When you accept this great love the Father has for you, Cassia, this love that gave us Jesus as our substitute, you are free. Free from your desperate need to have people love you, because you are loved so fully by God. Then you can love others without concern for their response. You can love them from your strength."

Cassia swallowed and studied the cell around them. "If we survive this night, Malik, I shall give your words more thought."

He turned her to face him. "It will be more important to consider if we do *not* survive this night."

"Why do they seek our deaths?"

"It has always been thus, child. In Jerusalem, in Rome, even here in Arabia. You remember I told you of my mentor, Paul of Tarsus?" She nodded. "Even he was not safe. Our own King Rabbel's grand-father, Aretas"—he broke off as Cassia winced at the name—"Aretas tried to have Paul killed while he was in your Damascus." Malik smiled, as though recalling a favorite tale. "We had to lower him from the city walls in a basket to get him past the gates." He squeezed her hand. "The truth, my child, always has enemies."

A shuffling outside their cell seemed an answer to Malik's dire statement. The believers scrambled to their feet around the cell, as if standing would make whatever was to come easier. Julian's hands tightened on the bars of their cell.

A face appeared in the gloom, peering through the bars at the inhabitants of the grimy chamber. Cassia recognized the long white-gray hair at once.

"Yehosef!" She scrambled past Malik to the front of the cell.

His eyes met hers. "I suspected. When they told me there was to be a group given to the beasts, a group disloyal to the royal house, I thought I might find you here." He reached a hand through the bars, and Cassia grasped it and held it to her cheek. Yehosef pulled his hand away and fished at his belt. She saw a flash of bronze a moment later.

"Come." Yehosef inserted a key. "There is little time." And then the cell door swung open and he was shoving them out, one after the next. "To the right, to the right." His voice was harsh in the darkness. She heard him unlock the other cell.

Cassia waited until only Julian remained, and he would not leave until she did. "Yehosef, what will happen to you?" She eyed the old gladiator as she passed him.

He shook his head, hair swinging. "Have no care for me, child. I can take care of myself. Always have."

They were shooed through the underground chamber, down a dank hallway Cassia had never entered.

"Keep going," Yehosef called ahead to the start of the group. "It is only a little farther."

And then the hallway turned, and ahead and above the night sky showed brighter than the corridor that slanted up toward it.

The pace of the group visibly increased, and Cassia believed for the first time that Yehosef had actually saved them.

In the moonlit street, the group huddled together and Yehosef brought up the rear. "Do not stay together," he whispered. "They will be searching for a large number. You must disperse."

Cassia gripped Yehosef's hands, then kissed his cheek.

He pulled her into an embrace. "I fear this must be good-bye, child."

"Thank you, Yehosef. Thank you for everything."

He pulled away. "Be safe, Cassia."

And then they were gone, melting into the night while the city still laughed and applauded the farce in the theatre.

Julian held her hand as they ran, none of them speaking. They reached the place where the steps to Zeta's home ascended the cliff, and Cassia knew that others followed.

Within minutes they had gained Zeta's home, stumbling into the dark front room.

Cassia stayed at the front blanket-wall. She swept aside one of the woven coverings and attached it to the hook driven into the rock, then stood in the opening, knowing the light behind her made her outline visible to the entire city. She imagined Hagiru down there in her palace, looking up at the cliff. Did she see Cassia? Did she even have a mother's heart?

Everything had changed this night.

The believers could not meet openly anymore.

She could not return to Yehosef in the amphitheatre, nor to her work on the tombs.

And Julian—she would not think of Julian.

But above all, Alexander's life had become nothing more than a token for the dark gods of Petra. Cassia did not know if Malik's words had been truth. If she could be a woman of both love and strength. But she would be strong. Of that she had no doubt.

The Festival of Grain would take place in five days.

But by then, she swore to the starry night sky, she and Alexander would be far from this evil place.

TWENTY-FIVE

———◆———

IT TOOK ANOTHER THREE DAYS FOR JULIAN TO BE
confident his plan was ready. For three days he hid in Malik's and
Zeta's homes, slipping through the streets at night and early morning
to see Cassia, to reassure her that although the Festival of Grain and
its accompanying horrific sacrifice grew close, they must wait to be
certain of success.

The church, for the sake of safety, had split into several smaller
groups and met in homes where detection would be less likely. Malik
managed to circulate among these meetings, assuring his flock they
would all be together again soon.

Indeed, today in the early-morning hours, nearly all of their number
were to assemble in Malik's grand home to finalize their plan. Julian
had left Malik in his still-dark courtyard, directing his servants in
hushed tones in the preparation of an early meal for the believers. They
covered cushions with clean fabrics and set out handsome dishes.

Julian crossed the city to get Cassia and passed Zeta and Talya on
the way, with only the slightest acknowledgment of each other. There
were eyes everywhere.

He glanced at the sky, judging how much time until the night sky would lighten with dawn. The morning call of the partridge already mingled with the chorus of the nightingales.

Many of their group who had secured work in the palace labored there during the day, but some needed to be present there through the night hours. This predawn meeting at Malik's house was the best time for all of them to meet together undetected.

The pale moon sat low in the sky this morning, and in its waning light he saw Cassia in the street below Zeta's home and quickened his pace. When they met, her upturned face, pained with anxiety, caught at his heart. Her head was bare, and the moonlight glinted off the reddish streaks in her hair.

"Will they all be there so early?" She gripped his arm.

He placed his hand over her cold one. "They will be there."

They crossed back to the east end of the city, and Julian held Cassia by the elbow, propelling her forward to keep pace with his longer strides. Halfway there, she pulled away and slowed, breathing heavily.

"I am sorry." Julian walked beside her, trying to match her pace.

"You are as tight as a lyre string."

Julian inhaled deeply. "I am anxious to be certain that everyone is ready."

Cassia shivered and wrapped her arms around herself. "Tell me this will work, Julian."

"Tomorrow you will have Alexander back in your arms, Cassia." He said the words with the conviction he truly felt, though he wished his words could somehow assure they would not fail.

They hurried through the housing district, with its stone homes nearly scraping against each other, and found the unassuming door that led to Malik's well-appointed home, then passed ungreeted into the front hall.

All was dark, as it had been when Julian left to retrieve Cassia, but he suspected the house held more people than it had earlier.

They slipped through the quiet hall to the central courtyard. Only one small brazier burned in the center of the flourishing gardens, but in its light Julian saw the faces of at least three dozen brothers and sisters ranging in a circle. They turned as one to Julian and Cassia, with joyous if strained smiles.

Malik bustled forward, took Cassia's hands without speaking, and led her to the circle, where he sat her on one of the wooden benches that had been brought from elsewhere in the house.

Julian followed, aware that the silence of the courtyard still spoke much of the hearts of the people.

He connected with the eyes of each one, nodding his thanks and acknowledging their sacrifice. Hozai and Rachim, Nahor the farmer and his grown son, Niv. Tabatha and Marta. He had grown to love each of them.

Beside him, he heard Cassia's quick intake of breath.

He looked down to where she sat on Malik's bench and found the old man on his knees before her, washing her feet.

Cassia raised stricken eyes to Julian.

He smiled. It was likely she had never had her feet washed by even a servant, and horror stamped her expression that this man of wealth and wisdom would stoop to perform this service.

She did not yet know whose example Malik followed, that he did this lowly thing to give her a message of truth.

But then Malik's gaze was focused on him, and Julian felt the blow of the message. It was as much for himself.

"If anyone desires to be great in the kingdom, he must be the servant of all."

Julian swallowed and nodded, suddenly feeling humbled by the older man's example.

In the days since their capture and escape, he had wrestled and nearly made peace with this idea of leadership. He had admitted, to himself and to God, that he had run from the disaster in Rome in part for the safety of his family, but also in part to avoid the call he felt on his life.

But it was these two things he could not reconcile in his heart. He had tried, God knew he had tried, in Rome. Tried to rise up and be a leader to the small group there, tried to make a difference. It had ended badly. Why would God ask him again to stand up? The thought made him feel as though ants crawled under his skin.

Would this endeavor end as the last one had?

Malik finished his ministrations toward a teary-eyed Cassia, then waved in his servants with their trays of food. Nothing hot this morning, as the cook fires might have attracted attention, but lavish platters of grapes and pears, of flatbreads baked the night before and fresh cheeses. The delicate, pure red clay pottery of Petra, hand-painted with floral and geometric designs, circulated among the group around the small brazier, and Julian watched their dark eyes, glittering in the firelight, as they were served from the finery. The open-air courtyard garden still carried the heady scent of night jasmine, and it would have been a lively party if not for the task for which they had gathered.

And Julian was anxious to begin.

He sat between Cassia and Malik, and the Elder of Petra dipped his head in deference to Julian, who first led the flock in a prayer of thankfulness for their safety thus far, for Malik's generosity, and for their food.

That finished, Julian leaned forward, braced his forearms on his knees, and spoke of the plan to free Alexander. "We could have used more time to place more people inside the palace. But as you all have heard by now, there is much more than Alexander's mere happiness at stake."

Cassia shuddered beside him, and he wished he could wrap her in his arms. A platter of fruit passed nearby but he waved it off. "The Festival of Grain is in only two days, and we must get the boy out of there before a great evil can be done." He sat back on the bench, crossed one leg over the other, and bounced his foot as he talked. "Let's trace the positions of each of you through the palace. Starting with Talya, who through God's mercy has been placed closest to Alexander." His eyes found Talya's and he spoke through the crowd directly to her. "Tell us what will be your challenge when your time comes."

Talya glanced around the group and she seemed afraid to speak.

Come on, girl. You are only the first.

He was about to hurry her along when Malik's hand touched his bouncing leg.

A radiating warmth from the man's hand quieted his muscles. Julian's shoulders dropped, it seemed by a full cubit, and he looked to the older man.

"Peace." Malik's eyes were a deep stillness. "Lead from your heart. From your spirit and from His. Not from your head."

The words were a soothing ointment on Julian's frayed nerves, and he accepted them with gratitude and nodded. He had much to learn from Malik, still.

He took a deep breath and turned back to the flock ranged around him. "Perhaps we need more time with prayer before our time with plans."

And it was the prayers of the people, lifted one after another with passion, that finally brought peace to Julian's anxious thoughts. The cries of their hearts for the safety of Alexander, their fervent entreaty against the evil that would overtake Petra, and their loving and compassionate pleas for Cassia filled Julian with a strength that did not come from well-laid plans.

Beside him, Cassia's tears wet her hands as prayer after prayer went up to the Lord on her behalf, sweet sacrifices from the lips of the saints.

Julian wrapped an arm around her, and she leaned her head on his shoulder, clearly spent with the emotion of the morning already.

When it was done, there was a confidence borne of the Spirit on each face. Julian knew they had each counted the cost of obedience this morning and had reconciled themselves to it.

Talya spoke first, of her plan to get Alexander alone, away from the clinging presence of Bethea.

One by one, each player in the drama that was to come rehearsed their part. Julian nodded, made a few suggestions, encouraged each one in their task, all the while holding Cassia beside him, trying to infuse confidence and peace into her.

When they had finished outlining the plan and Julian felt confident they were ready, Malik signaled his servants again, and more food was brought. Above them, the first pink flush of the clouds warned they could not remain much longer.

Malik drew Julian aside, leaving Cassia to be surrounded by others intent on loving her well.

"You have given good leadership this morning." He and Malik walked slowly through the columned portico at the edge of the courtyard.

Julian exhaled with some relief, realizing how much he valued Malik's approval. "I do not believe that God will allow the boy to be offered to the dark powers of the city."

Malik frowned slightly. "We must be careful that we do not insist that God agree with *our* plans. His ways are not our ways."

Julian said nothing, unwilling to consider that God would allow such evil.

Malik stopped their walk at the corner of the courtyard, deep in the shadows of the portico and out of hearing of the group. "Cassia will have a long journey ahead of her when she escapes Petra tomorrow." His voice was deceptively casual. "I will give her sufficient money to reach Jerusalem, but we must pray for her safety." Malik's eyes bore into his, and Julian knew well the man's words were more of a question than a statement.

"I am going with her."

Malik nodded once. "I thought as much." He turned away, braced a hand against a stone pillar.

Julian clenched his hands at his sides. "You do not approve."

Malik spoke toward the group, his back to Julian. "It is not the will of the Father that you go, Julian. This I know."

"I love her."

"Yes. And I believe she feels the same, though she is not yet ready to love, for many reasons."

Julian went to Malik's side until the man looked at him. His heart raced with the unfairness of what Malik asked. Had the man never felt what it was to love? "Then how can you ask me—"

"It is not I who asks."

Julian smacked the stone pillar with his open palm. "I am trying to be obedient, Malik. You say that God wants me to lead, and I am trying. But this—" He fought to keep his voice low.

Malik smiled, and his gaze drifted to Cassia. "I, too, have fought for these past weeks to accept what seemed to me to be illogical." With this, he looked pointedly at Julian, and Julian felt the wash of shame at his own immaturity. "And yet, His way is best. This is part of leadership, Julian. To learn that we do not control, we serve."

Julian looked over their flock, now dispersing with much embracing and kisses of farewell.

"Have you ever loved a woman like Cassia, Malik?"

He felt the old man's sadness swell beside him, and Malik laughed quietly. "Oh yes." His voice was full of memories, broken with emotion. "Yes, Julian, I have. Loved her and lost her." He leaned his head against the pillar. "The Lord gives and the Lord takes away. Blessed be the name of the Lord."

Julian's jaw clenched and he chose to remain silent, but his thoughts rebelled.

I will lead, old man. But I will not give up so easily as you.

TWENTY-SIX

THE DAY CRAWLED PAST, LIKE A HEAVY-LADEN CARAVAN inching through the desert sand. Cassia tried to keep her hands busy in Zeta's home, baking bread and tending a pot of spicy hare stew over the hot fire through the long day, but her mind and heart flew across the city to the palace a thousand times. She imagined Alexander's face when Talya would tell him tomorrow morning that he was being brought to his mama. She could see his bright, gap-toothed smile, his light eyes dancing. Her pulse beat at the thought of having him in her arms again.

She pounded dough against the smooth table, turned and folded, then pounded again. Would Alexander understand he needed to be quiet as he was passed from one servant to the next? A flash of memory, their last scheme with Aretas, left her standing over the dough lost in thought. Alexander's innocent delight in showing his father his loose teeth had resulted in their deception being revealed. Could something similar happen tomorrow? Her stomach roiled, and she put a floured hand to her chest.

"You are fearful," Zeta observed from the cook fire.

Cassia dug her fingers into the dough again and shrugged. "Julian will not fail." A brave, confident statement that did little to mask her anxious heart.

And I will be there to fight in whatever way I must.

Their cliffside fell into shadow at last, and Cassia helped Zeta prepare the evening meal of stew and bread.

"Go." Zeta shooed her from the table. "You should be packing for your journey."

Cassia sighed. "It will take very little time to pack all we have." She crossed to the low bedding that had been hers since that first night in Petra and took the traveling pouch Talya had sewn for her in her hands. The red-and-yellow-striped linen reminded her of the rock walls of Petra, and she knew that years from now, when she was safely living in Jerusalem or wherever she and Alexander settled, she would cherish this piece and remember her friends here.

With hands that trembled with anticipation, she folded the few tunics she had acquired, gathered her head scarves, and placed them into the pouch. Reluctantly, she took Alexander's beaded bracelet from her wrist and packed it. She would not take the chance of it being ripped from her in tomorrow's events. She wrapped Julian's carved white tiger in a scarf and buried it among her things.

The blanket-wall was swept aside and Cassia jumped, her hand over her heart. The balding head of Malik peeked through. "Greetings."

Cassia breathed again and shook her head at her own tension.

"Come away from that ledge before you fall, old man," Zeta called.

Cassia smiled from her side of the room. Did Malik have any idea how Zeta felt about him? Cassia had known since the first night she had lain here, when Malik's hands had somehow healed her shoulder.

He crossed the room to see what Zeta's firepot held, then dropped the pouch he had brought over his shoulder. Cassia let her memory linger over that first night once again.

Malik had healed her. In these many days since then, she had been so wrapped up in the revelation of Alexander's parentage and the horror that came of it, she had not dwelt much on the healing. But it came back to her now, and she studied Malik through new eyes.

She had thought him a religious old peasant that night, devoted to the gods of Petra by the way he had prayed over her. Tonight, as she watched him talk and laugh with Zeta, she saw a very different picture. A man rich enough to hire a dozen servants yet humble enough to play the part of one himself.

And his religion—this was something she had never known. A relationship with One God, a God he spoke with as a friend, a God who loved him, and supposedly her, enough to suffer a criminal's death in her place. A God she was beginning to wish she knew.

She finished her packing, then found the small box in which she had saved all the money she could. She wrapped the coins in one of her head scarves and pushed it in the bottom of the pouch.

So little. Would it get them to Jerusalem, the closest large city outside of Rabbel's realm and Hagiru's reach?

Zeta called her to the meal, and the three joined at the table.

"I thought perhaps Julian would come." Cassia tried to keep her voice casual.

Malik frowned. "He had some details to attend to before tomorrow."

The older man's wrinkled brow made her nervous, but Cassia chose to ignore it. Malik prayed over their meal and they passed the stew.

"Julian will come later," Malik said between bites, and Cassia could not hold her tongue.

"Is everything ready?"

Malik chewed the meat without answering for a moment, then swallowed and lifted his hands. "The plan is ready, the people are ready, the Lord is always ready. It is only Julian who cannot find peace."

Cassia breathed in relief. *That, I understand.*

But Malik did not seem to. "The boy still must learn to lead in the Spirit. He goes over the details again and again, as though he alone holds the future in his hands."

Zeta murmured her agreement. "But he is young, Malik." She smiled. "Perhaps you were as young once?"

"I know, I know." Malik reached for more bread. "He has many years ahead to learn how to be a man of the Spirit. The church in Petra will thrive under him, I have no doubt."

Cassia sipped at her wine, but it went down bitter, along with Malik's words. She had thus far tried not to focus on Julian here in Petra and she and Alexander in Jerusalem.

Malik's gaze found hers, reading her well. "It is the will of God that Julian lead the church here, Cassia." From his tone, one would think she had already voiced an objection.

She nodded. "His place is here. I know this."

Malik's attention was still on her, seeing through her. He grunted once and went back to his food. "And you, my child, still need to let Jesus love you."

Cassia wasn't certain how the two were connected, but she said nothing.

Malik and Zeta talked of church people and their burdens for the remainder of the meal, leaving Cassia to fret over tomorrow, and to wonder what Alexander was doing at that moment. Julian arrived as they cleared away the dishes, and Zeta sat him down to a bowl of stew before he was allowed to speak. Cassia sensed the tension between the two men.

While Julian chewed, Malik brought his pouch from the side of the room and pulled a linen-wrapped packet from it. "For you, Cassia." He embraced her quickly.

Her heart warmed at being given any sort of gift by this man she had come to love. She unwrapped it slowly.

Inside lay ten aurei, the equivalent of 250 denarii, and a letter. Cassia looked up at him and frowned.

"For your journey to Jerusalem." He patted her arm. "The money is for whatever you need. The letter is for you to give to Simeon—Elder of the church in Jerusalem and an old friend of mine. Ask for Simeon bar Clopas when you arrive. He is a weaver. Give him the letter. He will help you find a place to live, some work perhaps. People to help you."

Cassia fingered the money, more than she had ever seen in her life. More than any pouch of coins Aretas had ever brought home from his market swindles. But it was the letter that brought tears. She had not realized until that moment how fearful she was to leave these people and venture into the unknown yet again. But to have others, followers of the Way, to meet her in Jerusalem! Almost it made the parting bearable.

The tears spilled over and Malik chuckled. "None of that. Not yet. There will be time for good-byes tomorrow."

"Thank you, Malik," she whispered, then turned grateful eyes on Zeta as well.

The woman grunted. "Makes my contribution look like nothing." She produced another package. "No need to open it. It's only flatbread and sweet figs to take you through a day or two." She grinned at Malik. "In case you have trouble finding a place to spend the old man's money."

Cassia embraced Zeta, then went to Talya's striped pouch to store the gifts. Her earlier concern at the small store of coins there evaporated, and her nervousness began to lift, replaced by a tense excitement. Tomorrow they would be off!

Julian swallowed the last of his stew and stood quickly, knocking his bench backward. The three looked to him as though he would speak, and his face reddened. He scratched the back of his neck and looked to Zeta. "I thought perhaps Cassia and I could take a walk." He seemed to be asking her permission. "To talk over the details of the morning."

Zeta lifted her eyebrows and the corners of her mouth twitched. Cassia cleared her throat, feeling a little queasy. "Of course."

Zeta added, "Be careful."

Without a look at Malik, Julian extended his hand to the entrance of the home.

But Cassia looked to Malik, and the Elder of Petra seemed to send her messages with his eyes. She crossed to the opening and felt herself at the edge of a precipice, in more ways than one.

The sky was the purple sort of dark that came in the twilight hour. The street below was quiet, and Cassia and Julian descended in silence. Her stomach still felt knotted with excitement, and she forced her jittery legs to negotiate the narrow steps with care. "I am not certain it is a good idea to be walking about the city tonight." They reached the street.

"I know a place." Julian took her chilled hand. "Come."

They hurried across the wide street, behind the merchant stalls that dotted this end of the city, until they walked along the high rock wall opposite Zeta's home.

Cassia tipped her head back to try to see the top of the precipice. Somewhere up there, it seemed as high as the clouds, was the High Place where Dushara would be offered a sacrifice during the Festival of Grain. Cassia shuddered.

Julian read her thoughts. "Alexander will be well away by then."

He led her along the rock wall until they reached another set of narrow steps, twisting upward through scrubby tamarisk and nearly invisible in the fading light.

Cassia pulled back on Julian's hand. "You're *not* taking me up there."

"Only a little ways."

They reached a weedy outcropping of rock within minutes, and Julian led her along the narrow ledge to where it widened slightly, providing a comfortable place large enough for two people to sit. They settled themselves onto the flat stone, legs hanging over the edge, nearly touching.

The mountain brow across from them traced a jagged line against the darkening sky above it, and a crescent moon floated in the purple sea. To their left, a winding grove of tamarisk and acacia gave evidence of the Wadi Musa's wandering, and here and there a silvery gleam peeked through.

Cassia pointed down the street. "Zeta's home is at nearly the same height."

Julian laughed. "Between Zeta's house and the work site, I think we have spent nearly all the time we've been together perched above the street."

Together. The word brought with it a stuttering of her pulse, and Cassia looked away.

Below them, a farmer returned home late, leading a mule that kicked up dust and snorted.

She pulled her head covering down around her shoulders and let the evening breeze cool her neck. She tucked errant hairs behind her ears and felt the day's tension begin to relax.

"Cassia." Julian's voice was low, and she sensed anxiety. "There is something I want to tell you."

She nodded. "Yes, I need to speak to you as well."

He picked up a pebble and rolled it between his fingers. "What is it?"

Cassia inhaled and steadied her voice. "I am going with you, into the palace tomorrow." He began to object, as she knew he would, but she cut him off. "I know we had planned for me to be at the edge of the city, but I cannot be that far from Alexander when all of this happens. If he should need me—"

"I will be there."

"You are not his father!" The words were harsh and she regretted them immediately. "Julian—"

He shook his head. "You cannot come to the palace, Cassia."

Her hands balled into fists. "I will come—"

Julian threw the pebble into the night air. "If you cannot trust me, then you must at least trust God to keep him safe!"

She snorted. "And why should I trust this god of yours when even you cannot?"

His forehead creased and his lips tightened. "You think I do not trust—"

"All your plans and schemes—you think you can control all that happens, Julian. As though you hold the world in your own hands. That does not seem like trust to me. You are a hypocrite."

He closed his eyes, as though her words struck deep, and she regretted them, regretted her ability to see his heart. When he turned to her, his expression was sorrowful. He clasped her hands. "Don't you understand? I have to keep you safe. I cannot risk losing you."

Her hands trembled in his. "You will lose me tomorrow anyway, Julian, when Alexander and I flee to Jerusalem."

His fingers clutched at her, like a man drowning. "That is what I wanted to tell you. I am coming with you to Jerusalem."

Cassia's mouth went dry and her eyes burned with unshed tears. She tried to think, tried to find a reason to refuse. "You would leave Petra?"

His hand cupped her cheek. "What is there for me in Petra without you?"

She leaned into his hand and closed her eyes. How long since a man had touched her with tenderness? Her years with Aretas had been like living with a wild animal, his moods unpredictable and she was always wary, always careful. With Julian she felt safe.

She thought of her harsh words moments earlier. Could they truly be a family, the three of them?

Eyes still closed, Julian's whisper of her name was surprisingly close, and then she felt his kiss on her cheek, the greeting of a friend. Her eyes fluttered open, but she did not turn her face to allow him to kiss the other side.

And he did not intend to, for his next kiss found her mouth—and was not the kiss of a friend. She responded in kind, though her heart screamed a warning.

She pulled away several moments later, breathless.

"Cassia, you must know I love you."

She tried to smile, but her lips wavered with a confusing rush of joy and fear. She loved him as well, she admitted to herself, regardless of her determination to remain alone and strong.

"I know you need more time. Your heart is only with Alexander." He returned to gripping her hands. "But later, when we are far from here and he is safe, I . . . I hope you will let me care for you." He dropped his head, as if he feared her answer now that he had declared himself.

The evening smelled of cook fires and the smoke from a dozen homes wafted upward to their private perch, a smell of comfort and normalcy. And Cassia longed for what she had not known, had never known.

But she could not make promises. Not tonight, with so much still at stake.

"Tomorrow. When I leave the palace with Alexander, if you still want to join us—"

"When I bring Alexander to you at the mouth of the gorge," he corrected, his voice iron.

She shook her head. "I will be there, Julian. You cannot stop me. I will be near my son."

He released her hands. "That is not the plan, Cassia. Not the plan."

"I don't *care* about your plan!" He lifted his eyebrows and she spread her hands apologetically. "Of course I care about the plan. But it has a flaw!"

Even in the near-dark, Cassia could see the coldness of Julian's eyes. "You will not be there." His lips tightened. "You will be waiting at the Siq, and we will come to you!"

A strange feeling washed over Cassia then. A strange and yet familiar feeling. How many times had Aretas commanded her thus, telling her what she would do, what she would not do, regardless of her feelings?

Never again.

What had happened to her resolve? She had lost it all into Julian's dark eyes and generous mouth, and nearly let herself be controlled once again.

There was a time when she would have agreed, to please him. Agreed, to ensure he would love her still. But those days were over. She was stronger now. Both Aretas and Hagiru had seen to that.

"Do not think you can control me, Julian." She shifted away from him. "You are not a man I would give myself to." She searched for the words that would sever their connection. "You ran in fear from Rome, and now you are anxious to run again, to avoid what is asked of you. That is not the kind of man I want." Her inner sight served her well, for these were the words that would hurt him most.

Her declaration wounded him, clearly. But she would not call it back. He was not safe.

"It grows late." She covered her head with her scarf. "And Zeta will worry."

Julian stared into her eyes for a long moment, then climbed to his feet in the narrow space and pulled her to standing on the ledge.

She had not responded to his dictum about her plan tomorrow. Nor would she. Let him think what he liked.

When Alexander was snatched from the clutches of the queen, Cassia would be there to welcome him home.

TWENTY-SEVEN

———◆———

THE MORNING WAS STILL DARK WHEN JULIAN AWAKENED
to Malik's gentle nudge.

"They are here. They are ready."

Julian kneaded his eyes with his fists and swung his legs from the
bed. The night had been too short. Cassia's harsh words, her silence
when he left her, and his own anxiety about what this morning would
bring had kept him stirring on his bed far into the night.

And now they were to have a sort of repeat of yesterday's early
meeting, although today only those immediately involved in the plan
would be present.

Malik handed him a tunic from a nearby chair. "They are nervous."

"As am I." Julian dressed quickly, then washed his hands and face
at the basin beside the door.

"They want your leadership, your strength, Julian. But you must
come to them as a servant."

He nodded, impatient to meet the others, but Malik stayed him
with a firm hand on his arm.

"Today must not be about *your* plan, about impressing others to gain their approval, as you are prone to seek. Without the humility to allow God's Spirit to work through you, there will be trouble."

Julian sighed. Malik's words were true enough. But not so easily implemented. It seemed better to be in control than to focus on humility. Leadership and servanthood still seemed to conflict in his mind.

Malik frowned and studied the floor. Julian sensed a wrestling within the man's spirit. When Malik looked up, it was with the decision in his eyes.

"You will go. And you will lead these people. I am placing them in your hands."

Julian blinked slowly, the weight of it falling on him, along with the discomforting sense that Malik lacked confidence in him. He straightened. "Then we should go."

His people had assembled in a small room off Malik's courtyard this morning, unlike yesterday when there were so many. Julian strode into the room with Malik on his heels and blinked against the light of the oil lamps.

The faces of each turned toward him, and the murmured conversations ceased, replaced by looks of respect and confident smiles.

Compared to the warnings of Malik, the clear submission to his authority was a gift. He felt a strong, protective care for them flow through his heart, and almost a desire to gather each in a fatherly embrace.

Cassia stepped forward, her hands twisting at her midsection. She said nothing, but her eyes spilled over with anxiety. Malik remained behind him, in the corner of the room.

Julian tried to ignore the pain he felt in her presence and clapped his hands together. "We are ready?"

There were nods all around.

"We should have plenty of time to get in our places. Talya"—Julian smiled at the brave girl—"you will stay as near the throne room as you can, to wait for our arrival." Talya chewed her lip but nodded.

She will be there. She loves that boy as well.

"Nahor and Niv, you two are with me. Stay close and stay silent." The two muscular men, father and grown son, both folded their arms across their chests as one, and Julian smiled at their likeness. "Remember, I am not a friend, but a Roman who has paid you well to guard me."

Julian could feel Cassia trembling at the edge of the group and knew she felt helpless. "Cassia, you have all the provisions for the journey?"

She lifted a pouch slung over her shoulder. Julian chose to disregard her argument the previous night.

"Good. Hozai, you will have the horses waiting at the entrance to the Siq?" The short man gave a tight nod of his bald head. He had offered two of his fastest horses. A sacrifice, and Julian connected with his gaze for a moment and passed along a silent thank-you. The man dropped his gaze as though embarrassed.

"And the rest of you." Julian scanned the other three women and two men. "You will be in your place in line when the time comes."

They all looked to him still, as if he held their future in his hands. In a sense he did. The oil lamps had grown smoky, and Julian blamed them for the sudden tears that sprung behind his eyes. He cleared his throat, then remembered Malik still stood behind him.

He turned to the older man. "Can you think of anything else?" he asked, more from respect than fear of forgetting.

"We could pray."

Julian felt again his slight displeasure but brushed it off. "Yes, we should pray."

In the silent moment that followed, it was easy to hear the slap of sandals through the courtyard and the huffing of the servant Shamir as he pushed open the door.

Malik stepped in front of Julian. "What is it?"

"Palace guards, at the door." Shamir swallowed, and his eyes were wide.

Malik turned to the group. "Stay here." And then he disappeared behind Shamir.

Julian hesitated, nearly followed Malik, then decided to stay. They should not be seen together. Not today. He turned to the group. Should they pray now? It seemed wrong to begin without Malik.

Cassia trembled like a reed at the edge of the Wadi Musa. He crossed the room and gripped her arms. "We will get him, Cassia." He forced her to look into his eyes. "We will get Alexander out."

Her words were so faint, Julian could barely hear them. "They cannot kill him."

He pulled her into an embrace, uncaring that she had rejected him. "I know. We will not allow it." It was not difficult to promise. Every part of him believed it. "We must both trust God, Cassia."

Malik returned a moment later, and they all stood as though made of Roman marble, waiting to hear.

"The queen has sent for the leader of the church of Petra. She does not say why."

Julian's mind raced. How would it affect their plan if Malik was also in the palace?

"She also did not say who." Malik's gaze was on him.

Julian frowned. "What . . . what do you mean?"

Malik bowed his head slightly. "I believe she calls for *you*, Julian."

He took a step backward. "No. This is not the plan. It would change everything." His mind spun, trying to fit in the new information. "No. We are not prepared to go this way. We must stay with what we have already arranged."

Malik licked his lips, tilted his head to study Julian, then nodded. "Very well. Then I shall go." He moved toward the door.

"Wait!" Julian held up a hand and surveyed the room. "We cannot let you go in there alone. We have no idea of the queen's intent."

Malik waited, silent.

Julian debated for only a moment. "We go at first light." The eyes of his people widened, and they looked among each other. "Nahor, Niv, and I will follow Malik. The rest of you, you must go now."

Hozai piped up from the back of the room. "What if the king has not left his bed?"

Julian's hands formed fists at his side. "Then we will ensure that he does." He turned to Malik. "We will go in first. Our actions will bring both king and queen to the throne room, and your summons will be forgotten."

Malik said nothing, and Julian could not read him. "Well?"

The Elder of Petra dipped his head once, as though he was simply submitting to Julian's directive. *Infuriating man!* Julian half wondered if Malik believed he was being led to his death.

He spun to the group again. "Hozai, you can be ready with the horses earlier?" At the man's nod, Julian looked to Cassia. "Go with Hozai. But stay out of sight."

He met her eyes and her expression jolted him. She was not agreeing, not submitting, as Malik and the others had done. "Cassia—"

But there was no time. The blackness outside the chamber window had already turned to a light violet, and if Malik did not appear in the palace soon, none of what he had planned would come to pass.

He stalked to Cassia, wrapped his arms around her fiercely. She cried out and he loosened his grip.

"Go," he whispered into her ear. "Go and be safe."

And then they were all gone, all but Malik and Julian, and the father and son who would accompany them.

In the silence that followed the group's exodus, Julian felt like his own heartbeat could surely be heard by the others.

They had trusted him to lead.

Where would he take them?

TWENTY-EIGHT

Cassia passed into the street from Malik's home, but she did not turn east toward the road to the Siq. Instead, she lingered near the door watching Marta and Tabatha and the others hurry off to the palace and to their tasks. Gratitude washed over her and, with it, a determination to be part of this rescue. How could she simply wait while others cared for her son?

Hozai headed toward the market, away from the others, to fetch his donkey and wagon. She followed him at a distance until they reached the main street and he crossed it to slip between a spice stall and a shop of ceramics. Shop owners were beginning to lift their flaps, and the smells of grilled meats and honey bread wafted in the morning air.

Cassia hugged her traveling pouch, the one Talya had lovingly sewn, against her body and retraced a few of her steps back into the housing district and into a narrow alley. Already people were climbing to their flat rooftops to burn frankincense and offer libations to the sun god.

Cassia had more than traveling clothes in the pouch.

Talya had not noticed when one of the palace servant's robes had been missing from her mending basket. Cassia slipped it over her own simple tunic, then twisted and secured it at her waist. The string of beads she wove through her hair was an inexpensive one she had purchased in the market, but it would pass for something more at a distance.

When she felt adequately dressed, she pulled one more thing from the pouch.

The short dagger with its basalt handle and blade was a comforting weight in her hand. She pulled her robes aside, then fastened it to the rope that circled her tunic at her waist. She bent to test its placement and winced.

Must be careful.

The colorful pouch stood out against the white palace robes, and Cassia hurried through the alley toward the Nymphaeum, hoping she would go unnoticed.

She reached the fountain house in a few minutes, circled to the west side of the grand building, and found the large clay water pot she had placed around the corner late last night, still waiting for her against the wall.

With steady hands, she pushed the travel pouch through the wide mouth of the clay jar, then hefted the jar to her hip and strode through the Nymphaeum courtyard toward the street. She forced herself to slow. *You're carrying a pot full of water, Cassia.*

Eyes trained on the street ahead, she walked toward the palace, searching the market for Hozai and his wagon.

There. The man emerged from the shops, clucking at his donkey, and turned toward the palace. Cassia followed at a safe distance, knowing her disguise would not fool anyone who knew her. Julian would expect her to have reached the Siq by now.

Julian. Had he entered the palace yet? Did he stand before the queen?

She stepped over a wheel rut in the street and kept her gaze on the back of Hozai's brown wagon.

She felt strangely separated from Julian, unable to read him, and not only because she defied his wishes. Somehow that palace could swallow people, and it was as though he had disappeared into the underworld when he entered, lost to her. She tried to imagine him there in the throne room, strong and sure as he spoke to the king and queen, his head thrown back and those dark eyes fixed on the woman, daring her to defy him.

The street filled up with early-morning shoppers. It smelled of camel dung and the mixed odors of the market. Cassia moved forward on steady legs, sure of her plan.

A flash of memory seared her mind, of following Aretas, working his schemes with him.

But today I am the one with the scheme. The thought gave her confidence, and she touched her hand to the place where the dagger rested under her robes.

Hozai neared the palace and bore right, up over the sandy path that led to the back of the great house where deliveries were made. He had taken care to cover the back of his wagon, as though he bore goods for the royal family.

Now came the tricky part. Cassia would need to get past Hozai, into the back of the palace, without him recognizing her.

Julian's plan was a good one, detailed and careful. But it had a flaw. Talya would explain what was happening to Alexander and whisk him from the rooms where he spent his days, but she could not venture far with him without raising suspicion. Instead, she would pass him to Rachim, and then Rachim would take him to Marta, who had secured work as the palace washerwoman. Marta would put Alexander into the large basket she used to tote the washing to the banks of the Wadi Musa running behind the palace. Tabatha would join her in carrying the basket out the back of the palace, and once there, Alexander would be transferred to the back of Hozai's wagon, under the covering.

And this was where the problem lay. Cassia knew Alexander would be terrified by the time he reached Hozai and might refuse to get under that covering. He had never met Rachim, Marta, or Tabatha, and with Talya far behind in the palace, Cassia could not be certain he would cooperate with strangers.

She needed to be there when Marta and Tabatha brought him out of the palace in a basketful of dirty linens. They would ride together to the mouth of the Siq, then escape to Jerusalem on Hozai's horses.

And Julian?

Cassia pushed the thought of separation aside and plodded up the path toward the back of the palace, head low. She could see Hozai up ahead. He had circled to face the path, ready to flee. The morning sun had not yet climbed over the palace walls, and the path lay in shadow. Would he recognize her?

She kept to the wall of the palace, letting her arm nearly brush against its stone blocks. The sandy red path continued, and scrubby green bushes marked her progress.

Look away, Hozai. Would he be as cautious of discovery as she and avoid an interaction with a palace slave?

She walked on, her breath held, waiting for him to hail her. What would he do if he recognized her? But she heard only the snort and impatient pawing of Hozai's donkey, and then she was there, at the back entrance of the palace.

She slipped inside, breathing again. The immediate coolness of the limestone and marble was like a welcome drink of water, and the market street smells were replaced with the scent of floral gardens.

Cassia scanned the back hall in both directions, unsure of where Marta would appear. The halls were silent. Nearby, another corridor led deeper into the palace, and Cassia could hear the fountain that bubbled in the center of the courtyard.

A chamber door across the stone floor bid her to hide there, and she crossed and peeked inside. It appeared to be only for storage, so she slipped in still holding her traveling pouch filled with Malik's money and Zeta's provisions, and set her water pot on the floor. She stood near the door, her ears trained to pick up any sound in the hall. Each of her senses felt heightened, but her heart beat in an unbroken rhythm and her hands stilled at her sides.

A sound behind her in the storage chamber startled her and stole her breath.

A shadow shifted, then emerged.

Julian? She started forward, reaching for him.

But it was not Julian.

Her hand went to her chest.

The man hesitated as well, eyeing her warily. She sensed immediately that he was also hiding, that he feared detection.

"Who are you?" she whispered. Even dressed as a desert dweller, he resembled Julian, the dark wavy hair, the light skin, that Roman nose.

He didn't answer. His hand went to his side. So he had a weapon.

She had not imagined using her own dagger on someone who had never harmed her, who was not keeping her from Alexander. Could she?

He crossed the chamber before she had a chance to make that decision. In one trained move, he shoved her hard against the wall and covered her mouth with a rough hand.

Cassia stared into his fearsome eyes and tried to catch her breath. One thought forced itself into her mind.

No one even knows I am here.

TWENTY-NINE

JULIAN LEFT MALIK'S HOUSE ANGRY. THE MARKET STREET disappeared under the churn of his footsteps, and he felt the older man struggle to keep pace. Nahor and Niv hurried alongside him.

Why did the queen have to foul his plan with this unexpected summons of Malik? Did she somehow know they would take her prize from her today?

Did one of the several women working in the palace let something slip to another servant, and the gossip traveled to the ears of the queen?

The thought fired his blood, even though he knew he should not mistrust his Petra family.

It is of no consequence. His plan remained unaltered. He needed only to distract the king and queen long enough for Talya to begin Alexander's removal from the palace, then get himself and the two men with him out of the throne room safely.

He scowled. *Yes, only that.*

The sky lightened ahead, and dawn was upon them fully.

Had Hagiru spent the night awake, in communion with her gods? The idea drove a chill down his spine and Malik's warning echoed.

But he felt filled up with power himself this morning and was ready to face whatever the queen-turned-high-priestess delivered. Beyond the palace, the arched gate that marked the start of the sacred temple district only strengthened his determination.

He spoke over his shoulder, not slowing. "Malik, let us go in ahead of you. She will be too distracted by our presence to wonder where you are. You can go in after we have finished."

Malik said nothing, and Julian interpreted his silence as agreement.

They reached the palace, then marched up the two sets of steps, Julian leading the point of the three of them, with Nahor and Niv following. Malik remained in the street.

At the palace entrance, two guards stepped into the archway, and Julian held up a hand. "A message for the king. Word from Rome." He pushed his chin upward, giving them a good look at his Roman features.

The guards eyed each other, then one gave a quick nod and stepped aside to allow Julian to pass, though they filed in behind the three and stayed close as they passed through the front halls toward the throne room. Julian strode as though familiar with the palace, though in truth he had only followed Cassia to the central courtyard. But she had given him direction from her terrible moment before the king, and he attempted to look authoritative.

He passed through the doorway and did not slow at the sight of the lofty ceiling or marble pillars, would not appear awed by the rich fabrics on the walls, nor the superb sculptures that lined the room. The frescoes, the carved vines and medallions with their exotic animals, spoke of artists and sculptors trained in the best of Greek art centers, most likely Alexandria. An illogical jolt of jealousy surprised him, as though the enemy had found a chink in his protection.

Hagiru sat upon the throne already, purple robes spread around her, and she held out a thin arm when he entered, inviting his approach.

He stiffened and remembered he came as an invader, not a cowed peasant.

"You have returned."

Julian tried not to wince. He had hoped she would not remember him from their courtyard encounter. It made things more difficult.

"I bring a message from Rome. For the king." He stopped before the throne, legs slightly spread and back straight. Nahor and Niv pulled up behind him and he felt their solid presence.

"Indeed?" The queen's dark eyebrows rose and met in the center, under the peak of her hairline. Her bloodred lips pursed. "First you come as protector to the interloper's peasant mother, and now as emissary from Rome. Explain this."

Julian inclined his head as if he would oblige. "I shall explain all. To the king." From the corner of his eye, he saw Talya's small face, drained of color, behind a doorway at the side of the throne room. *Not yet, Talya.*

"The king is not receiving supplicants today." Hagiru's smile was amused, pleased perhaps.

Julian drew himself up, crossed his arms. "I am no supplicant! I have information for the king from the mighty Roman Empire."

Hagiru shrugged one shoulder and her gaze strayed to the side of the room. "So you said."

"Surely your soldiers have told you that an entire Roman legion waits on the other side of the Siq. Perhaps you wish me to bring these troops to bear on the palace, to prove that Rome has a word for the king." He began to sweat and tried to force his heartbeat to slow.

The first flicker of apprehension crossed the queen's face. *Ah, we have found a weakness after all.*

"The king is quite ill. He has taken to his bed."

Julian sensed it was the truth. Very well. A king in bed was no danger. He lifted his chin. It was time, and he would need to improvise.

"Perhaps I should simply remove the queen, take her to the other side of the rock where Rome waits. Perhaps that would get the attention of the king."

Nahor and Niv understood their cue and stepped forward threateningly.

Two palace guards were at their sides in an instant.

Julian laughed. "Do you think I would come here with only these two? And them not even trained soldiers?" He shrugged and folded his arms casually. "These are only two senseless thugs I hired for protection since I came to Petra. I have been here all these weeks, reporting your many weaknesses back to Rome."

Hagiru's glance shifted left and right, then over his head to the throne room's entrance. Clearly she felt concern that a contingent of Roman soldiers might burst into the chamber. She flicked an unspoken command to a guard near the doorway where Talya waited and he disappeared.

Julian followed the queen's glance and gave Talya a tiny nod. The girl vanished into the side hall.

Only a few minutes more. How long would it take Talya to convince Aretas's wife, Bethea, she should see what was happening in the throne room?

"I have told you," Hagiru said, "the king is unable—"

"Unable or unwilling?" In truth, Julian cared little whether the king appeared or not, but he needed to buy a little more time. It occurred to him now that he should have had Malik enter, for it would have stalled the matter further.

A new face appeared at the doorway. Bethea was dressed in crimson with her dark hair hanging about her face. She turned hateful eyes on Julian, and he felt that same chill the queen engendered.

Directly behind Bethea came a pack of palace guards, summoned to protect their queen.

Now we are ready. With the guards assembled in the throne room and Bethea taken from her post with Alexander, the way should be clear for the boy to be whisked from the palace, to the Siq where Cassia waited. He felt a twinge of uncertainty at that last thought but pushed it away and faced the queen. A murmuring circled the throne room from slave to servant to guard.

"Very well. The queen shall receive Rome's message."

But Hagiru's glance had not returned to him. Instead, she stared at Bethea, and Julian sensed a silent communication between the two, like a cold wind that poured out of the younger to the older, somehow giving Hagiru information.

What is happening?

He watched both women, trying to regain control of the room. Finally, finally, Hagiru brought her attention back to him, but something had changed.

The flow of power he had felt when he entered now ebbed as though it had met a dam, and then somehow, impossibly, he felt it reverse. Like a river running upstream, like a tide washing out, like air being sucked from his lungs. He staggered backward.

The queen stood and raised her arms, like some kind of dark bird poised above him. He half expected her to swoop over the throne room and knock him from his feet. His chest heaved, pressured by an unknown heavy hand.

"You do not represent Rome!" The queen's voice roared through the throne room. "You speak for no one but that old troublemaker and his peasant crowd of rebels!" She raised a pointed finger at Julian but spoke to her men. "Take him!"

The guards were on the three of them in an instant before Julian could ascertain how she had known. But the sense of another presence in the room, a heavy, sulfurous presence that whispered secret knowledge, made it clear.

Julian struggled in the grip of the guards, but his thoughts were on the last time he had breached the palace. The sense of power that had filled him, spreading protection over Cassia and Alexander.

He had felt powerful today, but it had not been the same. No, today had been only his own foolish confidence. Hagiru was instructing other guards to find Alexander and bring him to the throne room.

Julian reached out in his spirit for that filling of power, but it was too late.

Once again, he had failed.

THIRTY

CASSIA'S HEAD SMACKED THE WALL AS THE ROMAN'S ROUGH hand clamped her mouth and his body pushed her into the stone blocks. Her legs shook and her mind raced with thoughts of Alexander.

Her attacker was so like Julian, and yet this close she could see he was also unlike. His eyes were harder, his mouth tighter.

He had her pinned somehow so she could not move. Not bring up a knee nor twist away. She thought to bite his hand, but the fury in his eyes and the weapon she could feel pressed against her midsection gave her pause. She heard her own blood, a *whoosh* in her ears.

"Who are you?" His voice was harsh and guttural.

She could say nothing with his hand in place but opened her eyes wider and tried to look innocent.

He leaned in closer. "Do not scream." He edged his hand away from her mouth. "Who are you?"

"Cassia. I am also hiding. You are a Roman?"

His hand clamped over her mouth again. "Who told you this?"

She shook her head and he lifted his hand. "Only your appearance." Before he could stop her voice again, she asked, "Are the Romans attacking Petra?"

He pushed her harder against the wall, and she had the strange thought she would soon be one of Petra's sculpted figures in a wall niche.

His dark brows came together in a point over basalt-black eyes. "Why are you hiding?" Before she could answer, he shifted to reach between their bodies—for some unseen weapon?

Fear washed over her like heat, then receded, leaving her cold and shaking. "They have taken my son. I am trying to get him back."

She tried to read his reaction, but he seemed not even to hear. He was all nerves, as though he was attuned to every sound and every movement outside their hiding place.

Like a trained soldier.

He smelled of sweat and leather and cook fires, as she imagined a soldier would, and she suddenly feared her escape with Alexander might be complicated by forces she had not considered. *I have to know.* "Will Petra be taken today?"

His gaze roamed hers, as though he would read *her* and determine friend or enemy. "I do not wish to kill a woman." He acted as if that were an answer. Perhaps it was.

"I am no threat to you," Cassia whispered. "And I have no loyalty to the royal house."

He seemed to consider her words, then in a rush released her as he shoved himself back from the wall, retreated a few steps, and scowled at her. "Tell no one." He darted to the doorway, leaned out to scan the hall, and disappeared.

Cassia exhaled, leaned back against the wall, and tried to slow her heart.

But thoughts of Alexander soon overtook the aftereffects of the encounter. She left her water pot and pouch, slipped to the chamber doorway, checked the hall, then slid along the wall until she could bend her upper body around the corner and watch the hall that led into the center of the palace.

She did not have long to wait. At the far end of the corridor where she imagined it branched into the central courtyard, a pair of figures, one small and one larger, hurried toward her.

Cassia froze, willing the two shapes to become Marta and Alexander. Her heart seemed to beat in rhythm with their hurried steps, and then she dared to hope it was really him, and then she was certain.

Marta's head scarf had come loose and fluttered behind her. She held Alexander's hand in her own and her mouth worked silently as though she spoke to him, but her gaze was focused ahead. Alexander ran to keep pace, tripped over his own feet, and nearly fell. She slowed and righted him, then pulled him on.

Cassia felt a movement to her right and gripped the corner in fear. But it was Tabatha, speeding toward her and dragging a large woven basket. Her gaze connected with Cassia's and her mouth dropped open but she kept moving.

Cassia looked back to Alexander, tried to feel if he was afraid, tried to send him the messages of her heart. He looked so big. Had he dared to grow in spite of their separation? And yet he seemed vulnerable, too, and she longed to have him back in her arms.

As though he felt her love streaming toward him, Alexander lifted his eyes to the end of the hall and saw her. Her heart lifted and joined his, and his smile, she knew, matched her own.

And then there came more movement, behind the two, and Cassia's glance went beyond Alexander and Marta to the figures behind them.

It seemed to Cassia then that time had frozen like the ice she had seen one winter at the edge of a river in the mountains of Syria. It moved forward, one tiny drip at a time, with each moment suspended in a bead of clear water, magnified and distorted.

She saw the palace guards lurch into the corridor. Saw Alexander's hands reach toward her, unaware of the danger. Marta, too, with a joyous smile.

Then heard the pounding feet.

Marta turned, her eyes huge. The two guards lunged for them. Marta pushed Alexander behind her and raised her arms. The silence of the halls shattered with her shriek, and one of the muscled men swept her aside like an empty wheat sack. His forearm connected with her temple and she went down. The sound of her head as it smacked the marble floor was like a melon falling from a market table.

Cassia started forward, but Tabatha was beside her somehow and gripped her arm with claw-like hands.

Alexander screamed. The guard seized him, then turned and grunted something to the other guard, who picked up Marta's limp body, flung it over his shoulder, and followed the first.

Cassia strained at Tabatha's hold on her. The girl was stronger than she looked.

Two more guards rounded the corner ahead and took in the scene.

In that moment, Alexander twisted enough in the arms of his captor to connect with Cassia one final time, to reach his arms toward her and scream her name.

"Mama!"

The word echoed and bounced down the corridor and she slipped from Tabatha's grasp, tears streaming, and opened her arms as though she could capture the sound and have Alexander with it.

The two new guards focused on her, but she barely took note. Her attention was on Alexander as he turned the corner and was lost to her.

Arms extended and empty, she stared at the hollow place where her son had been.

A thousand kisses, shekel. A thousand kisses.

THIRTY-ONE

⸻

IN THE THRONE ROOM, JULIAN TRIED TO WRENCH HIMSELF from the guards who held him, but he did not know what he would do if they let him go. By now the others were racing through the palace in search of Alexander. Had the women gotten him out? Did Hozai have him even now, under the tarp in the back of his wagon, rumbling over the rutted limestone street to where Cassia waited?

Hagiru did not leave him to his thoughts. She stood on the throne platform above him, her eyes like two black bits of night spilling down on him.

"You thought to overpower me? To take what is mine?"

Julian expanded his chest. "He is not yours!"

"Ah, but he is." She smiled and rubbed her toe into the platform as though crushing an insect. "I do not know how you and your fellow Jew-lovers escaped from the amphitheatre. But the next time, I will not be so generous as to let you die gloriously as entertainment for the people."

Julian kept silent. His attention should be fixed elsewhere, not on the queen. *Father, I need Your power now. Not for my sake, Lord. Protect Your people.*

He felt the oppression lift a bit and leaned into his prayer.

But Hagiru must have felt the change, too, for a wave of darkness washed toward him from the throne. When he looked at the queen, her arms were raised toward him and her head thrown back. Her lips moved silently, and watching her pray to her god from the pit caused Julian to break into sweat and then grow chilled.

Movement at the edge of the room drew his attention. Two guards pushed in. One had a bulky arm around the waist of a small, wriggling boy. The other had a woman flung over his shoulder, as though he were a trader from the East carrying a bolt of silk. Julian could only see the lower half of her body, as her head and shoulders were draped down the guard's back. Even so, the muscles in his jaw bulged and his teeth clenched.

Hagiru laughed, low in her throat. "So, Dushara favors us after all." She turned on Julian. "Perhaps you should speak to *your* god, and tell him the god of Petra does not appreciate his presence."

Julian barely heard her. His eyes were focused on the second guard and what he carried. The man flung the limp body of the woman from his shoulder and dropped her to the floor.

Marta.

God, what have I done? Julian started toward Marta, though her bloodless lips and closed eyes gave him little hope. The guards who held him jerked him backward.

"We found her secreting him toward the back of the palace," the guard said to Hagiru.

The other set Alexander on his feet. Julian drank in the sight of the boy, trying to memorize every detail he could pass to Cassia if he managed to escape the palace. He looked healthy and was dressed as a prince, in the fine white robes of royalty. But his face was tear streaked and his lower lip trembled. He looked to the queen, not noticing Julian.

"I want to see my mother!" His voice was high and sweet, and it broke Julian's heart.

Cassia, I am so sorry.

How had it come to this? He had been so certain of his plan, so sure they followed the will of God in saving Alexander from the terror the queen planned for him. Julian felt the heavy crush of his failure, and it pressed on him in sharp contrast with the confidence he had felt when he entered. Some lessons were learned too late.

Hagiru turned on him once more, her eyes and her words cold. "I sent for the old man this morning. But I imagine you already know this. And it is just as well that you are here in his stead, for I am given to know the old man fancies you as his replacement." She licked thin lips, then sat on the throne and leaned back as though dealing with Julian was as trifling as giving direction on the morning meal.

"So I have a message for the old man, and you shall hear it as well." She paused, running her gaze over him as if to take his measure. "Dushara is the god-prince of Petra. And he will not be dethroned. I do not know why you and your band of rebels have aligned yourselves with the boy's mother, but I can promise you this"—she leaned forward on the throne and her eyes burned—"not one of you will survive your defiance of me!"

A wave of self-loathing washed over Julian, disgust at his failure and his foolishness, despair over the future. He swayed on his feet, believing the queen's words and half hoping she would immediately make good on her promise. At least if she did, he would not have to face Cassia.

"Julian?"

Alexander's small voice dragged his attention away from the queen. He tried to smile at the boy, to reassure him that all would be well, but the smile did not reach his lips.

Alexander cupped hands to his mouth and whispered, "Don't listen to her, Julian. She is very mean!"

The guard grabbed Alexander by the neck. Bethea started forward as though she would intervene, then stopped.

But Alexander's simple words took hold, and Julian faced the queen once more. A calmness swept into his soul, and he spoke words he knew were not of himself. "A time is coming, Queen Hagiru, when the One True God will make Himself known to you. And on that day"—Julian's voice rose to fill the throne room—"on that day, you will bow your knee to Him."

Her face contorted into a death mask of rage and she shot to her feet. *"Out!"* She pointed to the chamber entrance. "You will leave at once, and tell your people if they wish to wage a war, we shall see whose god is the stronger!"

Julian took one last look at Alexander, then nodded to Nahor and Niv and backed out of the throne room, through the front hall and onto the palace portico.

Malik still waited in the street, his face upturned to the palace steps, and as Julian studied the old man below, he knew it was only the prayers of Malik that had kept them safe. Certainly it was nothing Julian had done.

And now that they were out and all their plans had come to naught, he must seek out one small woman and tell her that her son was not yet coming home.

THIRTY-TWO

CASSIA SNAPPED, AS THOUGH SHE HAD AWAKENED FROM a frightful dream, and ran toward the end of the hall where Alexander had disappeared.

She knew the guards were there ahead, but somehow all else faded from view, and she ran through a dark tunnel. She heard herself yell something, she knew not what, as though the empty place inside had a voice of its own.

Somewhere in the middle of the hall she met up with the two guards. One of them, bigger and uglier, bent his head and drove it toward her belly. She fixed on his greasy hair and felt revulsion as his head burrowed into her stomach.

Air exploded from her chest and sparks ignited behind her eyes. She felt herself lift up, up, and over the guard, watched the frescoed ceiling pass under her, and wondered at such beauty and such ugliness in the same place. She hit the marble hall, dragged in one ragged breath, then remembered her training, leaped to her feet, and whirled to face them.

Her hand went instinctively to the dagger under her robe, and she said a quick prayer of thanks it had not punctured anything in the fall. It was slick and cold in her hand but felt like a caress. It was for this moment she had trained with Yehosef, all those long, sweaty nights in the theatre.

That surge of anger she had accessed so often with Yehosef came back to her, a welcome friend, to strengthen her arm and her mind to the fight.

She half crouched, dagger extended, and reveled in the flicker of concern that crossed the face of the guard who had flipped her onto the floor. They were brutes kept for their muscle, not their minds, and they had no weapons but their strength.

She circled, keeping them both in front of her, waiting.

The bigger one had a jagged scar that ran from his cheekbone to his hairline, and his eye drooped over the mutilated skin. He lunged first, as she knew he would, and she was prepared.

She lashed out with the dagger, a thrust and parry as Yehosef had taught her. The dagger found purchase on the guard's arm and drew blood. He howled, covered his arm with his hand, and backed off.

Cassia let the anger well up, a hot fountain of hate. She wished it had been the other eye instead of his arm. She flicked a glance to the second guard, daring him to be next.

Instead of fear, though, she saw amusement. A bubble of terror forced itself into her chest.

And then they were both on her at once. She felt the blows, heard the dagger *clink* somewhere on the marble floor, and realized in a flash that no amount of training would allow one small woman to take down two muscle-bound guards.

The big, greasy one wrapped his bloody arm around her waist like the arm of a lover and pulled her body to his, her back to his chest. The palace servant's robe she had stolen soaked up his blood at her waist like a red sash tied around her, and she tasted her own blood in her mouth and felt her lip swell.

He bent his thick lips to her ear and laughed. "Now we are having fun, are we not?"

His partner crossed the floor, scooped her dagger into his palm, and turned, a wicked smile playing on his face. Cassia's stomach churned and the anger drained from her, leaving her a brittle shell. Perhaps if the guard would squeeze harder, she would simply break into pieces and this nightmare would end.

The second guard sauntered toward them. He swung the dagger from a thumb and forefinger, still smiling.

"Cut for a cut, Lazar?" he said to her captor.

"Hmm," he murmured into her ear, as though the other fiend had offered him a ripe piece of fruit. "But it would be a shame to mar this beauty." His face was still buried in her neck.

His friend laughed. "Perhaps somewhere none but her husband would see, then!"

Cassia closed her eyes and fought the nausea that rose in her chest.

A shout from the end of the hall snapped her eyes open. Another palace guard hailed them, then waved a hand. "Bring the girl! The queen wants her—now!"

The bloody guard growled his disappointment, then kicked at her heels. "Walk." He loosened his grip on her waist only enough to step beside her.

The halls passed in a blur, and Cassia felt as though her feet slid over the marble floors, more carried to the throne room than arriving in her own strength. But she heard the slap of her own sandals on the white floor, heard it echo in the silent, lifeless room. After the violent struggle in the halls, the room seemed like the eye of a storm.

Cassia turned her heavy head in all directions, searching for a face she knew. Had Julian left her already? Where were Nahor and Niv? Malik? She scanned the doorways, hoping for Marta's face.

She knew without looking that Alexander was not there. She would have sensed him. The room was hollow and empty, save Hagiru's seething presence on the throne.

Cassia smelled incense and wondered absently if the queen had been offering sacrifices before Cassia had arrived. The thought brought a vision of Alexander on the High Place altar. It fell over her eyes like a hazy veil and produced a wave of dizziness that left her so sick, she expected to retch. She bared her teeth, stared at the queen, and strained in the grip of the guards.

"So, Aretas's plaything has not had enough?" Hagiru's chin tipped down and her eyes peered over her long nose.

Cassia's stomach settled and she drew herself upright to face the queen. "You will not kill my son."

Hagiru laughed. Her arms rested casually on the carved sides of the throne, and she lifted one hand at the wrist and gave the guard a small flick of her hand to indicate he should release Cassia. He did so with a shove, and she stumbled forward several steps before gaining her balance and facing the queen.

"And you will stop me?" Hagiru drew out each word as though the thought amused her.

Cassia knew the futility of it. She had nothing. No plan, no weapons, no army. She was only a mother. She had begged for the life of her son once before, but now her begging would accomplish nothing. No, it was a time for power.

And she had none.

She stood there, wishing the force of her hatred could melt the queen like a flame touched to candle wax. Hagiru met her look of hatred with a searing heat of her own, and Cassia felt the scorch of it build in her chest. It stole her breath and still it burned.

Black spots dotted her vision, and she imagined she saw a blackness hover over the queen like a cloud of malevolence. She felt the fumes of it choke her, and she swayed on her feet, fighting and knowing it was useless to fight.

Somewhere to her right there was a flutter of white, barely noticeable in her distorted sight, but then the white form was at the side of the queen and the noxious cloud dissipated, and Cassia was able to draw in a pained breath. She leaned forward, hands on her knees, and tried to regain the strength the queen had somehow stolen.

"It is the king." The messenger's whisper was loud enough for Cassia to hear. "He has taken a turn. You must come."

Hagiru's look of disgust flowed down over Cassia. "Throw her in a cell," she said to the guards at the edge of the room. "I will deal with her later."

Cassia sagged backward, exhausted beyond measure, and was nearly grateful for the guards when they caught her from behind.

Hagiru disappeared in a swoosh of purple, then Cassia felt herself dragged backward.

She would await the queen's good pleasure on the floor of a cell.

THIRTY-THREE

CASSIA'S STRENGTH RETURNED BY DEGREES AS THE GUARDS dragged her by her arms through the palace halls. First, the memory of Alexander's sweet face as he called out to her only moments ago lifted her head and opened her eyes. Then the hateful vision of her boy on the High Place altar strengthened her legs under her. She pulled herself to standing and held her ground.

The two men paused to spin her around to walk with them. She noted with relief these two were not the ones whom she had wrestled with earlier, not the greasy brute whose arm she had sliced open.

They pushed her along in front of them, down a corridor she'd never traveled, then stopped at a set of dimly lit steps. She could not see the bottom and knew they must end underground.

She had existed in a haze of despair since the guards had grabbed her, but now the reality of descending into the earth, far from sunlight and from Alexander, wormed itself into her consciousness and stirred up a new fierceness.

My last chance to save him.

She rocked back on her heels at the top of the steps and yanked her arms from the guards. They had not expected her defiance, and she slipped from their grasp.

A moment of triumph was followed by their angry shouts. They both reached out for her, and then she was fighting them, not with the trained moves of the arena Yehosef had taught her, but with a frantic, frenzied attack. She lashed out with arms and legs, kicked and clawed with the fury of an animal protecting its young. Her fingernails dug into flesh. The scene flashed light and dark before her as her hair tumbled about her face and blocked her vision.

She heard the guards' curses. Felt the rip of her clothes. Still she fought on, panting and thrashing. All the anger and futility of these past weeks exploded in a hundred pieces and she saw herself as from a distance, a tangled twist of tamarisk branches tossed in the wind.

But it could not last. Her strength ebbed, her arms slowed, and then she was soaring, flying, over open space—they had cast her off and thrown her down the steps. Time slowed enough for her to remember the first time she had been thrown out of the palace, the beginning of this nightmare, and to realize with a crushing sadness that this was the end.

The bottom of the steps rushed up to meet her and she thudded to the ground and lay still.

She heard the laugh of the guards as from a great distance and heard the word *jackal*. For a delirious moment she thought she heard Alexander's laughter float above their derision, but then it was gone and she knew it had not been real.

Cassia was conscious of nothing until she found herself being carried by her wrists and ankles through the darkness. A fire burned in her wrist and shot up her arm and into her heart.

Darkness again, then a scrape of iron and stone. The pain took her breath away.

She felt her body swing between them like a sack of barley being tossed onto a pile, then felt the weightlessness yet again and the hard smack of the ground beneath her.

When she woke, it was to solid darkness and utter silence.

The dirt floor was cold beneath her, and she lay still a moment, focused on her breathing. She tested her wrist, then cried out in pain and brought her hand to her belly, cradling it with her other hand.

The darkness was like the grave, complete and heavy, as though she had been buried while yet alive.

Am I alive?

The thought was like a wisp of smoke, and she fought to hold on to it. How could one be certain she still lived? Perhaps this was the underworld itself. She forced a picture of her cell into her mind, to hold on to sanity. Stone walls, no doubt. Iron bars across a small grate of a door.

In the end, it was the searing pain in her wrist, too real, too earthbound, that convinced her she had fallen only to the depths of the palace, and not to the depths of the earth.

And yet, what difference did it make?

She was useless here, as surely as if she were dead. The Festival of Grain began tomorrow. How long would Hagiru keep her here? Would she ever send for her?

If she ever frees me, it will not be before she has killed my son. This was truth.

Cassia rolled to her side and curled herself into a ball, still cradling the injured wrist. Her cheek lay in the dirt, but she barely noticed.

Memories washed over her, of happy times with Alexander, of her years with Aretas.

Cassia sighed as a tear slid to the dirt beneath her cheek. She had thought she had come so far, changing into a woman of strength. And yet what had it accomplished?

Strength had brought her to Petra. And Alexander was taken from her.

Strength had pushed Julian away so she could stand alone. And now she lay alone in a cell.

It would have been better to remain weak.

She had pushed Julian away, refused to let him into her heart, unwilling to rely on a man again. But if she had let Julian take control, if she had never come to the palace and simply done what he told her, she would not be here now, where she had no chance to help her son. Relying on herself only brought failure.

A scuffle in the darkness startled her. Something nearby and not human. She pulled herself to sitting and scurried backward, away from the scratching sound. Unthinking, she bore weight on her wrist. Flames shot through her arm and exploded in her head, and then the darkness grew even heavier and she slumped to the floor.

⚜

Cassia awoke, eyes blinking slowly. She felt only a slight surprise to find herself standing on the bank of a rushing streambed, her bare feet sinking into the mossy ground and ferns tickling her ankles. The smell of damp earth and leafy growth filled her, a smell she had loved all her life and had greatly missed since coming to the desert city of Petra, with its grand gardens all enclosed in the courtyards of the wealthy.

A huge acacia tree hung out over the stream, which she saw now was really a river. Its green boughs shaded her from the sunlight, still a pale yellow of early morning. The river rushed and tumbled here over smooth rocks, and somewhere nearby she believed she could hear it fall to a greater depth.

She sighed, feeling a deep contentment for the first time in many years. The feeling of holding a newborn Alexander in her arms, of watching him take his first steps, of the first time he wrapped skinny arms about her neck and clung to her.

"It is beautiful here," a low voice nearby said.

She sighed again, not caring to turn to the voice. "Yes, lovely."

The voice became the figure of a man beside her, but still she felt no curiosity about him, and rather than turn, she reached for the rockrose at her feet and ran her fingertips over its leaves.

"I planted that rose especially for you."

She smiled at him. "Did you?" He was not tall, nor remarkable in any way. She had never seen him before, and yet he was familiar. As though she had been hearing stories about him for many years and now at last was seeing his face.

He extended his arm along the riverbank. "Would you like to walk?"

Cassia did not answer but fell into step with him, and there was comfortable silence between them. She felt strangely as though her feet did not touch the ground, did not disturb the moss or plants, and yet the river passed by as they walked.

She tried to remember why she had been so sad earlier, but the memory eluded her, out of reach. She let it go.

"We will speak of that later," her friend said.

She sighed once more. "Where are we going?"

"To the truth."

They walked for some time without speaking again. A small wild hare darted in front of them and they slowed to watch. Another hare joined the first, and the two tumbled through the grasses like two siblings wrestling. Cassia laughed and her friend laughed with her.

The hares scampered away and her laughter went on, until it

swelled in her chest and turned to crying, as laughter sometimes did when one had held back tears too long.

She turned to gaze at her friend through blurred eyes, the tears building until she sobbed as though her heart would break and yet did not know why.

It was like—like something else . . . she tried to remember. Yes, like the time Malik had laid his hands on her shoulder and brought forth a storm of emotion she did not understand.

She did not know what her friend would say to such a display without cause, but he only wrapped her in strong arms and let her weep against his shoulder.

"We have reached the truth."

She nodded, ready to hear it.

"Cassia, you have spent many years seeking love through pleasing others. They have failed to love you well, for they were human and could not love you as you needed."

She sniffed against him, the sobs ebbing.

"You must find the love you seek before you can love others from your strength. And you must love from strength, not from need."

She pulled back, looked up into his warm eyes. "You sound like Malik."

He smiled. "Ah, Malik. He is a special friend of mine."

A light breeze lifted Cassia's hair and cooled her tears. She wrapped her arms about her waist. "How do I find the love that I seek?"

The light around them wavered and flickered, as though it were a candle flame blown in the wind. He grew serious, but it was still with the intensity of love in his eyes. When he spoke, his voice seemed to flow over her heart like a healing balm.

"Love has already found *you*."

She reached for Him then, because he seemed to be fading away, and because in that moment she knew His name, and the eyes of her heart opened and she wanted only to stay with Him and know Him more.

Jesus.

When she whispered His name and blinked again, she found herself back in the palace cell, still lying in the dirt, with visions of a grassy riverbank still hovering before her eyes.

THIRTY-FOUR

JULIAN LEFT THE PALACE TOO NUMB TO FEEL ANYTHING. Nahor and Niv followed behind, and somewhere Malik would be there, waiting to chastise him for his failure to trust in a power greater than himself. But he could only see Cassia's eyes, bereft of Alexander once more, and Marta's gray face and limp body sprawled on the floor of the throne room. He stalked down the main street, unwilling to speak.

They reached the housing district, and Julian slowed long enough to let Nahor and Niv reach him. Malik was not in sight.

The father and son pulled up and waited for his instructions.

Only a fool would look to me to lead.

"Go to the Siq. Find Cassia and tell her Alexander will not be coming."

"What will you do?" Nahor asked, his chin lowered.

Julian looked down the street to the tomb site where he and Cassia had spent so many hours together. "Go back to the tombs." *I am good at nothing else.*

He left them quickly, before Malik would appear, before they could ask any more questions, before anyone would rely on him to say or do or be anything at all.

It seemed to Julian the work site should have changed, should be different now that the world had shifted for him. But it was as he had left it, with little progress made in his absence. The crew worked near the middle of the facade, and no one had taken his place today on the highest stone ledge where his decorative figures would lend their beauty to the rock wall.

Here is where I should be leading. Where I can accomplish something.

He climbed the narrow steps carved for the sculptors and masons, ignoring the laborers who hailed him as he passed.

His hammer and chisel felt solid and worthwhile in his hands, and he took his rightful place facing the rock and hacked at the newest niche as though he could make it feel pain. The rock split and chips flew with no one to gather them, and the *ching* of his tools rang out across the narrow valley.

The physical release of attacking the rock did little to calm his spirit. Instead, his mind flew back to Rome, to the last time he had tried to take a stand and failed.

Why did I think it would be different this time?

No, it served no purpose to strive for greater things. Making a name for himself as a sculptor should be his focus.

The gouges in the orange-red rock deepened, and Julian did not pause even to wipe the sweat from his forehead. It beaded and ran into his eyes, but he merely blinked at the sting and kept pounding, pounding. The sun slid across the sky and the salt of his sweat mixed with tears, though he did not know if he wept or if his eyes simply ran with tears from the effort he expended. Nor did he care.

The midday call to eat echoed up from the ground and he ignored it. If he could keep up this pace, perhaps this niche would be hollowed out behind the small column of stone he left untouched, and he could begin the finer details of carving by tomorrow. Yes, that would impress the unskilled on the ground below, to see the newest sculpted capital, with its floral motif, take shape so quickly under his hands.

He heard his name called but assumed it was only for the meal and waved away the distraction. But then he realized someone was climbing to him, and he glanced down, ready to scold for the interruption—and found Malik, gasping for breath and clinging to the rock wall.

"What are you *doing*, old man?"

The sun reflected on Malik's balding head and his fingers scraped the stone for a hold. "Praying!"

Julian huffed. "You should not be up here."

Malik squinted up at him. "Then you come down."

Julian dropped his shoulders, then his tools. "Return to the ground. I will come down."

Malik picked his way slowly back down the rock wall and Julian followed, nearly stepping on the man's head. Finally in the street, Julian spoke. "I have much to finish before the end of the day. What do you need?"

"The tombs will wait." Malik's gaze on him was somber. "The Lord will not."

Julian barked a mirthless laugh. "What does the Lord want with me?"

"Everything."

Julian stalked away, not knowing where he walked but not wanting to remain. "I have tried that, and it has only brought others pain."

Malik kept up with him, panting slightly. "You have *not* given everything, Julian. Not yet." His voice held an uncharacteristic note of anger.

Julian slowed, then turned, shaking with the emotion he had held at bay since leaving the palace. "You have no idea what I have tried. You were not there, in Rome."

Malik gripped his arm and dug his fingers into Julian's skin until it hurt. "Tell me."

Julian pulled away, crossed the street to an outcrop of rock at the base of the cliff, and flung himself onto it. Malik lowered himself onto the ledge a moment later.

Julian searched for a place to begin, a place that did not feel like ripping open a barely healed wound. "The church in Rome is strong. I grew up there, in the midst of all of them, ready to take my place."

"Your parents are believers?"

"Yes. Since before my birth."

"A blessing."

Julian snorted. "Yes, as much as growing up in the shadow of a great man is a blessing for any boy." His father's tall, athletic form appeared in his mind's eye. "He is a senator, a well-respected one."

He felt Malik's surprise. "A Christian senator?"

"Exactly. It has not been an easy balance for him. But he has maintained his integrity, his witness, and his influence through all these years."

"Impressive, as you say."

Julian looked away, out over the sunbaked city. "Yes, until I managed to put all of that in danger."

"God is bigger than even our own impetuous mistakes."

Not surprising he assumes I was impetuous. "I did not believe that my father took enough of a stand when the persecutions began as a trickle. I felt if he were more vocal, he could stop it from becoming a flood."

"So you became more vocal for him?"

Julian rolled a stone under his foot, creating a track in the sand, following the track as though it carried him backward through time. The memories were there, hardly buried.

The arena, its thousands cheering, celebrating, as believers were torn apart. He saw the Flavian Amphitheatre filled to capacity, yellow-and-red pennants at its upper tier snapping in the warm breeze, and the white-and-gold togas of thousands in the seats.

And Vita, her blood soaking into the sand, nothing more than an afternoon's entertainment for them.

Later, when his father met with the others in the Senate House, Julian had burst into the building to speak his mind, convinced his father was too weak to say what should be said.

"They were *Roman citizens*!" His voice slapped back at him as if each of the senators were also made of stone. Even his father's face was unnaturally still. "We are not Gaulic barbarians!" he continued, his heart pounding. "We are Rome, and Rome has always shown respect for dissenting opinions, has always valued debate and discourse, as each of you in this room can bear witness to!"

His father was beside him in a few moments, his face still a mask of stone. He put an arm around Julian's shoulder and bowed to the Senate. "Forgive my son, gentlemen. He is young and hotheaded, with all the brashness that accompanies his youth."

"He shall make a fine senator someday!" one of his father's friends called out generously, and the room laughed. Julian felt his face flame. His father led him out of the Senate House, to the marble steps that overlooked the city.

"Go home, son." He spoke as though Julian were a child who had interrupted him at work.

"Father—"

But his father held up a hand. "This is not the way we shall win this battle."

Julian went home then. Back to his mother, Ariella, who had seen her share of grief in the arena and had an angry crisscross of a scar on her upper arm to prove it. She had always told him she was proud to bear the shame of her Lord's cross on her body as a reminder. That day she cried with him over the broken body of Vita, and the guilt that accompanied her death.

Julian came back to the present, to Malik's silent censure beside him. "My father has done much for the Christians in Rome. Not only despite his position but *because* of it, using his influence in elite circles."

"A wise man."

"With a foolish son. I brought undue attention and danger to my family through my actions."

"This is why you came to Petra?"

He laughed. "Yes. Ironic, isn't it? I fled Rome for the sake of my family's safety. And ended up here, where I have only done the same thing again. Brought danger and even death to the people I love."

The street had grown quiet, the noonday sun driving merchants and laborers under shade for a respite. Malik was quiet also for a few minutes.

"Julian, Vita's death was not your fault."

"She would not have been there—"

"Perhaps not. But she would not have been taken home to eternity if the Lord had not allowed it. The death of His saints is precious in His sight."

"Well, I see it differently. And I would imagine her family does as well."

"God has them in His hand, Julian. But there is more at issue here than even a family's grief. The question is whether you will become the man God calls you to be and allow Him to use your past and even your mistakes to further His kingdom rather than using them as excuses to hold back."

Julian shot to his feet and turned on Malik. "You have done nothing but push me into places I do not wish to go since I arrived here, old man! How many times must I explain that I am no great leader, nor will I ever be?"

Malik opened his mouth to speak yet again, but Julian was tired of talk, tired of guilt. Tired of Petra. He held his hands in front of him to stop the flow of Malik's words, then spun and walked away.

If only he could be anywhere but here, in this city of stone.

THIRTY-FIVE

—◆—

MALIK PICKED HIS WAY THROUGH THE MAIN CITY STREET, barely noticing the shoppers whose shoulders he bumped, forgetting to step around the piles left by rude camel drivers who did not keep their animals to the gutter. His feet carried him to the Great House, empty of council members today, but his thoughts carried him to the future and left him feeling despair.

How can this boy lead, Jesus? He is so young.

The answer came swift and sure. *Think of My ministry at his age.*

"Yes, but You were the Son of God!" Malik crossed the first courtyard of the Great House, drawing the curious look of a servant who scrubbed the courtyard floor.

He entered the quiet room where the council met and crossed to his customary place in the half circle of seats that rose around a central platform. The room was desolate, empty, and the sunlight filtered in without much strength, leaving the room gray and shadowy. Malik rubbed his knuckles across the rough stone of his seat and slumped backward.

He felt friendless and misunderstood in this place, and he thought of Julian's father back in Rome, taking his stand in the Senate. The thought gave him little comfort. Rome was a long way off, and here in Petra, Malik was alone.

I need more time, Lord. More time to establish Your church here, to strengthen the believers. I am not ready to pass it to another. Not yet.

He felt the Lord had things to say to him, but he didn't want to hear. He closed his spiritual ears to the small Voice and instead filled the council house with his own loud voice. "Not yet!"

The words echoed in the hollow shell of the room, and with the uttering of them, a deep and pervading sense of fatigue fell on him. Yes, he was tired, very tired.

Had he achieved all he had hoped in his lifetime? Had it been enough? The question brought him once again to Julian. The boy longed for impact and importance in a way that was different from his father's quiet influence in Rome. Not a better way, necessarily. But different. And Malik knew that God wanted to give Julian that desire, but only if he could surrender his own need for achievement, for acclaim and approval, that drove him even yet. Julian would have to become a servant before he could ever be a leader.

And he will.

Malik was unsure if the words were the Lord's or his own, or if perhaps they at last were speaking in harmony.

Step outside.

Malik obeyed. On the steps of the Great House, he paused, waiting for more direction.

The High Place.

Malik turned reluctant eyes upward, to the flat top of the nearest mountain, the place where evil acts were performed in the name of Petra's demon-gods.

The place where I will show Myself strong.

The red cliff of the mountain formed the backdrop of the amphitheatre on the other side of this city, but from this side, the cliff was a sandy incline of sparse trees and bushes, with a lone track weaving upward past carved tombs and family caves. Malik's gaze traveled the direction of the path until he scanned the flat surface of the mount. He was much too far away to see the altar he knew rested there, nor could he see the obelisks that had been carved as *betyls* for the gods, resting places for them where the people could worship.

He squinted when he spotted a puff of smoke rising from the lip of the plateau. Was there, even now, a sacrifice being offered on the altar?

The sun scorched his eyes, and he lifted a hand to shade them and watched as the smoke continued to rise, to become a billowing cloud that grew and spread over the High Place.

And then the feeling came, that feeling of the *knowing*, only it was not a prophecy, nor even words spoken to his spirit from the Lord. It was only the smoke.

Understanding filled him. A vision. He must watch and try to understand.

The smoke lifted and spread until it covered all of the mountaintop, and then flames ignited. Like a brush fire tearing across a field of dry wheat, the flames roared over the High Place in a mighty, purifying blaze. Malik watched, mouth agape, as the mountain's red stone ran in rivers like blood, as though the High Place had not only been burned but ripped open and now bled to death before his eyes.

The place where I will show Myself strong.

Yes, Lord. Yes.

The words lifted from his spirit like a song, and he felt a rending of something within him, something that had been tight and fearful and secret. *I am ready, Jesus. I am ready.*

The vision evaporated like a desert mirage and the High Place of Sacrifice returned to its solid form, but Malik's heart had become pliant and his soul rejoiced in the knowledge that Jesus' name would soon be proclaimed before all of Petra, and he was to play a part.

He needed to call the people together. They must be prepared for what was to come, for the time that would call on each of them to surrender, to speak, even to shout.

Malik hurried from the Great House steps, his feet light and his heart bursting.

He swept through the city as quickly as his feet would take him, stopping in shops and homes only long enough to poke his head through doorways and pass along the word that he wanted the church to gather as soon as possible in his home.

"Spread the word," he called to Alawin in the pastry stall as he passed, and the slight man lifted a hand in acknowledgment and lowered the flaps over the front of his stall.

By the time Malik reached his own courtyard, it was filling with believers and buzzing with conversation. Malik paused at the entrance, remembered his forlorn thoughts in the empty council house.

Forgive me, Lord. You are faithful, and You do not leave us alone.

He was embraced and kissed as he passed through the cluster of people. They wanted to hear firsthand what had happened in the palace that morning and were disappointed Julian was not present to give details. Nahor and Niv arrived and described the scene, and by the time they had finished their tale, there were tears at the loss of Marta.

Malik decided that enough had gathered and he should begin. He stepped onto a bench to be seen by each one. "Tomorrow, my friends, as you know, is the Festival of Grain."

The courtyard quieted at his voice, and faces turned toward him in respect. He felt that little surge of gratification at their submission to his authority, then forcibly handed it to his Lord. *I am ready,* he thought again, reminding himself that his days of leadership were coming to an end.

"The Lord has given me a vision." The people stilled, eyes wide to hear it. "A vision of the High Place, covered not with the evil of the powers and principalities of this earth, but with the strength and might of the risen Christ!"

He smiled down on them, their faces lit from within. "We will be part of this testimony, my friends. I do not yet know what God will have us do, but I know we must be ready." He grew serious. "Gather provisions, brothers and sisters, and prepare your families for travel. It may be that after tomorrow there will no longer be a place for us in Petra."

Faces before him became grave, but he sensed strength from them. "God will be strong for us and through us, but we may be called to sacrifice and suffering, as our Lord was."

He debated for a moment whether to tell them what the Lord had given him regarding Julian's leadership. That he himself would not be among them much longer, though he did not know where he would be. A twinge of sadness fluttered in his heart at the thought of separation from his dear flock. At the idea of them going on without him. He must have faith Julian would be there to lead them on.

No, it was not yet time to give them this burden, when so much was still unknown. Including the whereabouts of Julian, who still had not shown his face in the courtyard. Another entered, however, and Malik's attention went to the young girl at the courtyard entrance, whose stricken face brought a surge of concern.

"What is it, Tabatha?" He had not noticed her missing from the group but remembered now that she had been in the palace this morning, waiting to help Marta carry Cassia's boy in the basket of washing. Had she only now heard about Marta's death?

"I've just gotten free of my duties." Her eyes were full of unshed tears.

"Marta was a godly woman—" Malik hoped to give some comfort, but Tabatha interrupted.

"They have taken Cassia!"

Malik shook his head and looked to Hozai. "She was to be at the mouth of the gorge, waiting for Alexander. Did no one go to her?"

"She was not there. I assumed she had received word of our failure already and returned to the city."

"No." Tabatha wove through the crowd until she reached Malik's feet where he stood above her on the bench. "She was in the palace—she was there when Marta was killed and Alexander was taken to the throne room." She dropped her head. "I was hiding, and I saw the guards grab her. She fought with them, but they took her."

Malik stepped down and lifted the girl's chin. "You could have done nothing and would have only endangered yourself. Better for you to have escaped to bring us this news."

She smiled through her tears and nodded.

Malik scanned the group. "Is Julian still not among us?" Heads turned to search, but he was absent.

What had happened to Cassia? Was she a prisoner with her son in the palace, or had Hagiru already made an end of her?

A wave of sadness rushed through him. Cassia had found a special place in his childless heart, and his throat tightened at the prospect of her harm.

He sighed deeply over his people and looked once more to the entrance to his courtyard.

Julian, where are you?

THIRTY-SIX

CASSIA'S CELL GREW COLD, AND IN THE COMPLETE DARKNESS, she did not know how much time had passed. How long had she wandered along the riverbank with the One who seemed to still be present, even here in her cell?

She sat with her back against a dank wall, and the packed earth of the floor was rutted and bumpy, but she noticed little of the discomforts. Her mind wandered freely over the past, into the present, and even to the future.

So many years of relying on men, of remaining weak to keep their love. She had come to Petra believing that to be strong she must stand alone. But she had failed alone as well.

What if the strength she sought did not come from men or from within herself?

You must love from strength, not need. The words of Malik and the words of Jesus in her dream mingled and she was not certain who had told her that.

But how was she to do what they said?

She had always wanted people to love her, needed them to love her like she needed air to breathe. She had ordered her life to please them, and when they loved her, or even seemed to love her, she would cling to that love desperately until she had turned it into an object of worship and let it rule her.

But if she could believe there was One God who truly loved her . . . If the followers of the Way were right and Jesus was the Messiah for all people, who had come as the once-and-for-all sacrifice for mankind, then this was a love that changed everything. *Everything.*

Cassia felt the need to move, to walk. Something churned inside her and made it impossible to remain still. She climbed to her feet, careful not to put weight on her wrist, though the fire in it had banked.

With the fingertips of her good hand tracing the stone wall, she walked carefully along the length of the cell until she reached the corner, then turned and continued. The cell was not large, and she had mastered the circuit after twice around.

Her steps became automatic and her thoughts returned to what she was beginning to know was truth.

She could not say how she knew this, really. Was it the dream of Jesus beside the river? She had wished for a vision like Malik's friend Paul. But she was not a person to change her life based on a dream. Was it Malik and his joyful teaching of the One True God and the redemption he offered? Or Julian, always studying and learning and pursuing this God of his?

Her memory played over the faces of the believers, and she saw their smiling eyes as they sang together in the flickering lamplight, as they listened to the reading of letters from those who had gone before.

Yes, it was all of this, and it was the witness of her own heart as well, for once she opened herself to the One she had met by the river, a flood of assurance rushed in.

She lost count of how many times she had circled the cell, for her thoughts were racing down a path toward something better.

Jesus was the sacrifice for her. God wanted to love her, wanted a relationship with her, enough to do this marvelous thing. And she could be secure in that love, strong because of it. She could love others—from strength, not from need.

Warmth spread through her at the thought. To love others in the way she had always enjoyed, to understand their hurts, to help heal their pain, but to do it without wrapping tight fingers around the response and crushing the life from it—this would be true freedom!

Cassia slowed in her pace around the cell, turned a corner, and stopped. She lifted her face, eyes closed, to the roof above her, but felt as though she could see past it to the very heavens.

Jesus. My Redeemer.

She lifted her hands, her heart, her very self to the One who had come to set her free, who had died to give her life, and who lived even now to love her forever.

The warmth grew like an embrace, like she was beside the river once more, held by eternal arms. Silent tears flowed, and with them she let go of all that need, all the desperation that had been hers since her parents had given her up.

She had a Father.

And brothers and sisters! She smiled, then laughed aloud.

Oh, how she wished to see Julian! To tell him she had found his Jesus. Or had been found by Him. Her heart still ached for the pain she had caused him.

She leaned her back against the wall and wondered if she would have a chance to tell him anything, if she would ever be embraced by her new family. If she would ever hold Alexander in her arms.

All of it was important, so important. And yet she felt a deeper peace underlying the concerns, a peace that whispered, *All is well*, no matter what happened.

Sometime later, the slap of footsteps drifted down to her underground hole. She had been dozing against the wall, but now she sat upright, straining to detect whether it was a man or woman, friend or enemy.

A strange light played along the back wall of her cell, revealing jagged cracks in stones set haphazardly. Torchlight soon filled the cell, and Cassia blinked at a harsh yellow flame and smelled the bitumen that burned. Unaccustomed to the brightness, she could not at first make out who held the light.

But then it drew closer, until it was just on the other side of the narrow gate in the wall, and the face followed behind it, eyes peering into the cell, searching.

"Bethea!" Cassia stood and pressed her back against the wall. Had the girl been sent to finish her? Strange executioner, if so. Cassia had been expecting Hagiru herself. But perhaps that had been arrogant of her, to think the queen would bother to deal personally with someone as insignificant as she.

You are loved.

The words had come from somewhere both within and without, and she half smiled, even as Bethea's dark gaze roamed her face.

"She is going to have you killed."

Cassia sighed. "I am surprised she has not already."

"She has other pressing matters to attend to."

The Romans? Cassia remembered the soldier she had discovered in the storage room at the back of the palace.

Bethea looked over her shoulder, then brought a fearful glance back to Cassia. What was the girl doing here?

"You must get him out." Bethea gripped the bar of the gate with her free hand.

Had she found the Roman as well? How could Cassia possibly help? She squinted at the girl's haunted gaze. "I don't understand."

"I cannot do it. I . . . I am too afraid of her." Bethea swallowed hard. "I am not strong like you." The admission seemed to cost her something. Her vulnerability called out to Cassia. She read Bethea's heart as though it were written in clay tablets, and the hurt there was one Cassia knew well—that desperation to belong, to be loved.

She went to the cell gate and laid her hand over Bethea's. "Tell me what is happening."

Bethea looked down at Cassia's hand on her own, then lifted hungry eyes to her. "Rabbel is dead."

The news sent a wave of shock through Cassia and she dropped her hand.

Bethea continued, her words coming in a rush. "I had thought that when she heard, the queen would forget her plan for the festival, but now she seems more fearful than ever that without a king in Petra, the Romans will attack. She is desperate to put Obadas on the throne with herself as regent, but fearful the people will object because of Alexander."

Cassia fought to focus, to hold on to each detail, though she ached to think only of Alexander. But at the mention of his name, Bethea's whole countenance softened, and Cassia knew.

Bethea had come to love her son. How could she not?

"What can we do?" Cassia breathed deeply, trying to free her lungs from the crushing pressure.

A tear slid from the corner of Bethea's eye. "She is intent on going through with the sacrifice tomorrow night. She says that when the sun sets on Petra on the first day of the Festival of Grain, a human sacrifice to Dushara will ensure the Nabataean kingdom remains free of Rome."

If Rome does not come in and slaughter the entire royal family before that. Cassia kept the thought to herself. The girl was already terrified. "Has word gotten out that Rabbel is dead?"

Bethea shook her head. "Only those closest to him know." She shifted the torch to her other hand and fumbled at the gate's latch. The heavy beam that lay across the door and extended down the wall could not be lifted from the inside, and even from the outside, Bethea struggled with it.

"Let me hold the torch." Cassia reached her hand through the gate. Bethea passed it off, then used both hands to lift the beam. It took a succession of passing the torch between them to get the bar lifted past it, but in a moment Bethea swung the cell gate open and Cassia was free.

Her thoughts tumbled and she tried to formulate a plan.

"You must get him far from here before the sun sets tomorrow," Bethea said.

Cassia nodded, but her mind rebelled. What could she do that had not already been tried? She could not break Alexander out of the palace alone, nor with the help of her friends. It would take an army to get him out of this place.

An army.

"Bethea, I have need of two more things from you." She struggled to keep her voice calm. "First, you must help me get out of this palace unseen." The girl nodded, eyes wide. Cassia touched her face, overcome suddenly with empathy for this woman who had been Aretas's victim even before her. And it was a love that came not from a place of need within her, but from a place of strength.

"And then you must find me a water pot."

THIRTY-SEVEN

——◆——

CASSIA FOLLOWED BETHEA THROUGH THE BACK HALLS, staying close to the girl and to the wall. She led Cassia through tiny rooms with doors on the other side, down steps and through dark corridors, then back into the light and through narrow halls. Had Bethea done nothing in her years in the palace but explore all of its crannies? Perhaps she had made an art out of remaining unseen.

Cassia was breathless by the time they reached an underground chamber where sunlight outlined a tiny door on the far wall. Bethea crossed the room, sure-footed, then bent and shoved the door open.

"Quickly," she whispered, but Cassia held back.

"I can't fit through there!"

Bethea waved her over. "You are smaller than I, and I've done it many times."

Again, Cassia wondered at the life Bethea had led here in the palace. "Why did you stay, Bethea? All these years since Aretas left?"

The girl hesitated, then sighed. "Aretas always thought he had a better way to do everything, even rule the kingdom."

This, I know.

Bethea pushed Cassia toward the small door. "It was such a small disagreement he had with Rabbel. I always believed he would return." She dropped her chin. "I would have given up long ago if I had known he had you."

Cassia paused only a moment to give Bethea a quick embrace. "You remember what I need?"

"Yes, yes. Now go!"

"I will see you behind the palace."

Bethea nodded, her eyes full, but Cassia was unsure whether she wept over Alexander or because Cassia had embraced her. How long had it been since anyone had shown her love?

She bent to the narrow opening, pushed one arm out, then her right shoulder and her head. A moment later she was wriggling onto the sandy ground on the back side of the palace, away from the street. Her wrist gave her some pain, but not much.

The door closed behind her without a word from Bethea, and she was alone.

From the sun she guessed it was late afternoon. Not much time before nightfall to accomplish her plan. Scanning the ground that rose slightly behind her, she saw no one. The Temple of al-ʻUzza to her left would be busy at this time of day, as people finished their workday, but from here she should go unnoticed, even in her dirty and torn palace-servant robes. She straightened and tried to look as though she belonged behind the palace.

It seemed an age since she had entered not far from where she now stood, sneaking past Hozai to find Marta and Tabatha inside. Her heart thudded with a dull ache at the memory of Marta on the throne room floor.

How long would it take Bethea to retrace her steps through the palace? It would have been simpler for the girl to have come out with

Cassia and enter through the back, but she was not willing to risk being seen outside with Cassia.

She walked along the back wall, still trying to appear nonchalant, until she reached the back entrance of the palace where she had broken through so many hours ago. It was not safe to venture farther, but she was loathe to remain still.

She watched the sun with some anxiety and tried to speed Bethea with her thoughts.

"I will never leave you nor forsake you."

She had heard Malik read those words from one of the accounts of Jesus' life with His disciples. It was Jesus who said it, she remembered, to His faithful ones. Were the words also for her, even today?

A harsh whisper caught her attention. Bethea stood at the back entrance, Talya's colorfully striped pouch in her hands.

Cassia rushed to her, took the pouch, and embraced her once again. "Thank you, Bethea."

The girl nodded, stark fear in her roaming glances.

"Tell Alexander I love him. Tell him I am coming soon."

Bethea gripped her arms one last time. "Be sure you do."

And then Cassia was off, strapping the pouch over her head and shoulder to secure it and thinking through the route she must now take.

Down the main market street of shops, past the grand Nymphaeum where she had first met Julian. Past the houses of friends built into naturally occurring terraces or cut into the sandstone cliffs. She would have to pass the tomb work site, where her fellow workers would be toiling. Would Julian be there? She could not allow him to see her. If he didn't stop her, he would no doubt follow her, which would bring disaster on him.

She would have to sneak under Zeta's home, past the amphitheatre where Yehosef was probably training his gladiators.

As her feet carried her through the city, she realized how many people had grown dear to her in Petra.

If she made it out of the city now, she might be able to save them all. If things did not go well on the other side of the Siq, she might not return. The thought quickened her steps. She kept her head down and stayed in the crowded parts of the street.

The familiar landmarks passed behind her, and when she cleared the amphitheatre, she felt some relief. There should be no one to recognize her between here and the Siq.

The rock wall that cradled the city bent to the right, and she rounded the cliff and saw the traders and their market laid out before her, the first scene she had witnessed when she and Alexander emerged from the mighty crack in the mountain all those weeks ago. It looked the same yet very different now that she was no longer an outsider.

How hopeful I was that day. And yet how different the present was from what she had imagined.

But there was no time for reminiscing. As on that first day, the sun would not linger in the west much longer, and the market had slowed its business.

A quick scan of the area and she found what she sought. A horse trader with several decent mounts. She approached with a bold confidence and asked the price of a black mare.

The horse dealer, a runt of a man with broken teeth, looked her up and down, took in her palace robes, albeit ripped and filthy. "Seventy-five denarii."

She laughed. "Do you think I am the queen herself?" She halved his price, then looked away, as though searching for another trader. In truth, she had very little time for bartering, but to act the foolish buyer might draw more attention than she wished.

The scrawny man patted the horse's side. "Fifty denarii, I could not let this fine one go for less."

"Fifty, then." Cassia pulled the pouch from her neck and fished out some of the money Malik had given her.

Seems so long ago.

She hoped her barter had brought the price down enough that she would not be noted.

When the money was exchanged, the horse trader handed Cassia the frayed rope that hung from the horse's halter, but she shook her head. "Help me up."

His bushy eyebrows lifted, but he cooperated.

Cassia had not ridden much, and she felt unsettled on her mount, but she had no time for training either. With a kick to the horse's haunches and a pull on her head, she directed the mare toward the narrow crack in the cliff wall, where all who entered and left Petra passed. She trotted obediently, but once they had entered the slit in the mountain, she urged the mare to something faster than a trot.

The crowds traveling out of Petra were not so heavy today. Most travelers headed into the city.

For the Festival of Grain.

She kicked the horse into a full gallop, then clung to the reins. Her teeth came together in a jarring snap and her hair loosed and flew behind her.

The pounding of the horse's hooves on the limestone paving cleared the way of pedestrians. She wove through camels and donkey carts, giving the horse direction but mostly giving her her head.

It had taken such a long time to walk through the Siq, she remembered. Each bend in the rock wall promised to be the end, then revealed another length of road to walk. But the swift ride in the other direction sped by, and she barely noticed the water channel along the wall, the sculpted facades, the djinn blocks that had all been so fascinating.

The cliff walls spread apart and she flew out of the gorge onto the wider road that led toward it. Here the travelers thinned, and as the hour grew later they would disappear.

She rode out of the protection of the city alone, into the open desert, at the worst time of day.

Straight toward the enemy camp.

How long until she would see signs of the Roman encampment that lurked at the edge of Petra, waiting to swarm the city? She had not seen it when she and Alexander came to Petra, and this fact guided her direction now. It must lie somewhere they didn't travel.

Certainly the Romans would have a challenge in taking the city, protected as it was by its natural walls. Roman legions must be positioned near every major Nabataean city, but if they could take the capital, perhaps they would have no need of other sieges.

The sun bid the desert good night at last and sank into its bed. The sky grew violet and a tiny crescent moon hung over the horizon, partnered with one bright star.

Cassia slowed her mad rush from the city, scanning the desert for signs of Roman life.

Where are they?

Seeing nothing, she continued east, though she did not drive the horse so fast. There was no sense in galloping in the wrong direction. The steep and rocky hills, pierced everywhere with caves and fissures, stared down at her like hollow eyes, and the pale strip of desert stretched like a barren carpet before her.

Slowed now, she had time to reflect, though she didn't want to. Her palms grew sweaty in their grip of the reins, and she forced her thoughts away from the festival and the sacrifice.

Scrubby grasses poked out of the red sand, and her horse bent for a mouthful. She did not stop her. Her errand seemed foolish now. How had she thought she could save a city?

A wave of exhaustion settled on her, catching up with her from a day of tension and fear. She swayed in the saddle and half closed her eyes, wishing she could slip to the desert sand and sleep.

But the thought of sleep and dreams brought back her riverside walk with Jesus, and the tentative and newborn faith she had claimed in her cell.

Jesus, are You with me even here?

She wished for Him to walk beside her again but then realized the Spirit of God Malik spoke of so often had taken up residence within her and God was closer than a heartbeat. She smiled, filled again with the warm love that gave her strength.

On the horizon, Cassia thought perhaps she saw a fire. She dug her heels into the horse's flank and leaned over her neck, as if she could reach the flame sooner.

Yes, it grew as she advanced! She urged the horse to full speed and soon saw that the fire blazed atop a sentry tower, built at the edge of a square-fenced camp.

The Romans.

She had no hopes of arriving unseen. With the sentry tower's torch blazing and her a lone rider across the twilight desert, she only wondered how long until she was hailed and stopped.

The irony of the situation fell upon her. Early this morning Julian had entered the Petran palace claiming to have a message from Rome. And now she stormed the Roman camp with a message from Petran royalty.

Only this time, it was true.

THIRTY-EIGHT

As Cassia expected, a yell went up from the posted sentry at her approach to the Roman camp. She tilted her head back and met his look, wanting him to see she was a woman. There was, perhaps, less chance of a javelin being thrown at her if he knew.

The enclosure was built of wooden pickets—scarce in the desert so they must have been brought far—easier to build than a stone wall. She had seen the old Roman military camps in Syria. If the soldiers stayed long, they would indeed build stone walls. For now the wooden pickets sufficed as protection in the middle of a desert where attackers could not approach with stealth.

There was no gate, only a narrow opening in the wooden fence guarded by two soldiers who lowered their *pilum* at her approach in the dusky evening. Their red-plumed helmets and leather-and-iron breastplates seemed so foreign, so formal.

She slowed her horse, then slid from it, giving up any advantage she may have had and allowing them to see that not only was she a woman but a very small one, and unarmed.

"I have come to speak with your commander. I have a message from Petra."

The two soldiers eyed each other, then laughed. "They have sent a slave to pass their messages? Rome will not be pleased."

Cassia smoothed her robes and lifted her chin. "I am the mother of Petra's next king, fleeing for my life and thus disguised."

The other soldier inched his pike toward her, as though he would poke her to see if she bled. "And I am Emperor Trajan, come to check on my troops." He jerked his head at his fellow soldier and grinned. "You there. You work too hard. Take the night off."

His companion laughed and saluted. "Thank you, Emperor. You are most observant."

A voice behind her turned Cassia's head. Another on horseback approached and called out to the guards, "Are you two on duty or on holiday?" Cassia studied the newcomer's horse, certain it had been another she had seen with the horse trader.

The guards looked over her shoulder at the new arrival. "Aw, Decimus, we're only having a bit of fun with an Arab slave."

Cassia whirled back on them, glaring. "I told you—"

"What did she tell you?" the man, Decimus, asked from behind her.

The leaner guard laughed and Cassia wanted to smack him. "Something about being the prince's mother—"

"Turn around."

His command was low but authoritative. Cassia turned.

The Roman! The one she met in the palace storage room. Clearly he recognized her as well. "Who are you?"

She inhaled courage and licked her lips. "My name is Cassia. I am the mother of Alexander, son of Aretas, son of Rabbel, king of Petra. My son is next in line for the throne of Petra, and I have come to speak with the Roman commander about the future of our city and our kingdom."

"You told me this morning they have taken your son. Who has taken him?"

"The new queen. She wishes to kill him and put her own son on the throne."

Decimus shrugged. "What does any of this have to do with us? Before long there will be no king of Petra, only a governor of the new Roman province of Arabia."

"That is what I wish to speak about. I believe it can be done without bloodshed. With no loss to your troops or the people of Petra."

Decimus's eyebrows lifted, and Cassia sensed strength in him but no danger. She would not say more. Not to him. "I wish to speak to your commander."

"Search her." Decimus slid from his horse.

When they were satisfied she was unarmed, the two guards led her into the compound, with Decimus at her heels.

The camp was large, with row upon row of leather tents pitched in a grid and a street of rocks and broken potsherds leading from the front entrance straight through the camp. A larger tent sat at the center, the destination of this impromptu street in the desert. She assumed this was the commander's residence.

And it was there the guards led her. Heart pounding and legs shaking, her resolve slipped. Could she do this? Did she dare? She spoke for all of Petra. All but one power-mad queen.

The guards yelled through the leather tent, its flap was lifted, and she was pushed inside. The two sentries did not accompany her, but Decimus drew up behind her, a solid wall at her back.

Jesus, give me the words. Give me the wisdom.

The inside of the tent was considerably darker, as the commander had not yet had enough lamps lit. One brazier burned in the center on a small marble column, and Cassia marveled at the luxury inside this central residence. Did his soldiers know their commander slept on soft bedding and reclined on couches to dine from delicately painted bowls?

The man himself reclined even now, a bowl of wine on a low table before him and a small scroll in his hand. He looked up, attentive to his visitors.

"Ah, Decimus, you have returned." He thrust the scroll aside and pulled himself to standing. Cassia studied him, from balding head to leather boots, and tried to read him quickly and well, waiting for any telltale throbbing in her head that always warned her of danger.

In his forties. Still fit. He was attractive and knew it, confident in his authority. Not unkind or cruel. But determined, and perhaps ambitious. Her assessment gave her hope.

"Yes, Commander," Decimus said, above and behind her.

"And I see you have brought something back from the city in stone." His gaze traveled the length of Cassia, clearly curious.

"She arrived before I did, Commander. Though I did meet her while reconnoitering."

"Hmm." The commander circled in front of Cassia, still taking her in. "I do not know what to ask about first. The state of the city or this pretty little thing."

Cassia lifted her chin. "They are one and the same."

"Ho, ho! She speaks. And with fire in her eyes." The Roman commander laughed and met Decimus's look over her shoulder. "Perhaps you should leave us, Decimus."

"As you wish, Commander Corvinus. May I only say that when I encountered her hiding in the palace this morning, she was telling the same story as she now tells, and I have reason to believe she speaks truth."

The commander pursed his lips, looked between the two of them, and then dipped his head toward Cassia. "High praise from my most valuable scout. Let us hear what you have to say." He flicked his hand toward Decimus, and the soldier bowed and backed out of the tent, leaving Cassia alone with the man who held her future in his hands.

Not so, the Lord whispered to her. The thought gave her boldness and the fluttering of her heart slowed. She found her fingers twisted together and forced them apart.

"Come, sit." The commander extended a hand to his couch.

Cassia hesitated. She did not come for his hospitality and could see he had other things on his mind. She could imagine that months and even years away from their wives did not make Roman soldiers trustworthy in these situations.

In the end, she favored her first reading of him, that he would not be cruel. Lascivious, perhaps. But not cruel. She went to his couch and perched on the edge.

"You have traveled far." He reclined beside her. "Please, rest. Have some wine."

Cassia shook her head. "Thank you, no. I have urgent matters I must discuss with you."

"Ah yes. The state of the city." He sipped from a Petra-red clay bowl, painted with a leafy design with red berries along the lip.

"The people are informed. They know of Rome's march across the world, of the way in which it has swallowed even more than Alexander did, and made subjects of kingdoms far and wide."

Corvinus smiled over his wine. "Indeed? I would not have thought even news could penetrate through the crack in the rock."

"They are ready. Ready to also become a Roman province. And they would see it happen peacefully rather than at great cost to them, to their families, and to their land."

He set the bowl down on the table with a slight *thunk* and leaned toward her. "Who are you? Do you speak for the royal house?"

Cassia swallowed hard, bit her lip, and stared at her hands. *Yes. And no.* "My name is Cassia. My son will be the next king of Nabataea."

Corvinus took in her servant's robe once more and lifted an eyebrow. "Indeed."

She did not back down. "His father was the eldest son of King

Rabbel. The king's second wife also has a son, and since discovering Alexander existed, I have been in hiding and my son has been in jeopardy. The queen plans to kill him." Cassia's voice caught on the last two words, and she fought to control the tremor.

Corvinus sat back and used his tongue to work at something between his teeth, regarding her through half-closed eyes. Did he believe her story?

"How can you be certain that your son would be king and not hers?"

"It is the Nabataean way. Eldest son to eldest son."

"Still"—he shrugged—"none of it is of any consequence, for Rome will soon rule the Arabian province and there will be no king in Petra."

Already there is no king in Petra. But she would not speak of this yet.

"The people desire peace. And I believe that you and I can give it to them."

He smiled, clearly amused. "I am listening."

Cassia breathed a quick prayer to the God who heard all, then folded her hands in her lap. "I want to strike a deal with you. The queen, Hagiru, holds my son in her grip and plans to kill him tomorrow night at the Festival of Grain, as a human sacrifice on the altar of the High Place in Petra."

Corvinus's nose wrinkled. "Disgusting. What kinds of gods do you serve here?"

Cassia chose to ignore the complicated question. "I want you to send in enough soldiers to retrieve my son and remove Hagiru from the palace."

"Hmm." He reached for a bowl of figs on the table beside them and his hand grazed her leg. "Shouldn't be difficult. And what do you propose to offer me in return?"

Cassia thought back to Rabbel's courtyard, when she had offered her very self in exchange for Alexander's life. "I offer you Petra."

He popped a fig between his lips and smiled before biting down. "The entire city?"

"My son is too young to rule alone. I would act as his regent. And as his regent, I would follow what I know is the will of the people of Nabataea. I would abdicate my son's kingship and peacefully become a province of Rome."

Corvinus chewed slowly, his eyes on her, but his mind clearly playing with the idea. She waited.

"How could I be certain that you would keep your agreement?"

Cassia shrugged. "I suppose you cannot. But you have little to lose and much to gain. I would guess the acquisition of Nabataea without the involvement of your troops would reflect well on your command to those who watch from Rome."

He sat up, grinning. "You would make a formidable politician, my girl."

Cassia had aimed correctly, at his ambition.

He stood and paced the tent before her. "I can see only one reason not to agree." He stopped and turned to her. "I am under orders to take Petra soon. From all I have learned, the king has no such desire to abdicate. And I cannot wait until your son is made king in his stead."

Cassia stood as well, not wanting him to be looking down on her when she answered.

"The king, Commander Corvinus, is dead."

THIRTY-NINE

_____•_____

HAGIRU SAT ON THE EDGE OF RABBEL'S DEATHBED, HER gaze roaming over his composed features.

His personal servants had dressed him in a clean and simple robe of white and folded linen over his body, with a sharp crease of fabric across his chest. Hagiru watched his chest, waiting for it to rise or fall.

Is he truly gone?

The room smelled of death, though it was the aroma of embalming spices, already brought and sprinkled around the body even before preparation had begun.

She had not expected it to take so long. Over the months of his illness, she had second thoughts and even third about her course of action. And even now, now that it was over, she couldn't help but think back over their years together and wonder if they couldn't have done better.

She had hoped for so much when they first married. Believed they would rule side by side, that she would make him happy. Bear him children.

Hagiru had not anticipated that she could not compete with her predecessor, who could do no wrong now that she was dead. And her childbearing had nearly been a failure, until the gods had intervened and given her Obadas, for which she owed them her loyalty.

She smoothed the linen that covered his lifeless arm, then studied her own hand on the fabric, the loose skin and crisscrossing lines. When had she aged so? Rabbel's face seemed to have lost enough years that he looked as she remembered on their wedding day, as though he had been wrapped in the cares of a kingdom like grave clothes, and in death he had finally shed them. But the years were evident in her hands, and more so in her heart. It was time to claim the power she had yearned for since the day she realized she would never have love.

Angrily, she swiped at a stray tear that had stolen from her eye as she had grown morbid about the passing years. In the hall outside the chamber, she could hear the muffled keening of palace servants who had heard the news of the king's death. She had given strict instructions that it was not to be told outside the palace, but it would not be long before all of Petra heard. And then the Romans, camped outside the city.

Yes, it had taken longer than she expected for him to die, and yet the gods were with her, for the timing was fortuitous as well.

She feared that Rabbel would change his mind about the sacrifice of Aretas's son, but now there was no danger. She worried the boy's mother would become even more of a problem, but as soon as Hagiru heard of her husband's death, she sent guards to the underground cell to make an end of the girl. That effort had not turned out as she planned, but her spies were everywhere. Already they scoured the city for word of where the escaped woman was hiding. She would be dead before morning.

And then nothing would remain in her way. Obadas would be named king and Hagiru would rule from behind him with an iron hand, ready and able to quash the Roman occupation and keep her people free.

A slave appeared at the door, eyes downcast in respect for the dead. He was one of the few allowed access to the king's private chamber. "Someone to see the queen."

"Who is it?"

"One of your guards, with a message he says is urgent."

Hagiru nodded, and the guard appeared a moment later. He also bowed low as he entered and spoke quietly.

"I have received reports from throughout the city, my queen."

"Where is she?" Hagiru half expected him to say the girl was still in the palace, still crawling about trying to save her son.

"She has left Petra."

Hagiru narrowed her eyes and looked up sharply. "You are mistaken." Though she had ignored it, Hagiru had seen the mother-love in the girl's eyes. She would not have left her son the day before the festival.

"She has gone to the Romans."

Hagiru shot to her feet. "Traitorous little—"

"I also have reports that a Roman soldier may have been in the palace earlier today."

She paced, her thoughts spinning. "Do they know the king is dead?"

"You were most clear that no one was to speak—"

"People talk! Do they know?"

He shook his head. "I have no idea."

She stalked back and forth across the death chamber, and her sandals slapped a rhythm on the stone floor. "What does she hope to accomplish?"

Her trained guard did not speak, presumably because he had nothing to offer.

Hagiru stopped her pacing in front of him and let him feel the weight of her anger. "She must be killed. Immediately."

He nodded once.

"I don't care how many you have to take to get past the Romans. She must not return to Petra."

"As you say, Queen."

She clapped her hands together twice and pointed to the door. "Go!"

Hagiru returned to Rabbel's bedside, but she had no desire to continue to sit with his body. There was still much to be done before Obadas would be king, and an indulgence in memories of the past would do nothing to secure her future.

It was time to act.

FORTY

———•———

WHEN JULIAN LEFT MALIK IN THE STREET BELOW THE tomb work site, he had little idea of where he could go to get away from the old man and from his own thoughts. Petra was a thriving, teeming city, but at times it seemed its placement inside this natural gorge was like being held in a great stone fist, with nowhere to go.

And so he climbed. Not to the tomb site, nor to any of the rock-cut homes in the cliff. He wished to be alone, and there seemed no lonelier place in Petra, at least for today, than the High Place of Sacrifice.

Since hearing about the horrific sacrifice planned for tomorrow's festival, Julian had been curious about the cliff-top holy place, and so this evening he would satisfy both his curiosity and his need for solitude.

The sun hung low in the west when he began his ascent, and he pushed away the thought that it was a foolish errand at this hour. Sometimes foolish action was better than no action.

He had already wandered to the west end of the city, past the palace and Temple of al-ʿUzza, past the Great House, and under the Sacred Gate that marked the beginning of the religious sites, including the Great Temple of Dushara. From this end of the city, the path to the High Place was longer but not as steep as it was beside the theatre. He trekked up the winding path, avoiding the scrub brush and rocks, and not pausing to examine the elegantly carved tombs he passed.

Halfway up he was already sweating and breathing heavily. He fought a great sadness more than any other emotion. Sadness at what had happened and what he had become, both a failure and a coward. The past and the present merged to condemn him together, as though they had joined hands and then pointed fingers of accusation. Cassia and Vita. Malik and his parents. He had not won the love of either woman, nor the respect of his elders.

And Alexander.

His heart felt tender and raw at the thought of that little boy calling out to him in the throne room, with Julian unable even to speak words of comfort to him. In only the few brief times he had encountered the boy, already Alexander had become dear to him. Perhaps it was only that he saw him through Cassia's eyes.

My mother would love Alexander.

The thought came from nowhere and felt like a blow to the stomach. He paused beside a large rock and put out a hand to steady himself at the wave of emotion.

The city had begun to fall away, and the path hugged the cliff now, with narrow ledge-steps grooved into the rock in places and winding natural paths in others. Julian passed one tomb with a large interior, its *triclinium*'s three benches large enough to hold a huge funerary banquet for the deceased. The rock ribbons were especially beautiful inside, even in the fading light, and Julian wished Cassia were here to see the silk-like formations. Wished that he could show her every beautiful thing in the world, from now until the end.

Not far from this beautiful chamber he passed a lion sculpted into the rock wall, with a fountain of water pouring from its mouth. It reminded him of the carving he had seen in the Siq when he first came to Petra.

Why *had* he come here? He climbed higher, trying to go back to his first goals, trying to forget what had happened since he met Malik and Cassia.

He wanted only to hide from the long arm of the emperor, to keep his family safe back in Rome. To forget about Vita.

He could sculpt here, pursue the talent he had always enjoyed. What better place to make a name for himself than a city made of rock?

He paused a moment to catch his breath, his back against the rock wall to fight the dizzying height. The city crawled with ants now, not people. And the sky, though darkening, seemed close enough to touch. Lodged between earth and sky, Julian felt himself the only person alive.

And he began to fear the solitude he had sought. For in solitude, it became easier to hear the voice of the Lord.

Had he thought to come up here and avoid that Voice? As if the evil of the plateau would frighten away the One God? He nearly laughed at his foolishness, however unconscious it had been, and remembered the story of the Hebrew prophet Elijah, hiding in the cleft of a rock while the wind and the fire rushed past, then hearing God in a quiet and still voice.

He was not ready to listen. He climbed again. One foot higher than the next, grabbing at the narrow ledges of orange-red rock as the wind increased and the city dropped farther out of reach.

And then at last he had reached the plateau. He waited for some sense of victory, of accomplishment at the climb, but felt only the pervading sense of evil that spread over the High Place like a dark and heavy blanket.

From the ground, the top of the mountain had seemed like only a ridge, a narrow point. But now that he stood on it, he realized it was more like a wide plain, broken by small variations of rocks, rising and falling to differing levels but still a vast area. Toward the north he could see the promontory that jutted over the city. No doubt the actual altar and holy site were there. But to his right he saw two large obelisks carved from solid stone. Sacred rites must occur there as well, far from the altar.

Again, a wave of heaviness pushed at Julian, and he pulled away from the side of the cliff, fearing it could somehow knock him from the High Place.

He crossed the rock top to the far side, looked down on the east end of the city, and far below could make out the large complex of huge tombs where he worked every day.

Where I belong.

And yet going back to the tombs felt like failure too.

What am I to do, Lord?

Once a call from the Lord was heard, could he turn his back and ignore it? Could he go back to sculpting rock when his heart told him his work was carving out a church?

The wind picked up, and once again Julian backed away from the edge of the cliff and crossed back to the two obelisks that stood like the lone pillars of some fallen temple.

It was nearly dark now, and he still would have to climb down.

Passing the second obelisk, Julian felt a deep vibration shudder through him. He paused and put a hand to the tall rock, curious and fearful at once.

Yes, there it was. Like an earthquake but confined only to the column of stone, radiating out from it, through his hand, across the ground, up and through his feet.

And with the vibration, there was an almost audible rumble. A low growl, angry and threatening.

Julian yanked his hand from the rock as though it burned him, and in a way it did, for he felt pain, both physical and in his spirit at the sense of hatred that flowed from the stone.

A bitterness rose in his throat and he stumbled away from the pillar. *God, what is this?*

But even as he asked, he knew the answer. The obelisks were said to be the resting places of the gods, like the large black cube in the Temple of al-'Uzza. The faithful worshippers of Dushara circled such monuments religiously, in hopes of gaining the favor of the gods housed within. A guttural voice wormed its way into Julian's mind, and he could not tell if it spoke aloud or only inside of him.

THE PRINCE OF PETRA DEMANDS YOUR OBEDIENCE.

A hand seemed to clamp onto his chest, and Julian gasped and bent at the waist trying to release it.

The entire plateau seemed to buck and rock now, as though caught in the throes of an angry storm. Julian himself felt like a piece of wood on the waves, a shipwreck tossed high, then plunged to the depths.

He put out a hand to steady himself, then yanked it downward when the only solid thing was the obelisk.

The crush of the unseen waves on his lungs grew unbearable, and Julian half walked, half stumbled to the narrow steps that had brought him to the plateau.

I must get down.

When he reached the edge, a sickening urge to throw himself off swept over him and he tripped on the first few steps, his hands scrabbling over the rock wall for something to keep him from pitching downward.

It was too dark to see the steps. His foolishness had caught up with him.

Somehow he kept moving down the path without falling to the rocky ledges that outcropped below.

The minutes stretched on and still he fled downward, the pressure easing slowly on his chest and the city growing larger beneath him.

Halfway down he could go no farther without resting, and when the ground leveled out before a small grouping of tombs, he found a flat rock and stretched himself on it. He stared at the purple sky, his breathing labored.

And lying there, halfway between the city and the High Place, far from Rome and far from friends, the past and his failure crushed down on him like the evil on the plateau, only instead of stopping his breath, it welled up inside and he found himself weeping for all that had happened and all he had failed to achieve.

All his life he had worked to gain the approval of others. To see admiration in their eyes, to hear them praise his work. Yet here he lay, on a rock in the desert, a disappointment to everyone he knew.

You are not a disappointment to Me.

Julian threw an arm over his tearstained face and listened, longing for the Voice to speak again.

You are My dear son.

His heart reached out, desperate, wanting the words to be true. Wanting them to be more than his imagination.

You are My dear son.

Just that, no more. No mention of what he had accomplished, what he could achieve in the future. No conditions, no demands.

His heart stilled. *If God is for me, who can be against me?*

Was it presumptuous to believe that God was *for him*? Was it a promise he could claim?

The darkness had come fully now, heavy and black. Julian sat up on his rock and searched the sky, counting the stars as they appeared, then losing count.

And there, caught between the city and the High Place, a change came upon him.

Evil was up there, of that he had no doubt. But it was an evil that had no power in the face of the One God. And it would be defeated.

This is a work that God wishes to do. And He wanted to use Julian to do it.

He climbed from his rock and looked down toward the city.

What would happen if he gave up his need for approval, if he walked away from the safety of praise and admiration? If he rested in the acceptance gained through Jesus' death for him? Risked everything to answer the call to lead through humility, to be a servant?

He searched the plateau above and thought he saw a wisp of smoke waver above the rock, as though the altar consumed a sacrifice already.

It is time.

He heard the words from outside himself and knew the final call had come, and he must make his decision now, in this moment.

Follow . . . or deny.

He thought of Cassia, of her accusation that he had once run in fear. And he thought of Vita, given the chance at life if she would renounce her Christ, and the way her face had glowed with something like heaven as the lions were released from under the theatre's seats to rush across the sand toward the huddled band of believers. Could he do any less?

And you will do much more.

The words filled his heart, assuring him he had new things to accomplish, to achieve—unseen things that would outlast even his stone sculptures.

Julian breathed deeply of the night air, filling his chest with it, breaking the bands that had tethered him for longer than he had realized. *Yes, it is time.*

The path down to the city seemed to be only a few cubits long, and as his feet found the road to Malik's house, Julian knew he had left the guilt of the past on the High Place, where the evil that dwelt there could do nothing to hurt him again.

FORTY-ONE

◆

CASSIA SLEPT FITFULLY IN THE BACK OF COMMANDER Corvinus's tent, one eye open most of the night. He insisted she stay there, with him sleeping in the front on one of his couches, telling her there was no safer place in the encampment. This she believed to be true, but she still did not sleep easy. Her night was split between nightmares about the festival and waking thoughts about being the only woman in a garrison of nearly a thousand soldiers.

But the morning came, slicing without mercy through gaps in the leather tent and searing her eyes with its arrival. She dragged weary limbs from the bed and rubbed her temples. Her head felt as heavy as a djinn block.

Corvinus had promised her last night that she would ride today with a *contubernium*, ten of his best men, into Petra to rescue Alexander. They would ride without Roman uniform, stagger their entrance into the city to avoid notice, and meet at the palace. Corvinus assured her his men could get into the palace and back out with Alexander before the queen even knew they had arrived.

The commander was gone from the tent already when she straggled to the front room, but a breakfast of grapes and goat cheese had been laid out. Alexander's favorite. She ate greedily, realizing she had not eaten since yesterday morning.

"Ah, good, you are awake." The commander's voice filled the tent before his body fully passed the front flap. "I have been selecting your men and briefing them on their mission."

Cassia tried to smile but found herself suddenly nauseated. She put a hand to her stomach to quiet the rolling.

"No fear, my girl," Corvinus said. "You go with the best-trained army the world has known."

She nodded. "How soon do we leave?"

He snatched a grape from the table. "As soon as you are ready."

It was the answer she had hoped for, and Cassia stood, her breakfast forgotten.

They were saddled and ready within the hour, and her horse stood at the point of the ten men, including Decimus, as though she would lead them into battle.

She circled the animal to face the *contubernium* and frowned. They wore the robes and head scarves of Arabs, but everything about them, from their profiles to their bearing, screamed *Roman*. Could they pass into the city without notice?

Corvinus strode in front of the group and gave his final instructions. They were to get in and out quickly, remove the boy, and dispatch the queen.

At this last bit, the heat drained from Cassia's face. It was clear Corvinus wanted Hagiru dead by the end of the day. Could Cassia be part of this and bear no guilt?

It is Hagiru or Alexander. She knew this to be true and was only glad it would not need to be her who stood against the queen.

Corvinus patted her leg as though they were old friends. "Courage, girl. Courage."

She nodded and gave him as much of a smile as she could muster, and then they were off, trotting across the red sand with the early-morning sun warming their heads.

The men behind her spoke little, and the horses' hooves made no noise as they sank into the soft sand. The only sound was the scrape and swoosh of saddle and leg, leaving Cassia time for her thoughts.

She expected to feel more anxiety as they neared the Siq, but it seemed to her the desert stretched before them like a victory processional. The cliff that hid Petra from view seemed dwarfed compared to her first entrance into the city, friendless and unknown. She straightened her back and lifted her head, then gripped the reins of her horse with steady hands. For the first time in many weeks, she believed Alexander would truly be freed from the queen. Whether it was the Romans behind her, the God who had adopted her, or the strength she had found within herself, she could not say. But while the entrance to the Siq was still far off, Cassia felt as if success was in her hands.

Decimus talked to the soldiers about splitting off. They would separate long before any travelers or traders heading into the city could notice ten Romans dressed as Arabs riding together.

The wide desert narrowed, and they headed between two low-lying hills, one of the many roads that led to the King's Highway, the main trading route from Egypt to Syria. It was still early, but even in the mornings, these trade routes were unsafe. Bandits could waylay unsuspecting travelers, relieving them of their money and goods. Cassia remembered her fear the first time through one of these straits, but this morning she passed with ten trained Romans with little concern.

She should have been more wary. They had entered the narrow pass and were traveling in a single column when the first marauder came screaming from a small cave, a sword held aloft as he ran. The rest of them flooded in, surrounding the group in a moment.

Cassia's heart quailed at the screams and she spun back into the group of soldiers.

The ten of them clustered at once in an organized defense, evidence of their training, and brandished weapons.

Cassia watched in horror as the bandits and soldiers engaged. The thieves would have little interest in her during the battle, but they would not leave her unhurt if she was without the protection of the soldiers.

The Romans had the immediate advantage of being mounted and used it fully. She watched, shaking in the saddle, as Decimus hacked and thrust at the attackers. Her horse whinnied and pawed the ground, and she tried to keep the mare steady in the center of the circle while watching the battle that swarmed around her.

And then as she watched, a startling thing became evident. The bandits were not going after the men, trying to steal whatever they had on their horses or their persons. They were trying to get *past* the men, to the center of their circle.

To her.

The soldiers seemed to realize this at the moment she did, for she had only a moment or two of panic before they tightened around her in obvious protection.

"Hold, Cassia!" Decimus yelled, as though she had the notion to go running off alone.

Though grateful for their protection, her heart pounded and she struggled to breathe. Had the attackers thought she would return alone? Had they waited in the caves for her to approach, then attacked before they realized how well protected she was?

Clearly they weren't prepared for the *contubernium*. Decimus and the others slashed and stabbed, and the attackers fell in turn, bloody and lifeless in the sand.

It all happened so quickly, and yet time stretched out as she saw each one fall, saw necks sliced open and chests mauled by a Roman *gladius*. Watched as one fell with his face hitting the sand first, and another drop to his knees and clutch his chest before slumping to the ground.

And then there was only one. The man looked around and saw he was alone—and clearly thought better of his intentions. His gaze roved the group of her protectors, his face filled with indecision and then fear, then he dropped his weapon and fled toward the end of the pass.

Decimus said nothing but flicked his head in the direction of the fleeing man. Two of the soldiers kicked their horses and took off after him.

Decimus urged his horse forward until its head matched Cassia's mount. "Are you hurt?" His tone had little of concern and more of a leader taking stock of his men after a battle.

"They were after me." Her voice shook.

"Sent by your queen?"

Cassia huffed. "She is not my queen."

He examined his men. There were a few injuries, but those not serious. They waited in the pass for the two sent ahead to return. When they did, their faces spoke for them. Cassia read anger and frustration—the last of the queen's men had eluded them.

"That cursed gorge," the one in front called. "It's as full of people as the Forum on market day."

"He disappeared into the rest of the Arabs." The other drew alongside his partner. "And they all look alike."

Humorous as it was coming from these Romans, all pressed from the same mold, Cassia could not laugh. "He will tell the queen I am not alone."

Decimus scowled. "If she is alerted, we will be unable to find our way into the palace unseen." He seemed to debate a moment, watching the end of the pass that led to the Siq. "We will return to camp. Give Corvinus this information. Wait for his decision."

"No!" Cassia pulled her horse to face his. "We cannot turn back. The Festival of Grain begins tonight!"

Decimus shook his head. "It is a failed mission. We must regroup and plan another."

The ten men circled and started back at full gallop. Cassia hesitated, torn between her need for their help and protection and her desperation to return before anything happened to Alexander.

But what could she do alone?

I will never leave you or forsake you.

She kicked her horse into a run but did not catch up with the soldiers until they reached the Roman encampment.

They were in the commander's tent within minutes, and he had the full report from Decimus soon after.

Corvinus spoke when Decimus finished. "If we go in now, we are expected."

Cassia had hovered at the edge of the group, but now she pushed forward. "We must go in now!"

Corvinus considered her, then his men. "If we do this thing today, it must be with more men, and with the troops at the ready here in camp. Their defenses will be prepared, and we must be ready to engage in full."

"Then do that!" Cassia knew her voice sounded ragged and tearful, but she did not care. "We have only a few hours before the sun is down and Hagiru will sacrifice my boy!" She gripped Corvinus's arm. "Have mercy, Commander."

He patted her hand. "We will get ready as quickly as we can.

There is good strategy in going in during a holiday anyway, but it will take some time. You must be patient."

Cassia nodded, grateful. But as the afternoon wore on and still Corvinus would not send out the troops, the separation from Alexander grew impossible.

So ignoring the commander's warning that she acted foolishly, as the sun started its descent in the late-afternoon sky, Cassia saddled her horse, swung herself onto it, and turned it toward Petra.

She knew not whether the Romans would arrive in time, but she would be there.

And when darkness fell on the High Place, Cassia would face Hagiru with God alone if that's what it took to save her son.

FORTY-TWO

———•———

CASSIA BROUGHT THE HORSE ALL THE WAY THROUGH THE city. It might draw attention, but hiding had done nothing. Hagiru's people must be everywhere, reporting on her actions and those of her friends.

Friends.

This was where the horse took her, to her friends, though she slipped from its saddle and used the lead rope when she reached the housing district. She wandered the streets slowly to judge whether anyone followed.

When she believed herself alone, she directed her steps to Malik's house.

Would Julian be there? She had not seen him as she passed the tomb work site, though it was a holiday and the site would have gone quiet hours earlier.

Cassia thought back over her encounter with Jesus in the palace cell, her new seedling of faith in Julian's Savior. She longed to tell him of it, and to heal the wounds between them.

The servant Shamir met her at the door and embraced her as

though she had come back from the dead. "We did not know what had become of you." He took the horse's rope. "Everyone will be relieved." He inclined his head toward the courtyard.

"They are here?"

He nodded. "The whole family, or almost. Still a few work in the palace, to watch over Alexander."

Cassia fought back the rising emotion.

"Go," Shamir said. "They will rejoice to see you."

Not all of them, perhaps. Julian's words and his face the last time she had seen him left her unsure what he would feel at her return.

She walked slowly to the courtyard, hearing Malik's voice as she drew closer. He was teaching from Paul's letter to the church in Rome, Julian's favorite. His teaching seemed strengthened in some way, more passionate, more alive. What had happened to fire his voice in such a way?

She rounded the corner, coming upon the group in the verdant courtyard with their backs to her, ranged on benches and the floor with their faces upturned to hear their teacher.

Julian!

She watched in wonder as Julian's voice carried to her on waves of power. He did not see her there, so caught up was he with the truth of what he taught.

"Do you see, my friends, there is now no condemnation to those in Christ Jesus, who walk not according to the flesh, but according to the Spirit? For Christ Jesus sets us free from the law of sin and death! The law is not able to do this, but God sent His own Son in the likeness of sinful flesh, that the righteousness of the law may be fulfilled in us!"

She searched the room for Malik, concerned for a moment that something had happened to him, but he was there, along the back wall, his face glowing with the warm pride of a father.

She turned her eyes back to Julian, and his words poured forth and seemed to come from heaven itself. His face glowed with passion, and his dark eyes shone so bright she could feel their heat from across the courtyard.

His words spun a cocoon of silk around her, leaving her breathless with the living, shining truth of what he spoke. And then those blazing eyes turned on her and widened. He paused, midsentence.

As one, the group followed his attention to the back of the room, and though Cassia could not take her eyes from Julian, she heard her name called out by a dozen voices and felt the surge of brothers and sisters scrambling to their feet and pressing toward her with much embracing. The crowd grew thick around her, and she lost view of Julian, who had still been standing at the front with a pleased but remote smile.

So many questions. They all wanted to know how she had gotten free of the palace. When she mentioned to Zeta that she had escaped the day before, a ripple of shock went through the group.

"Where have you been then, girl?" Zeta asked.

"I spent the night in the Roman encampment."

The declaration silenced the room as though a death shroud had fallen upon them, and then it erupted again in a burst of more questions and consternation.

Cassia answered their questions distractedly, still trying to catch a glimpse of Julian. Was he still there, listening? Had he left already, not wanting to be in the same room with her?

At last the questions quieted, and Malik pushed into the group and put his arm around her waist. "Let's give Cassia some time to rest." He led her from the courtyard, into the front hall of his home. Cassia allowed him to remove her because the questions and attention had begun to make her head swim, though she had no intention of resting. Not with Alexander still in the palace.

"In here." Malik extended a hand through a wide doorway. "Some privacy."

The room was a luxurious bedchamber, larger than the home she had shared with Aretas. "I cannot sleep, Malik." She turned to the older man.

He patted her cheek. "Perhaps not. But you can prepare. We have reached the final moments of this battle."

She nodded, fighting down the wash of useless emotion.

He tilted his head, as if to examine her. "Something has changed. You are different."

She smiled, her eyes misty. "I have met your Jesus."

He gripped her hands and his face grew somber. "He is your Jesus now, Cassia." It did not surprise her that Malik somehow knew all that had transpired in her heart.

"Julian has changed as well." She searched for words to describe what she had seen.

Malik bowed his head and squeezed her fingers. "We are all changed, Cassia. All of us changed because of your coming to Petra. And this night, this night God will show Himself mighty here through us."

Her heart tripped over itself at Malik's words. "Through me as well?" She waited, afraid he would say yes, then afraid he would say no.

He bent to kiss the top of her head. "It is only the beginning. But first"—he turned his face toward the door, where Julian stood, his hands on the door frame—"first you must make things right."

Julian stood aside to let Malik slip from the room, then brought his attention back to Cassia.

Words failed her, and she felt herself blush under his steady eyes. He did not smile, but neither did he scowl. Cassia could not read his emotions. It was almost as if he felt nothing at all. The idea made her tremble. The days without his friendship had made her realize how important it was to her.

"Julian . . ." She searched for a way to begin, came up with nothing, and fell to silence once more, wondering why he only stood there watching her and did not speak. He still had that fiery look about him, and it seemed he had gained both height and years since she had seen him last.

"Julian, I am sorry."

He smiled and finally spoke, coming into the room. "There is no need."

"Oh, but there is." She took a step toward him, then another, but then backed away again. "I . . . I treated you very badly, said things—"

Julian held up a hand and shook his head. "We do not need to speak of it. It is behind us now, and it matters little."

"It is important to me! *You* are important to me. I value your friendship, and I cannot bear the thought—"

He drew close to her, but for all his fiery teaching, she felt little warmth from him. It was as though he were one of his sculptures. "You have my friendship, Cassia. And my respect."

She searched his eyes for some sign of more. "I want you to know that those things I said—"

Again, he held up a hand. "Please, Cassia. There is no need to speak of it again."

"But—"

"And it is of no consequence. Not any longer. There are other things."

She had thought him cold when he first entered, but now she saw his face light from within.

"Other things?"

"The flock here." He turned his head to the doorway. "They are about to be called forth to a great challenge and a great showing of power. I must focus on them, on helping them stand firm."

"You are . . . you are leading them." The wondering words fell from her lips.

Julian's back straightened, and again the glow of something other-worldly, something heavenly, shone from his eyes.

He does not need me.

The thought rocked her, even as she saw he had become every-thing she had wanted.

All those years with Aretas, she had been drawn to his strength, his confidence. And yet it was a layer of stone over a core that crumbled with a lack of integrity, and in the end it had been their undoing.

But Julian . . . She looked up into those dark eyes, the full lips, alive with a smile that was no longer for her, and she saw he had become a leader with both strength and character.

The effect on her heart was shattering, and she reached out for him, wanting him to know she loved him.

"Cassia." He held her hands far from him. "You will always be dear to my heart. But God has shown me that I do not need the approval of others, nor their praise, for I have His acceptance and His call. And that is where I must turn my life."

"But—"

"Rest awhile, if you can. The night will be long and it will be fierce." He dropped her hands. "I will be here when it is time."

And then he was gone, and she stumbled backward, sank into the generous bedding Malik had provided, and felt the heavy weight of a great loss.

FORTY-THREE

———◆———

HAGIRU HAD NOT IMAGINED THIS DAY AS IT HAD UNFOLDED.
When the gods first whispered to her that the boy must die, she
thought the Festival of Grain would arrive with sacred celebration
and a resolute certainty that she acted in accordance with the will of
Dushara.

But as the time for the sacrifice drew near, Hagiru found herself
in the Temple of al-'Uzza, kneeling before the massive black cubic
stone, beseeching Dushara to guide her acts.

Rabbel's body grew cold in the death chamber, Cassia had escaped
every attempt to dispose of her, and from what Hagiru's assassin
reported, she was returning to Petra with a contingent of Romans protecting her.

She whispered a prayer, a powerful supplication that called on the
gods to give her success, then laid her hands on the black stone—a
presumption for which she would have executed anyone else.

"Dushara, strengthen me. Al-'Uzza, guide my hand."

Surely the sacrifice of Alexander would assure the gods' favor and
keep the Romans from annexing Petra and her kingdom. When the

boy was out of the way, Obadas would sit on the throne, with her behind him. And a new era of strength would come to Nabataea.

The crackle of dry tinder and a smoky scent drew her from the stone *betyl* to the outer chamber where a priest prepared a sacrifice. She swept across the chamber to the altar and circled it, staring into the flames and seeking knowledge.

Why did the Romans come with Cassia?

She could think of only one answer. Instead of a provincial governor, they intended to place their own king, nothing more than a puppet of Rome, on the throne of Petra, as they had done in Judea. The long line of Herods, the first of whom had been born right here in Petra, had kept relative peace for Rome for many years, until some sixty years ago.

And if the Romans meant to put their own king in Petra, somehow Cassia had convinced them it should be Alexander.

Hagiru stopped before the altar as the priest threw pinches of incense into the flames, which popped and sizzled over the flesh of a young lamb.

She breathed deeply of the burning scent, letting it dizzy her and carry her mind to a place somewhere in the heavens, as though she floated above the temple.

The sense of power that came with this mental flight comforted her for only a moment, before thoughts of the Romans, of Cassia and her brat, invaded and brought her earthbound once again.

The surging hatred for the girl and for Rabbel's grandson was like flames in her throat.

What did she have if she did not have Petra? With Rabbel gone, power was all that remained. And if that was taken from her, she would have nothing.

Be nothing.

The silent priest offered her a chunk of the lamb's cooked flesh, and she snatched it from him and chewed it angrily, uncaring that it scorched her mouth. The flesh was fatty, and she could do little to destroy it. The lack of cooperation angered her further, as though the meat also defied her and refused to be controlled. Could she not even rule over a piece of meat?

She spit the mouthful into the fire.

Enough.

She turned from the altar and stalked to the temple entrance where one of her slaves waited to escort her back to the palace. "Fetch the boy. Aretas's son. Bring him to my chamber."

The slave bowed and ran to do her bidding. *At least someone listens to me.*

Hagiru strode back to the palace, unheeding of anything around her. Only one thing concerned her. Was her desire to do away with the boy truly in obedience to the gods, or was she only motivated out of a selfish desire for her son to rule? She almost feared to seek the answer of the gods on this matter, and yet she feared even more doing something that would not please them. She could not take that chance.

So once in her own bedchamber, where her personal shrine for the household gods burned with its own small sacrificial fire—an oil lamp and incense—she braced her hands against either side of the wall niche that housed the small figure of Dushara, with his grape-leaf garland and curly beard, and opened her heart to whatever the gods might say to her.

Hagiru had not realized how much she had been holding the voices at bay until this moment of opening herself. The voices rushed in, like air into an unused chamber, feeding a flame within her.

She put her hands to her head, trying to still the clamor and the matching chaos that overtook her physical body and seemed to turn her organs in upon themselves.

It was always like this at first, as though the gods themselves fought over which of them would reign in her mind, which of them would speak. And when one voice would speak louder than the others, still she often felt they were all there even yet, pacing behind the leader like an angry pride of desert lions, waiting for their king to fall.

The competing growls faded as she stared into the lamp's flame, and one voice spoke, low and soothing.

Destroy the child.

Hagiru sighed and closed her eyes. So simple. So definite.

The door to her chamber swooshed open and she turned, ready to take possession of the boy and enact the will of the gods.

A slave bowed at the waist, his wide and fearful eyes still on her. "The boy cannot be found."

Hagiru huffed. "He is about somewhere. Look in the courtyard. Find Bethea."

"They are both missing. No one has seen them for some time."

Her blood ran colder, like an icy wind had blown across her veins. "The pathetic little thing cannot have gone far. Find her."

But in the end, it was not the slaves who located Bethea. They came to Hagiru in the palace courtyard, where she lounged beside the fountain, watching Obadas draw pictures of tigers on the flagstones with a sharp rock.

"We have searched throughout the palace." The slave was clearly terrified to bring the news to the queen. She rose from her chaise, tried to burn a hole through the slave with the force of her glare, then strode past him into the front halls.

Here, in the fading daylight, she closed her eyes, let her head drop backward, and breathed a prayer. "Gods and goddesses of Petra, hear

me." Her scratchy whisper diffused through the hall. "I am your servant, here to do your bidding." She let the silence build, then issued
her request.

"Show me the boy."

Dark thoughts and fearsome images tumbled through her head,
visions of fire and blood, screams of terror, and she welcomed them
in, glorying in them, for she believed she saw the near future and it
would be good. And then the face of Alexander, at first blurred and
distorted but then growing sharp, appeared before her, and she saw
him, huddled and frightened, in the cell where Cassia had spent too
little time the day before.

The messenger slave still cowered behind her, and she whirled on
him. "Below the palace," she barked. "In the cells. You will find him
there."

His eyes grew large at her certainty, but he fled toward the steps
at the end of the hall.

Hagiru went to the palace entrance, ignored the two guards who
offered to escort her anywhere, and stood on the portico, her gaze
trained upward to the cliff top where the altar waited. The sun had
nearly dropped behind the westernmost cliff of Petra, and already
Hagiru could see that a line of citizens snaked up the back side of the
cliff, a procession that would continue until the High Place had filled
for the festival. Even then, people would be perched on ledges and
sitting on the paths that led upward, as close as they could get to the
holy sacrifice.

A scuffle in the hall behind drew her attention and she turned to
the palace.

Two guards dragged a woman and a child toward her.

Bethea. Hagiru stared at her protégé and shook with a hatred
borne of betrayal. *She was never good enough.*

Bethea would not meet her eyes, but Hagiru had little interest in her at the moment. She would deal with the girl later.

But the boy . . .

She towered over Alexander, who looked up at her with the innocence of a lamb. *Perfect.*

"Bind him," she said to the slaves, then looked toward the High Place again. "It is time."

FORTY-FOUR

———◆———

"Cassia. Cassia, it is time."

She jolted awake, disoriented. Had she slept in Malik's extra bedchamber? How could she sleep when the moments of Alexander's life were disappearing like grains of sand blown across the desert?

Malik smoothed her hair and smiled. "It is good that you rested."

"No, no, I must do something." She swung her legs from the bedding, then paused, dizzy.

But do what?

This question had plagued her since she returned to Petra without the Romans. She had no confidence they would arrive in time, for although Corvinus had agreed to help her, he could as easily take the city by force without any agreement from her.

So she had no plan. Nothing but the certainty that she would be on the High Place before the sacrifice took place.

Her glance shot to the small square window in the bedchamber. It was not fully dark, but it had grown late as she had slept.

She stood, then gripped Malik's arm, trying to draw strength from him. He laid his hand over hers.

"Remember who goes with you, Cassia."

She nodded. "I know. You and Julian will be there. And the rest of the church."

"Jesus walks by your side. The very Spirit of the Christ is within your heart."

She searched his eyes, wanting to believe he spoke truth. "I think I finally understand what you have been telling me, Malik. About not needing the love of others if I could understand the love of Christ."

He smiled, though she sensed a sadness there as well. "And so you have found the strength you sought. Not within. And yet it is within. For you are not only the mother of a king, you are the child of a King as well."

She faced him fully, looked more deeply into his eyes, saw into the depth of his heart. "What is it, Malik? I see—I believe you are afraid." Her voice shook a bit at the observation. If Malik was afraid, how could she be brave?

He inhaled deeply, then looked away, to the darkening sky outside the window. "The Father will use this ability you have, Cassia. This way of seeing to the heart."

She bowed her head. From the time her parents had called her "Little Sorceress," she had sought to use her ability only to protect herself. But she thought now of her words on the rocky ledge with Julian. "I do not always use it fairly. Sometimes it is a way to wound others."

He shook his head. "It is a gift, you will see. A gift from the Father, to guide you in how to love others well."

She caught his hands in her own, drew them up between them, and kissed the gnarled fingers, remembering the first time they had met and the way he had laid these hands on her injured shoulder. "Tell me why you are downcast."

"I do not fear the queen." He spoke as though confessing secrets.

"Nor do I fear that God's power will be defeated tonight. But—" He sighed and dropped his head, then lifted it again and met her eyes. "I have told no one this. Not even Julian." He smiled but his eyes watered. "The Lord has given me to know that my time here in Petra is coming to an end."

Cassia frowned. "Where would you go?"

"To glory."

Her breath caught in her chest and she dropped his hands.

"It is well, Cassia. The church here will thrive, the Lord tells me. Under capable leadership, as you must know."

She pressed her hands to her chest, as though that could ease the heaviness in her heart.

"And I do not know when. Perhaps I will live to see many more years."

Cassia could see he did not believe this, and in fact the heaviness of his own spirit came from the belief that tonight would be his last night. She did not know what to say.

Malik saved her from speaking by embracing her, suddenly and fiercely. "Go, Cassia. You must go. But know this"—his voice deepened, as though it came from a well within—"you will rise up to be a mighty woman for God, and many will call on His name because of you. Go in this strength, and go in the love of Christ your Savior."

She dropped her head onto Malik's shoulder. "You are the father I never had, Malik," she whispered, and felt his gentle cry in response. "I love you."

He pulled away, kissed both her cheeks, and released her.

Cassia crossed to the doorway but turned before leaving. "Malik." She paused as he swept tears from his face. "Tell Julian—tell him to be careful. The Romans, they are coming. Not for him, but still"— she faltered and bit her lip—"tell him to be careful."

Malik nodded once, smiled, then lifted his hand in farewell.

She had not expected the swell of people that glutted the streets and headed for the High Place. Somehow when she had allowed herself to imagine this night, to picture facing Hagiru on that cliff top, she had imagined it as desolate and lonely. The two of them, and Alexander, and the demon gods Hagiru served. But as she crossed the city and turned toward the amphitheatre, she realized the Festival of Grain must be a much-venerated holiday, for it seemed all of Petra pressed forward to the single, narrow steps that led upward to the overhanging plateau.

But as she wove through the crowd, trying to squeeze between tight family groups, it was not a holiday spirit that pervaded the people. Rather, a tense and even angry mood seemed to hold them captive. Cassia heard snatches of conversation as she pushed forward, talk of Rabbel's death and of the coming Roman occupation. They feared the queen's stubbornness would bring destruction on them all.

All of Petra sought the favor of the gods on the High Place, to protect them from the blade of the Roman army. The thought sent chills through her body and quickened her steps. She knew how they believed they would gain such favor.

She passed the amphitheatre at last and pressed forward into the single line that twisted upward into the night. There was barely enough light to see where to put one's feet, though some carried torches, held aloft for safety.

Cassia avoided thoughts of the last time she had climbed this path, only to the first ledge where she sat under the moon with Julian.

It is too long. She had not thought it would take such time to reach the top, not known there would be so many people.

Her foot missed a step and she went down on her shin, scraping the skin. She cried out but picked herself up quickly and pushed upward. No one asked if she was hurt. The mood of the people had gone from tense to hostile, and angry shouts could be heard up and down the side of the cliff as they all moved upward, like an avalanche flowing the wrong direction.

In spite of the falling night and the coolness it brought, Cassia began to sweat and then to feel a chill over her skin. Her legs trembled with fear and with the effort of the climb, and the flow of people slowed as all of them tired of the steep incline. Cassia let her fingers trace a path behind her along the rock wall for balance but still felt the strangeness of the height. Her breathing grew rapid and shallow and her fingers numb.

At last, at last, there seemed to be no more rock above them. The wall at her side fell away and the plateau stretched out before her.

So large! She had not expected that. People crawled over the surface of the mountain like a plague of locusts, and she paused to get her bearings, wondering how she would find Hagiru, and Alexander.

Torches had been thrust into the ground, dozens of them over the space of the plateau, and people wandered, talking in groups, or sat in clusters on the ground, spreading blankets with food they had brought up the mountain. The smell of cooked meat turned Cassia's stomach.

A shove from behind nearly sent her to her knees. She moved forward on wooden legs, scanning the crowd for her son.

But there was no altar here. No place for a sacrifice. Only a wide outcropping for the crowd to congregate and a strange pair of obelisks, standing impossibly atop the bedrock as though dropped there from the heavens. Off to the right and in the distance she could see the plateau climbed even higher, and some of the crowd headed that direction.

She put her hands to her temples, where the blood pounded furiously. The sense of evil she had discerned in the city, in the palace, was nothing compared to what she felt here on the High Place. As though all of Petra's darkness was funneled out of the night onto this barren plateau.

If there was a higher place than this, the altar would be located there, as close to the gods as possible. She wove through the people of Petra, her gaze on the sloped path that bent and the higher plain above it, also lit with torches that edged it like fiery columns around a courtyard.

It took so long, too long, to reach the upward path. The dry desert was in her mouth, and her lungs burned with the effort of pushing through the people. But at last she reached the highest level of the mountaintop, still crowded with worshippers, and searched for a face she would know.

On a rise above her, the flat top of the cliff had been shaped into the proper function of a place of worship. No actual temple had been built here, but a squat, square enclosure had been cut into the rock floor, with gutters and slight platforms for various activities. She saw now that what she had thought were torches placed around the perimeter were actually bowl-shaped braziers on stone pillars no higher than her head and filled with burning oil.

Along the left edge of the squared open-air temple, where the High Place dropped off into space, stone steps led up to an altar. Cassia could see from where she stood that the altar was laid with dry wood and brush. At the side of the altar, the stone had been hollowed into a shallow bowl, and a channel ran downward from the bowl. The basin was for libations of both blood and wine. Cassia's stomach rebelled at this sight, and she fought to keep from retching.

One hand on her mouth and one gripping her robes, she turned in a slow circle, head still pounding. *Where are you, Alexander? Where are you?*

But it was not her son she saw first. The crowd that had gathered on the stone platform parted as though a royal procession approached, and Cassia found herself at the end of the open path, looking up.

And then Hagiru was there, above her, her eyes flashing in the firelight, her hair pulled back from her face, and the dark downward peak of her hairline highlighted against the paleness of her skin.

As she had been the first time she saw the queen, Cassia was struck with the unearthly beauty Hagiru possessed, encased though it was in a shell of cold fury.

The queen's eyes lowered to Cassia's. Her mouth curled into a wicked smile.

Cassia's hands went to her chest, fluttery and fearful, and she forced them to her sides and steeled her muscles.

"Cassia." The queen drew out her name like the hiss of a snake.

Cassia felt as though her tongue had been cut out, so unable was she to speak a word.

And then the queen began to laugh.

FORTY-FIVE

———◆———

Returning to the High Place in the company of the believers carried none of the hopelessness that had plagued Julian the night before. Indeed, as the band of followers trekked up the mountainside with the rest of Petra's worshippers, Julian studied their faces and admitted he felt something akin to excitement. The word of the Lord was strong on him tonight, assurances that a mighty display of power awaited, and he had hopes that many would turn to the power of Christ through what they witnessed.

And Alexander . . . Julian prayed the boy's life would be spared and tried not to dwell on the idea that the Father at times chooses to bring some home for His good purposes.

The darkness grew as they climbed higher, and their progress slowed. The narrow steps gouged into the rock allowed a mere toehold in places and were wide enough for only one person. Only the most tenacious desert plants survived here, but they poked from crevices at unexpected moments and tore at sleeves and legs.

Julian's excitement also tempered as they climbed, and he felt the oppressive weight of evil that roamed the High Place unhindered.

Not for long.

They cleared the cliff face at last, and when Julian pulled himself up the final step, he found the believers who had been ahead of him arranged in a half circle on the plateau a short distance away, waiting for instruction.

Julian paused, strengthened by their faces, each one filled with what seemed a holy light in this place, a serenity that belied the circumstance and stood in contrast to the fear that permeated the rest of the crowd.

He went to them, and they waited for the rest to straggle up the cliff. The plateau filled with citizens as they waited, and the multitude of yellow torches ringing this side of the mountaintop lit the crowd as though it were still midday.

When they were all assembled, Julian looked to Malik, who had been one of the last to arrive, aided in the climb by Nahor and Niv. Malik shook his head, still winded, and held out his hand toward Julian.

Julian nodded, and a trickle of sweat chased down the center of his back. He pointed to the flat area between the two obelisks that stood sentry near the ledge and called out instructions. "We will assemble there. Between the pillars."

Some turned to the stone columns, then to other believers around them, their eyes large and fearful, and many shrank back.

"There is power there, yes. And we will break that power through the word of the Lord." He pressed on, lifting his voice so they could each take strength from the truth. "Remember, we do not wage war as the world does, my friends. The weapons we yield are not the weapons of the world. No, they have divine power to demolish strongholds! And we will demolish everything that sets itself up against the knowledge of God. The prayer of the righteous is powerful, brothers and sisters!"

Heads lifted then, and Julian felt the strength return to them. People of the city pressed around their band of faithful, no doubt wondering what little sect had drawn apart in this way.

Julian turned, confident that each one would follow him, and strode through the crowd toward the flat place between the stones.

Talya caught up with him and tugged at his sleeve. "Where is Cassia?"

He scanned the plateau, but there were too many thousands and the night outside the torches too dark. "I do not know. We must trust that God has her in His hand as well as us, and we must do only what He calls us to do."

She dropped back, and Julian knew his words sounded uncaring. In truth, his heart felt split in two pieces, and one of them was with Cassia.

He reached the pillars, searched out the spot, and found there was a rise in the ground, with a flat-topped rock about thirty cubits from the two pillars. He positioned himself on this rise and beckoned Malik to join him. The older man was at his side in a moment.

"Here is a good place from which to speak to the church," he said to Malik. "You will be seen, but you may have to shout to be heard in this crowd."

Malik patted his shoulder but did not look at him. "My shouting days are over, son."

So Julian lifted his head to take in the flock, with their faces turned to him, but also all those beyond, who milled around in fearful groups, or shouted and laughed in a spirit of celebration, or pushed and shoved through the crowds to gain a better place from which to see the sacrifice.

He loved this church, Julian realized in that moment. Loved it in the way he had loved those in Rome, with an affection he had not thought he would feel again. But above them and beyond them and around them were the people of Petra, and a wave of compassion washed over him for these souls as well.

How many they are. And how lost.

His heart swelled with the unexpected emotion. He had thought the actions of the church here this night would be about conquering, about showing the might and power of the One God, greater than any demon-gods the queen could conjure. Instead, he felt a deep and soul-wrenching desire to show the glorious love of Christ to each of those lost in darkness.

Was this how Jesus felt when He had looked on Jerusalem and wept?

And with the emotion came something else, even deeper, like a vibration in the core of his being, words to speak that were not of himself and yet were true. A *knowing* that rose and burst from his lips as though he had prepared the words in advance.

"In the last days the mountain of God's temple will be established. It will be chief among the mountains. It will be raised above the hills, and the nations will stream to it. Many nations will come and say, 'Come, we will go up to the mountain of the Lord, to the house of the God of Jacob. He will teach us His ways, so that we may walk in His paths.'"

The believers were not the only ones to hear, not the only ones to turn their faces and listen, wide-eyed, as this man, neither priest nor Petran, spoke as one with authority.

The words poured from Julian like a mighty flow that could not, would not, be held back. He heard himself speak but also heard and saw everything around him. The white eyes of all those who listened, the orange-yellow of the flaming torches set into the ground, and the black smoke that rose from each into a purple-dark sky.

Around them, the red rocks became dark shapes, filled with

mystery and portent, and the wind rose and howled through cracks in the rocks. It tore at his tunic and whipped it around his legs.

The wind pushed at him, gusts so hot they seemed borne from the fires of Hades. He tried to anchor his feet to the rock where he stood but staggered. Hands braced him from behind as he continued. The gnarled hands of Malik.

Something had changed on the plateau. When they had arrived it had been a gathering of the citizens of Petra. No longer. They had been joined by a legion of unseen dark powers. He felt it in his soul and saw it on the faces of the believers.

"Our struggle is not against flesh and blood," he called out to them, "but against the rulers, against the authorities, against the powers of this dark world, and against the spiritual forces of evil in the heavenly realms!"

He looked to Talya, to Nahor and Niv, Tabatha and Hozai, and prayed for the power of God to flow into them. "Put on the whole armor of God, my friends. So that you can take your stand against the deceit of the evil one."

The truth seeped into their faces, but as it did, there came a clear separation, one Julian could see as if each person on the plateau were visibly marked. Their circle tightened, a circle of joyful confidence, and all around, a chaos beat against it with poisonous wings.

The believers joined hands, all prompted by the Spirit at once, and stepped forward until Julian stood in their center, with Malik still holding him steady.

He felt as though he were caught in the center of a sandstorm, a pinpoint of calm while all around them the storm swirled with a ferocious howl.

Indeed, the howl of the wind had turned to an audible shriek of voices now, and the sound chilled his blood.

The dark powers had fallen over the people of Petra.

Some of the crowd lifted their hands to welcome this dark anointing, heads thrown back, voices raised in unearthly screams.

Julian felt the surge of evil, like a thousand tiny insects biting. He lifted his voice above it all, to call to the people. "If God is for us, who can be against us?"

He felt a mighty oppression, whispering, accusing, berating. And he knew his people must also feel the weight. "Who will bring any charge against those whom God has chosen?" He wept in earnest now, overcome with compassion for the people, with a fiery jealousy that God's name be lifted above the darkness, and with the knowledge he was powerless and could only be effective if God chose to work through his frailty.

"Who shall separate us from the love of Christ?"

At the name of Christ, the earth shook beneath his feet and, in the same moment, the light of a hundred torches extinguished.

Terrified screams shot to the heavens and bounced back, as though the sky above had turned to stone. People turned on each other in a blind panic. Thick smoke rose from the useless torches and the plateau filled with it, held low by the stony sky.

The ground shook again. Julian felt a shift in the power, as though God's might were flowing away and the darkness would smother them all. The thousands massed on the plateau shrieked as one and struck out at each other.

"Pray, my friends!" he shouted to the believers. "Pray for the people of Petra! Pray that Jesus would free those who all their lives have been held in slavery!"

And then he felt the prayers go up from the tight circle, saw them rise from the lips of the faithful like wisps of light in the darkness, heard the murmured name of Jesus on a hundred tongues.

The smell of burning sulfur beat against them, unable to penetrate, and Julian threw back his head and knew the angel army of the Lord battled in the unseen realms with the prince of Petra and his legion.

Only God could save them now.

And though Julian wanted nothing more than to keep his flock huddled tightly together, he felt the word of the Lord on him strongly.

"Go out among them, my friends." He knew that only through the Lord could they do such a thing. "Go out to the people and show them the love of Christ!"

Wide, startled eyes lifted to him, but he spread his arms and urged them outward. "We are more than conquerors through Him who loved us, friends."

And as they drew strength from his words and from the Word of the Lord spoken in each of their hearts, one by one they turned their circle outward to face the darkness.

Julian lifted his hands above them as they dispersed, in the same way he had spread protection over Cassia in the palace so many days ago, and he called a benediction over them as they went forward, his voice echoing over the plateau, riding somehow above the terror, above the fear.

"To him who is able to guard you against stumbling and to set you in the presence of his glory . . . without fault and with great joy—to the only wise God our Savior, be glory, greatness, power, and authority, before all ages, now and forevermore!"

In that moment, the moon itself turned to blood.

FORTY-SIX

MALIK DROPPED AWAY FROM JULIAN, HIS EYES ON THE bloodred moon.

The boy had done well thus far, but the powers rising around them were stronger than any Malik had ever encountered. As though Dushara, the unseen prince of Petra, had called forth every demon of hell to aid him in his domination of the High Place and the people.

Could Julian withstand such an onslaught? Malik was not certain he himself could do it, and Julian was largely untested and so young. Malik listened to Julian's voice above the wind, above the screams of the people, and thought perhaps the boy's strength faltered even now.

I should speak to them. I should tell them to have faith.

Malik's skin twitched. His fingers tightened into fists, his fingernails dug into his palms.

The torches on the other side of the High Place, where the altar stood awaiting its gruesome offering, still flamed. Cassia would be there, Malik knew. He could do nothing for her, could not even call out words of assurance she would hear. He must entrust her to God alone.

And the rest of them.

Malik's heart reached out to the word of the Lord, such a quiet voice amid the chaos that swirled around them. *Say it again, Lord.*

My child, you are not trusting the flock to Julian. You are giving them to Me.

Malik had visited Mount Hermon in Judea once, when he was much younger. He had seen the snow and ice atop the heights. And in this moment before the Lord, he felt as though he were that snow, melting under the heat of the love of God, dissolving and pouring downward. He closed his eyes and loosened his fingers, his hands open as though releasing at last his grip on the church.

The turmoil on the plateau grew louder, more frantic, and Malik opened his eyes to trace the cause. His people had gone out to the citizens of Petra, the word of the Lord pouring from each of them, the light of the love of Christ shed abroad.

But the powers of darkness would not lie still at this assault. One citizen after another seemed to be filled with an evil so palpable, it shot venom from their eyes and mouths.

Malik had seen this before. In his youth he had been present when Paul cast demons out of the very bodies of people who had become inhabited by a foul presence. He saw those afflicted tear at their own skin, rip out their own hair in an agony of confusion, their own bodies becoming their enemy. Paul lifted the name of Christ over these demons, their backs arched and lips drawn back over their teeth, then the evil spirits left the bodies behind, like empty shells, nearly lifeless in the dirt.

Malik swallowed hard, fought against the fear in his chest, tasted ashes in his mouth. His stomach turned at the smell of burning flesh, as though the demons fed upon those they had invaded.

The wild eyes of both men and women who had given them-selves away darted left and right, up and down, looking for someone to devour. And Malik heard a wrenching sound, as though the very earth had been torn open and shrieks erupted from the deep.

He turned to Julian, fearing an attack on the boy, for the wild-eyed ones turned on anyone who approached.

Julian stood with his arms upraised, his eyes closed, and Malik saw the Spirit of God on him, a shield of defense. He breathed in relief, but the breath was cut short by a sharp pain, like the prick of a small needle, in his lower back.

He turned a slow circle, confused, and put a hand to the pain.

Behind him, a young man, his eyes impossibly large and dark, hissed through clenched teeth, "You will not win here." He waved a short dagger. "You are *nothing* here!" Then he was gone.

When Malik brought his hand before his eyes, he saw it was covered with blood, and his legs grew wobbly.

He turned back to the battle. Although it raged on, for Malik all had grown quiet. The sound of the clash of heaven and hell was replaced by a sweet silence, and perhaps soft music far away.

His vision blurred and he decided to lie down on the rock, for that would be much better.

A thousand stars looked down on him in that sweet silence, and Malik thought, strangely, of Moses dying on Mount Nebo, not far from here. Of Aaron, also called home on a mountain, some said here in Petra.

It is an honor to die thus, on a mountaintop before the Lord.

He felt no pain, only some sadness that like Moses, he would not live to see the end of his battle.

The battle is the Lord's, Malik.

He nodded to the dark sky, to the stars watching him.

You have done well, faithful servant. It is time to enter into your rest.

Malik smiled and turned his head slightly on his rock-bed. There was only one thing left to do.

As though Malik's desire had carried on the hot wind and lodged in the heart of the boy, Julian looked down, saw Malik there on the ground, and dropped his arms.

Come, Julian. It is time to say good-bye.

FORTY-SEVEN

—◆—

Cassia thought perhaps Hagiru could cause the earth to open and swallow her as she stood before the queen on the narrow promontory of rock at the highest part of the plateau. Below and to their right, an unearthly shriek had begun, and when Cassia glanced that way she saw that darkness reigned over the area. All the torches had gone out.

Hagiru saw it, too, and Cassia felt a flash of something like fear in the queen, but it was gone just as quickly and the queen's gaze was back on her with a fury that could burn through rock.

As though the citizens feared this battle could also take them down, they cleared the stone-outlined rectangle that served as the holy place. Only a few held their places, and behind Hagiru, Alexander was held by a palace guard. A rope circled his wrists and the sight of it caused Cassia physical pain, wracking her body with a trembling chill she fought to control.

She forced a smile for Alexander, who rocked back and forth as if to calm himself. She wrenched her attention back to Hagiru, who had crossed to stand before a rectangular slab on the ground, stained with the blood of many sacrifices.

Cassia climbed over the few rocks that separated her from the enclosure, then stepped over the low stone wall and faced Hagiru.

"You cannot stop this," Hagiru screamed. "The gods will have their offering!" A fierce wind blew across the stony plateau, and Cassia trembled again. She was exposed here on top of this rock, vulnerable and unprotected, and she longed for Zeta's cozy cave or the tomb where the church met and sang and prayed.

At the thought of the church, her gaze strayed to the darkness where masses of people seethed over the mountain. The torches sent an inky smoke toward the heavens, but from here it seemed that a hundred tiny lights moved through the crowds, too small for torches, a glow too soft to be flame, too bright to be only a reflection.

She turned back on Hagiru, but in Cassia's distraction the queen had summoned Alexander to be brought to her. The guard who held him shoved him forward, and he stumbled and fell onto the stone slab, unable to break his fall with his bound hands.

Cassia cried out, reached out, and again felt physical pain, this time in her empty arms.

Hagiru held out a hand to a nearby priest.

He shook his head. "The priest must be the one—"

"And I am high priestess!"

At Hagiru's shriek, Alexander tried to crawl off the slab. The queen clamped a jeweled sandal down on his neck, pinning him to the stone.

Cassia's body shook, her trembling uncontrollable. *Jesus, save my son.*

The priest brought the blood basin, his face a mask of anger at the queen's presumption.

Hagiru bent to Alexander.

"No!" Cassia's scream echoed across the rock and Hagiru lifted her eyes—and smiled.

Behind the queen, a pubescent voice called out, "Do it, Mother! Do it!"

Cassia lifted her eyes to see Obadas, his face aglow with a cruel delight. She held out her hands as though she could stop this thing.

Hagiru's glance went to her son, then back to Cassia. "You see? *That* is true strength. Already the boy is stronger than his father. He sees what must be done and does not shrink back. We will have a true king of Petra at last!"

Cassia shook her head. "Cruelty does not make one a fit king. Rabbel was a good man."

Hagiru straightened and laughed, the knife held loosely in her hand. Cassia took a shallow breath, her eyes on the blade.

"A good man?" She pointed to Obadas. "That is the only good thing that ever came of him. He was weak from the day he was crowned. It is a mystery to me how he stayed alive as long as he did."

The truth flashed upon Cassia, as clear as a drop of water. "You killed him."

Hagiru shrugged one shoulder, her thin red lips turned up at the corners, then pointed again to her son. "There. There is the reason I have done what I must. It is all for him."

Cassia lifted her head and inhaled. "It is all for yourself."

Hagiru's face blanched, as though Cassia had named her secret, and it seemed the skin of her face tightened over her bones. Her lips drew back from her teeth and she raised her knife to point it at Cassia.

She said nothing, but Cassia felt a darkness, inky and black, slither into her chest and climb up into her mind. She put a hand to her head but could not rid herself of it.

Hagiru's laugh caused the darkness to swell inside her. The wind rose, billowing the queen's robes around her and pressing Cassia's dress to her body, like a second skin that was no protection.

Insects crawled in Cassia's mind, biting at her thoughts, chewing on her emotions, whispering in a thousand insect voices. She clutched her head with both hands.

She must get away from those insects.

She looked around, at the rocks, the torches, the people. Beyond Hagiru, beyond the stone altar laid ready, the open air called to her, promised her freedom.

The drone of the tiny insect voices merged into one loud voice, commanding and not to be ignored.

THROW YOURSELF DOWN.

FORTY-EIGHT

Julian saw Malik lying prone on the ground. His heart lurched with the certainty that after this night, this mountaintop, everything would be changed.

He ran to Malik. Fell to one knee beside the dear man. "Where are you hurt, Malik?" His voice was nearly lost in the screams and the howling wind.

Malik shook his head slightly, his eyes focused on Julian's own. "There is no pain." He smiled a bit. "I hadn't realized until now that it was the pain I feared most."

Julian searched Malik's body. If he was not hurt, then why did he lie on the rock? "Come." He tugged Malik's arm. "Come and stand with me for the people."

The elder reached a shaky hand to Julian's cheek. "It is your turn to stand for the people, son."

Julian clutched at Malik's shoulder, fear chilling his hands. "Not yet, Malik. Not yet."

Malik dropped his arm and it fell across his chest. "There is not time to argue with the Lord, boy. Nor is there any purpose in it. Believe me, I have tried." He laughed at his own words but then looked up earnestly at Julian. "Listen, my dear son in the faith. It is a good thing that you do not feel ready. Let it remind you that you must not act in your own strength. You cannot. The Spirit will teach you how to lead from the heart of a servant, and you must listen."

Julian nodded, unheeding of the storm around them, focused on Malik's every word, to draw from them everything he would need in the days ahead. "I will listen, Malik."

The older man smiled, and Julian grasped his hands resting on his chest.

But there were no more words of instruction. Malik's eyes widened, and Julian feared for a moment that he felt great pain. But his gaze had gone to the sky above, and it was wonder reflected there, not pain.

"The hosts of heaven, Julian! The hosts of heaven have come!"

Julian followed his gaze upward but saw nothing but the dark sky, though he thought perhaps he heard the distant beat of wings. When he looked back to Malik, the man's eyes were raised to heaven still, but they were unblinking and glassy.

His body and mind numb at the loss, Julian pulled a hand free and closed Malik's eyes. He gripped Malik's hands again, unwilling to say good-bye.

A strange feeling began in Julian's hands then. As though Malik's grip on him, still tight, was a fire that warmed him, a heat that traveled the length of his arms, into his chest, through his entire body.

When he was a child, Julian's mother had told him stories of when she had been a young woman in Pompeii, of the day the mountain had exploded and rained ash down on the countryside, and of the molten rock that had flowed into the towns like a river of fire, then hardened into a solid thing.

This was what he felt now. A molten heat flowing into him from Malik's hands, filling up his body and hardening into a strength that drew him to his feet and turned him to the battle.

Malik had gone on to his reward.

And, Julian, you will lead My church.

With the words, the torches on the plateau once again blazed.

There were more screams from the people, but Julian saw the faces of his own people in the torchlight turned to him and full of power and joy.

It was as though heat and light shot from his fingertips. The smell of sulfur receded, replaced by a sweetness that tasted like honey on his lips, and the voices of his people rose around him, part song, part prophecy.

The evil fell away, peeled back from the mountain like the sloughing off of dead skin. And the power of God fell heavily from the sky on the people of Petra, an invisible wave of strength.

One after another they fell to their knees, weeping with the bitter sorrow of conviction, crying out to the One God, lifting hands of repentance.

All among them his people moved, grasping people's hands, laying hands of blessing on their heads, singing songs of joy, their faces like beacons of light on a distant shore.

Julian lifted his voice in his first words as Elder of Petra. "On every side there is tribulation, but we are not crushed. We are perplexed but not in despair, persecuted but not forsaken, struck down but not destroyed. We carry in our bodies the death of Jesus, so the life of Jesus may also be revealed!"

FORTY-NINE

A THUNDEROUS WAVE OF LIGHT RUSHED OVER CASSIA and sucked the voices from her head. She swayed on her feet, dizzy but aware.

Something had changed. Something had turned. A filling of power that was not of herself.

Bethea had arrived and stood with Obadas, behind Hagiru.

The queen's attention went to the plateau beyond, where the torches were again alight. A strange wail ascended from the people, like the sound of a thousand in mourning. Her gaze came back to Cassia, and a flicker of fear sparked there.

Cassia took a few steps forward, and it seemed as though she grew taller with each step—and Hagiru grew smaller before her eyes.

"You cannot stop this." But Hagiru's voice seemed feeble now, like a little girl, petulant and selfish.

And then Hagiru's whole life seemed to open before Cassia, unrolling like a scroll of pictures she read in an instant. She knew every hurt that had ever come to Hagiru, every disappointment, all the futility.

Cassia reached out hands of compassion, shocking even herself.

"The love you have always longed for is here, Hagiru. Jesus' death is the redemption for us all, from least to greatest."

Hagiru drew back as though she had been slapped. "Stop!" Her eyes lit with fire. "Do not speak that name!"

"You have spent a lifetime yearning for love yet seeking power." Cassia took a step closer. "Let it go. The One God seeks to save that which is lost."

The queen seemed to shrink in upon herself at Cassia's words. Her knife clattered to the stone at her feet, a hand's breadth from Alexander. She backed away, her attention never leaving Cassia, but her fists going to her ears. Cassia moved toward her again, until she stood beside the stone slab, with Alexander at her feet.

The queen fled backward to the altar, grabbed one of the two torches at its side, and waved it in front of her. "Do not come closer! Do not speak!"

But Cassia had finished with speaking. Instead, she bent to Alexander and searched his eyes.

He gave her a quick smile. "Hello, Mama."

Her heart felt as though it would burst with relief and joy. She picked up the knife Hagiru had dropped and, in one quick move, sliced the rope that bound Alex's wrists and lifted him to his feet. He wrapped thin arms around her waist, but she fell to her knees and buried her face in the sweet smell of him. "Alexander." She was whole at last.

The sight of the two of them seemed to infuriate Hagiru, and she raised the torch above her head. Cassia thought she would fly at them but strangely felt no fear. It was as if the entire High Place had become a platform for the power of God. Nothing could fall on them without passing first through His hands.

Hagiru's eyes were bloodshot and red-rimmed. "You have no power, peasant."

At the weak words, Cassia smiled. "There is power in the mighty name of Jesus."

At this, Hagiru dropped to her knees before the altar.

Cassia became aware of the sudden surround of people and stood, hoping to find Julian and Malik. Instead, she saw Decimus and his Roman *contubernium* in a half circle behind her, swords at the ready.

"Step behind us, Cassia," Decimus said, and she complied, leading Alexander by the hand.

The Romans faced the queen, but Cassia bent to her son, bringing her face down until their noses touched. Alexander grinned.

"You were very brave. I am proud of you."

He shrugged. "The tall men told me not to be afraid."

Cassia tilted her head. "Tall men?"

He nodded and looked around, as though searching for someone. "Yes, the shining ones that were all around. Did you not see them?"

Cassia pulled him to her, pressed his warm body against her own, and wept.

But the joy of the moment shattered in an instant as Hagiru gave a hideous shriek and rushed at the Roman contingent, the burning torch still held aloft.

The soldiers moved forward as one, and Cassia could not see which of them ran her though with his *gladius*. Hagiru bent over the blade, her eyes bulging and flecks of foam at her mouth.

Cassia covered Alexander's eyes and turned his head.

The soldier yanked his blade from Hagiru's belly. She still stood upon the altar steps, but now she staggered, the torch tracing a fiery circle in the air above her.

And then she fell, not to the steps, but backward, onto the altar. The torch fell with her, onto the oil-soaked wood. Flames leaped into the night sky, raced in an orange-red line along the length of the altar, and engulfed Hagiru's body.

The queen did not cry out, and Cassia prayed she had been dead before the first flame touched her body.

Cassia glanced at Obadas, but Bethea hid his face from the blaze.

The Romans turned as though the hideous, unplanned sacrifice meant nothing to them. Decimus approached her, and she pushed Alexander behind her.

"There is work to be done. Papers we will need you to sign, oaths to swear."

The Romans had not kept their part of the bargain, for it was God who delivered Alexander into her hands, not them. But a peaceful annexation was best for the people of Petra. And she would give it to them.

She nodded, and a strange and settled peace seemed to fall upon the High Place.

If only Julian would appear. Cassia was tempted to call out for him, but it would not do for him to come now, when the Roman soldiers still ranged around her.

But then he was there anyway, down below the low stone wall, his eyes alight with relief and a magnificent smile on his lips. She smiled in return and lifted a hand.

Decimus followed her gaze, and she felt the crush of what she had brought upon Julian as the soldier drew up in surprise and held his sword out before himself. "Julian!"

His glance shot to Decimus. His mouth dropped open and he took a step backward.

Cassia looked between the two and in the frightful silence she said, "You are known to each other?"

Decimus turned his body toward Cassia, but his eyes did not leave Julian. "He is my brother."

FIFTY

——◆——

IN THE BEATS OF SILENCE THAT FOLLOWED DECIMUS'S declaration, Cassia looked between the two and remembered how she had mistaken Decimus for Julian when she first saw him in the storage room of the palace. It was not simply the Roman profile, the wavy dark hair, she saw now. They did indeed resemble each other as brothers would.

So this was the brother who had not embraced the faith of his parents, who had gone his own direction.

"You are part of this?" Decimus's eyes on Julian were at once curious and accusing.

"I am. And I have matters to which I must attend."

Decimus scanned the plateau, taking in the thousands of people, the burning torches. "We saw things—" He broke off, as though unwilling to continue, but then inhaled and pressed on. "Fire and smoke coming from the mountain, and the rocks ran like rivers of blood."

Julian nodded once, his gaze never leaving his brother's.

Cassia held her breath, unsure of how this would end.

But then Decimus turned to her, as though Julian had not come. "Perhaps we should go to the palace to conduct our business."

Julian's eyes narrowed at the words. She took Alexander's hand in her own. "I am ready."

They walked past Julian, and Cassia allowed herself only a brief touch of his arm as they passed, though the touch sparked beneath her fingers and she longed still to speak her heart to him.

They climbed down from the High Place, she and Alexander, surrounded before and behind by Roman soldiers, as though to ensure she would not change her mind and defy them.

By the time they reached the palace, Cassia's legs felt like quivering mud and she wished for a bed. But she led the way into the throne room, where word had already spread that both king and queen were dead, and palace slaves and servants thronged the room awaiting what would happen next.

The commander, Corvinus, arrived not long after, signaled by his soldiers that the city had been taken.

A table was brought, scrolls spread on them, and Cassia's signature placed on one after the other. She read each document carefully, in spite of her burning eyes and the barely familiar Latin figures that swam across the parchment.

Alexander sat beside her on the platform for a while but soon succumbed and slept, his cheek pressed to the cold floor.

And then at last it was done, and Cassia lifted Alexander in her arms. Decimus offered to carry the boy, but she did not intend to give him up. They moved through the palace halls behind two slaves until they reached an empty bedchamber.

Cassia laid Alexander beneath a warm blanket and crawled under it beside him. He stirred awake and looked at her with sleepy eyes. "A thousand kisses, Mama?"

She pressed her lips to his soft cheek. "A thousand kisses, shekel."

Now and always.

❦

In the darkened street outside the palace walls, one Roman stalked before the steps, waiting for another Roman.

In the time it had taken to bring the church down from the High Place, to restore the believers to their homes, and to care for Malik's body properly, Julian had ceased to wonder at the chance intersection with his brother. God was at work in this place tonight, and the appearance of his brother was part of that plan. Still, he paced as the commander, Corvinus, was summoned and rode in to sign treaties with Cassia. Julian longed to be at her side but knew better than to insert himself into a military matter.

When at last Decimus and the rest of his *contubernium* descended the palace steps, torchlight reflecting from their metal aprons and studded sandals, Julian stood his ground in the street and lifted his chin to his older brother.

"It is time we talked, Julian." Decimus clapped him on the shoulder. "You live in this place?"

"Come." Julian extended a hand. "I have somewhere we can go."

In Malik's *triclinium*, Julian stretched on one couch and his brother on another. Exhaustion swept Julian, and he pulled himself up to sit, for fear he would fall asleep. Thankfully, slaves brought salted bread and wine. The brothers did not speak as the slaves served them in silence.

"She asked about you," Decimus said when they had gone. "The prince's mother, Cassia."

Julian half smiled and bit into his bread.

Decimus laughed. "If I had any question about your feelings, that answered it."

Julian swallowed, then flexed the tight muscles of his shoulders. "She does not come from noble birth—"

Decimus waved a hand. "I have been too long away from Rome, in the lands of barbarians, to care about such things. She is an amazing woman. Don't let her go."

Julian grinned. "I do not intend to."

"I have had letters from Rome." Decimus grew serious and propped himself on one elbow. "Mother told me of Vita and the others."

Julian lowered himself again to the cushion, unable to stay upright, his appetite gone. "I did nothing, Decimus. If you had been there, you would have stopped them."

His brother lifted his cup. "You are wrong. I could have done nothing. Nor could you. It was not your fault, Julian."

"They were innocent."

Decimus set the cup on the table before him and scratched his unshaven jaw. "You know I have never ascribed to this faith you and our parents have embraced, this Jesus who provokes so many enemies. But I saw things on that cursed mountain tonight. Things I cannot explain."

Julian nodded, eyes closed. "You saw the power of God, Decimus. The very hand of God."

"Perhaps I have been foolish."

"It is not too late."

They talked long into the night then, and Julian's exhaustion fled as he shared truth with Decimus, as he watched his brother open his heart at last. Joy filled him as the dissension of many years evaporated in the light of the Father's love.

But when sleep came in the early-morning hours, Julian's last thought was of Cassia.

FIFTY-ONE

———◆———

CASSIA AWOKE TO BRIGHT SUNLIGHT AND AN EVEN BRIGHTER smile from Alexander.

"Will we stay together now?" he asked when she rubbed her eyes and pulled herself up to sitting.

She kissed his cheek. "Always, shekel."

Slaves brought them a tray of food, but Cassia ate little. Her mind had traveled through the city streets, into the housing district, to the home of a wealthy man and the one he was training to lead.

After they had eaten and dressed, Cassia took Alexander's hand and they headed for the city. Soon she would need to speak to the people of Petra. To announce to them that last night the kingdom of Nabataea had become the Roman province of Arabia, peacefully and without bloodshed.

But for now, she wanted only peace with one person.

Alexander pulled his hand from hers as they walked, and she saw he had grown while apart from her, that he was finding his own strength. The pang in her heart came from both a mother's loss and a mother's pride.

Malik's home was filled to overflowing when they arrived. People she did not recognize crowded the front hall, and the courtyard was packed with more bodies than she could count. The previous night's wonder had added greatly to their number. Across the courtyard, Cassia was only half surprised to see that Bethea had searched them out. Niv loomed over her like a protective older brother, his eyes locked on her face. Cassia smiled.

Julian spoke then, from the other side of the enclosure. The crowd quieted, and Cassia led Alexander forward until they could see Julian through a gap in the people.

Cassia's heart clutched at the sight of a bier in front of him, laid out with the body of Malik.

He knew. He knew.

Julian was speaking, but she heard little of what he said. A shadow loomed at her shoulder, and she looked up into the face of Decimus. She narrowed her eyes, but he smiled.

"I've decided it is time to listen to my little brother."

As Julian finished his tribute to Malik, his gaze fell upon Cassia.

She had thought to speak to him privately, but somehow in this moment it seemed she should speak her heart in front of the people she loved, in front of those he would lead.

The crowd parted to allow them to see each other.

Julian smiled. "Cassia, we thank God for your safety and for the deliverance of Alexander."

She nodded. "As do I. For your God has become my God."

He breathed deeply, as though a heavy weight fell from him. But she was not finished.

"It was you who showed Him to me, Julian. You who helped me

see that I could trust Him." She stepped through the crowd, leaving Alexander in the care of Decimus. "You are a good man. A mighty man of God."

Julian bowed his head, and she saw again how her words had hurt him once, and she sought to heal the wound.

"I was afraid of your strength. Afraid it would swallow me up, for I have given myself away to strength before." She stopped before the central fountain, looking over the bubbling stone pillar to Julian's face, still turned to the ground.

"But you are different, because you are a man of integrity. And God has shown me that when I trust myself to you, I trust myself to Him. And so I will."

Julian looked at her then, his eyes full. He circled the fountain and took her hands in his.

Alexander ran to them and put his arms around their legs. Julian ruffled the boy's hair and grinned.

"Will you show me the best places to climb now, Julian?" Alexander asked.

Cassia laughed, but the laughter caught in her throat and she thought she might cry instead.

Julian circled her waist with his arm. "First I must speak to your mother." He turned his dark eyes on Cassia. "Alone."

In a tiny room off Malik's courtyard, Julian pulled Cassia into a crushing embrace and rested his chin on the top of her head. "I feared for you. For him."

She closed her eyes and leaned into his strength. "I meant nothing of what I said that night, Julian. I wished to be strong, and somehow I believed that you and Aretas were the same sort of man, and that even your God could not be trusted—"

Julian tipped her head back with a gentle hand and silenced her rambling with his lips. When he broke away, he bent to whisper into her ear. "I am not running, Cassia. Never again."

She laughed at his words, and the sound was strange in her ears. "Is that a promise?"

His gaze on her was intense, serious. "It is only the first of many promises I will make to you." He smiled. "And to Alexander."

Sometime later, after whispers of family and future, Cassia led Julian back into the crowded courtyard, where Alexander and Decimus sat on the paving stones playing with a tiny green lizard.

Julian stood behind her, his hands on her shoulders. "There is much work to be done here, Cassia. A different sort of work than we have yet done together. There are many new converts, and they will need much from us."

Cassia took in the face of each person, felt the challenge of knowing each of them, and her heart filled up with both purpose and passion.

"We will love them all, Julian. In the strength of God, we will love them all."

THE STORY BEHIND THE
STORY . . . AND BEYOND

———◆———

In AD 106, the city of Petra became part of the
Roman Province of Arabia, and soon after it began to fall into decline.
Before many centuries, its exact whereabouts between the towering
cliffs had been lost to all but local Bedouins and faded into the stuff
of legend.

When I traveled to Petra in the country of Jordan, our guide,
Aladdin (yes, really!), had us shut our eyes as we took the final steps
through the two kilometer-long Siq and rounded the corner to get our
first glimpse of what is known as "The Treasury"—that amazing rock
facade made famous in the movie *Indiana Jones and the Last Crusade*.
It is indeed a marvelous site, as is the entire rock-carved city of Petra.

In 1812, adventurer-scholar Johann Burckhardt, disguised as a
Bedouin, convinced the local inhabitants of a nearby settlement to
lead him into Petra. His initial visit opened the way for other travelers and mapmakers, and eventually archaeologists, to document and
study this fascinating culture and location.

A note about Scripture translations: In bringing you a picture of
the early church in Petra, I wanted to convey the sense of how critical

Paul's letters were to these people. I chose to paraphrase rather than use a modern translation that would not have been in use at the time.

There is so much more to share with you about the city of Petra and the people of Jordan! Please join me at TracyHigley.com to escape into the music, food, and feel of this place, to discover what is fact and what is fiction within the book, and to skim through my travel journals. I'll also have a short story for you there, free for the taking. Come and share your heart with me!

Tracy sitting on the steps of "The Treasury," typing her notes.

READING GROUP GUIDE

1. At the start of the story, Cassia has been involved in an un-healthy relationship for many years. Why do you think she has stayed with Aretas?
2. Have you ever struggled to walk away from an unhealthy situation? If you were able to get free, how did you accomplish it?
3. In what ways is Cassia's tendency to find her identity through what others think of her challenged by the events of the story?
4. Cassia is confronted by the truth of the gospel in the course of the story. How did you feel about her acceptance of it? Did you feel there should have been more of a traditional "conversion" scene? Why or why not?
5. In what ways do the locations of the valley of Petra and the High Place mirror Cassia's emotions and challenges?
6. What character did you most identify with? Why?
7. The events of the Roman conquering of the Nabatean king-dom and its capital, Petra, are historically accurate. How did you feel about the Nabateans submitting to Roman rule? Did you expect something different?
8. This story takes place in AD 106. How familiar are you with

the church's history in this period? What new things did you learn about the history of Christianity through the story?

9. The end of the story involves some specific intervention by God, showing His power. Do you believe God still works in this way? If so, where have you seen or experienced it?

10. Cassia learns that true strength does not mean resisting connections to other people or refusing to rely on others for help. But what does it mean? How does Malik challenge her to find strength in the right place?

11. How difficult is this truth? Do you struggle with finding your identity and security in what others think of you? What can you do to break free of this?

12. Julian's home church in Rome was the direct recipient of Paul's letter to the Romans, and he loves this epistle as a letter from a good friend. How did his view of the book of Romans, and his use of its familiar passages, give you a new perspective on this New Testament book?

13. What does Romans 5:8 teach us about our identity?

14. Romans 8:38–39 talk about God's love for us. How do these verses directly challenge us to break free of our bondage to the opinions of other people?

15. Petra is considered a "lost city" because its existence was unknown to the scholarly world for many centuries, and only a handful of Bedouin locals knew of its whereabouts. Why do you think we have such a fascination with "lost cities"?

16. In what ways do you feel that the author's travels through Petra and other ancient lands have informed her writing? Would you like to travel to Petra, in the Muslim country of Jordan? Why or why not?

ACKNOWLEDGMENTS

WHILE WRITING BOOKS IS OFTEN SOLITARY, IT WOULD also be impossible without all of the people whose names aren't on the cover but who are a part of every page. I am grateful especially to each of the following people for their support and their help.

Thank you to the team of people at B&H Books, whose hard work to put my words into print is so appreciated: Karen Ball, my extraordinary editor; Julie Gwinn, marketing genius; Aaron Linne, digital marketing guru; Diana Lawrence, art director, and all the rest of you who are such a joy to work with!

Thanks to my agent, Steve Laube. You are always excited, supportive, and most of all, interesting! I appreciate your input. Thanks for sharing your love of history with me.

Thank you to my fellow "Pilgrims" who journeyed through Israel, Jordan, and Egypt with me: Carl Green, Bob and Ann Sloan, Kay and Barry Graham, Steve and Eilene Bauer, Tom Fink, Cindy Davies, Diane Hershey, Gloria Snyder, Sean Fox, Theresa Lambert, Wayne Rissmiller, Richard and Faye Simpson, Steve and Eileen Swymer, and my husband, Ron Higley. Thank you for waiting patiently as I lagged behind to madly type my research notes and document every ruin with photos and video. What a great trip we had!

Thank you to each of my children: Rachel, Sarah, Jake, and Noah. Rachel and Sarah, you are so patient and supportive as I write and travel, and I appreciate both of you and your input to this effort. Jake, your book cover suggestions rock! And, Noah, someday when you're older and read this book, I want you to know that every adorable and wonderful thing about the character of Alexander was inspired by you! I love all four of you very much!

Thank you to my husband, Ron, for your continued partnership with me in books and in life. You are my best friend, and I can't imagine navigating life's adventure without you!

THE QUEEN'S HANDMAID

ONE

Alexandria, Egypt
January, 39 BC

Lydia detached herself from the surge of chaos in the palace kitchens and slipped along the shadowed corridor, to a door in the south wall where a few coins would finally find their way into her palm. If she was not caught.

The shouts had come thirty minutes earlier. The Idumean governor of the north-country province of Israel was navigating his ship into the royal port. Slaves assigned to watch the darkening harbor scuttled back to the palace.

In the kitchens, Banafrit was barking commands at her frantic staff, her voice a whip-crack over slaves and servants alike who scurried to do her bidding. But Lydia's presence was neither needed nor expected there, and her secret errand would not wait. She risked a beating, or worse, but it was not the first time.

From somewhere in the cavernous palace came a haunting melody plucked on lyre strings, but the gray walls of the darkened corridor tunneled away from the sound to the south wall. Lydia sped forward on sure feet, sandals scuffing the stone floors. She could navigate these halls in darkness, and often did, to be alone with her thoughts.

The blue glaze of the jug she carried was smooth, but her fingers instinctively sought out imperfections, any trapped air or roughened clay that would render the piece less valued. A figure in the narrow doorway ahead shifted, the moonlight outlining wide shoulders and brawny arms.

At his sudden appearance, her back stiffened.

"You are late." He spoke in a whisper. The light behind him left his features undefined, but the voice was familiar.

In the harbor beyond, the eerie sound of a cat yowling for its next meal raised the hair on Lydia's arms. "I had difficulty getting away. We have a guest arriving—"

"Yes, Herod. The whole city is aware. But one politicking Arab need not disrupt all of commerce!"

Lydia bit back a sharp reply. Her small jug was hardly the stuff of exotic trade. She held the piece to the moonlight. "I gave this one shaded striations of blues and grays, and you'll see that the neck is quite delicate—"

"Girl, you know I care nothing about beauty." He snorted. "The only beauty I know is the lovely color of the obols your pieces fetch me." He jingled a pouch at her eye level. "Pity you can't work faster. Your work is always in demand."

Lydia handed him the jug and took the pouch from his outstretched hand. "Someday." She shook the coins as he had done. "When I have saved enough of this."

Though at the pace she found time to make pieces, she would be older than Banafrit by the time she broke free of palace service to open her own shop. If she survived that long. "Someday."

He shrugged and disappeared into the night with a disinterested wave and a muttered, "Until next week."

Lydia's free hand lifted of its own accord, as if to bid farewell to the jug that was a part of her, as all her artwork became.

She turned back into the corridor, and a flutter of white caught her eye. Her pulse jumped. "Who is there?"

Silence met her question. She tucked the money pouch with its scant obols under the folds of her outer robes and hurried forward, sliding her fingers along the length of the damp wall. Around the first corner a smoldering torch painted the corridor in a smoky half-light. Her quarry vanished around the next bend, but not before the jade-green robes and pale flesh had given her away. Andromeda.

Had the girl been watching? Seen the transaction in the shadows? Lydia paused in the hall, one hand braced against the wall and the other clutching the meager pouch. Cleopatra's anger knew no limits and was as unpredictable as summer lightning.

The scent of smoke watered Lydia's eyes and a chill breeze snaked through the hall and sputtered the torch, mimicking the beat of her heart. She swallowed against a bitter taste. She was so close to her goal of six hundred obols. She needed only to keep her head down and stay safe from Cleopatra's wrath until she earned a bit more. But if Cleopatra found out . . .

She would not follow Andromeda. Better to tuck the pouch's dismal contents into the carefully concealed pocket of her sleeping mat, in the lower level of the palace she shared with two other servants, than to try to figure out the girl's plan. Lydia passed the smoking torch, rounded the corner hesitantly, but Andromeda was already gone, off to spread gossip, no doubt. The girl was younger even than Lydia, perhaps only fifteen years old, but never missed a chance to outshine her. Lydia escaped to her bedchamber, secreted away the coins in the straw, and hurried to the kitchens to assess the damage.

The palace kitchens bordered a spacious atrium with a central *impluvium* beneath the open sky catching rainwater. Tonight, at the four corners of the *impluvium*, four large bronze pots were suspended by chains over cook fires. The overflowing pots pitched and heaved like ships on tempestuous waves of fire. Heat radiated through the courtyard, barely escaping into the night air. No expense, no effort would be spared to impress Herod. Cleopatra had made her desires clear.

Around the fires, palace staff stumbled, shoved, and shouted. The raised arms of pretty serving girls rushed past with platters of delicacies, and new-muscled boys shouldered amphorae of wine in a parade of luxury marching toward the spread tables.

Lydia weaved through the bedlam to the huge kitchen off the atrium, following the sound of Banafrit's roar of impatience.

"What do I care about such nonsense tonight, girl?"

Lydia hesitated in the doorway, jaw tightening. Andromeda had already found her way to Banafrit, to pour her poison into the woman's ear and try to curry favor. But Banafrit elbowed the girl away, bustling around a table littered with the remains of radish and carrot tips and greens and scowling at the noisy kitchen staff all at once.

The woman's gray-streaked hair was struggling free of its combs, and in the fire-heat, strands plastered her pink cheeks. Flour coated her left eyebrow, and she wiped the back of her hand across her forehead, the tan smudge like a scar.

Blustering as she was, Banafrit was the closest thing to a mother Lydia had ever known, though Lydia would never admit to the woman that she had constructed the role for her. Lydia belonged nowhere, but at least in this kitchen, she was acknowledged.

The older woman eyed Lydia in the door frame, glanced from her to Andromeda, and scowled once more. The younger girl seemed to understand where Banafrit's loyalty lay and slunk off to complain to a servant boy who was always hanging about her.

But it was another who greeted her, rising unsteadily from a chair against the wall. "Lydia, at last." He ringed a table of servants arranging pale-green melons on platters and came forward to greet her.

"Samuel." She held out welcoming hands to her friend. The aging man's usually laugh-crinkled face was somber, his white beard uncombed. "What brings you to the palace on a night such as this?"

"I—I need to speak with you—"

Banafrit waddled between them and swatted at Samuel in a familiar gesture born of years of acquaintance. "Be gone, old man. We've no time for lessons and studies here tonight. Herod will be wanting his food and his comforts, and we've nothing but slow-witted servants and lazy slaves about."

She cast an evil eye over Lydia, though a fondness lay behind her expression. "And you—why is it everyone wants to speak *about* you, *to* you? Haven't you duties of your own tonight? I should think that brat—"

"Cleopatra is readying her son herself this evening." Lydia idly rearranged some pomegranates and green grapes on one of the serving dishes into a more pleasing display, with complementary colors better balanced. "She wanted to remind him of the proper manners before a Jewish Galilean governor."

Samuel grunted. "He's not Jewish. And as for proper manners . . ." He left off, with a glance at the ceiling and a shrug.

Samuel's hostility ran deep. Although he had been born in Susa, in what had once been the Persian Empire, he was intensely loyal to all of Israel, from whence his people had been exiled centuries ago. And Lydia was equally loyal to him. If Banafrit was mother, then Samuel was father. Though it was best to remain independent, to keep some distance. A battle Lydia continually fought.

"Banafrit is right, Samuel. I should make myself available for whatever is needed tonight. Our lessons must wait."

"Hmph, lessons." Banafrit poked a servant girl and handed her the fruit platter. "Why you want to learn to be Jewish from this man, I'll never understand. You're not even a Jew."

Lydia raised her eyebrows. "How do you know?"

Banafrit's glance flicked to Samuel, then away, as though the two held a confidence between them. "I told you I've no time for chatter."

But Samuel grabbed her hands, dwarfing them in his own large grasp. "No lessons tonight, Lydia. There is something important I need to tell you. Something has happened—"

"Ly—di—a!" The screech echoed through the kitchen chamber, familiar enough to freeze every servant and slave at his task.

Cleopatra sailed into the kitchen, raven hair unbound and streaming, dressed only in a white sheath. Her dark eyes were wild with anger or excitement, perhaps both. "There you are! I have been calling for you all over the palace like a peasant woman chasing down a wayward husband! I need you at once. Caesarion has hurt himself, and I am not even *close* to being ready to meet Herod." She gave a glance to Samuel, his hands still wrapped around Lydia's, and frowned. Then she spun and departed, her expectation clear that Lydia would follow on her heels.

Lydia tried to pull her hands from Samuel's grasp, but he held firm. "Not yet, child. I have something vital I must tell you. Something of your future— something that is past the time for telling."

Banafrit's never-ceasing activity stilled.

Lydia bit her lip at the intensity in his eyes. "What do you mean, past the time—?"

"Ly—di—a!"

She snatched her hands from his. "I must go, friend. I will find you later." She fled the kitchen, but his declaration thudded inside her mind like an omen of destiny. Her *future*. And perhaps her past? She wanted to reach back for the knowledge, but it was like grasping at a wave and finding only sea spray. When would she have another chance? The deep ache, with her always and all the more these past months, swelled against her chest, full and yet desolate.

She shook her head against the emotion and crossed the flame-lit kitchen courtyard. Her mistress was already gone. She hurried down the front hall of the palace, up the massive stairs, to the chamber suite of Cleopatra Philopator, reincarnation of Isis, Pharaoh of Egypt.

The white-kilted Egyptian guard nodded at her approach.

She rapped her knuckles twice against the wooden door but did not wait to be invited. Caesarion's wailing penetrated into the hall, and Lydia's instinct propelled her into the room.

"What is it, little cub? What's happened?"

She pulled up short. The boy sat inconsolable in the lap of Andromeda. The girl's green robes were smirched with wetness, and her dark and stringy hair hung over his head.

Andromeda shifted her eyes toward Lydia and gave her a tight smile of challenge. It was no secret that Andromeda sought to replace her in Caesarion's affections. Already the girl cared for Cleopatra's newborn twins. Was that not enough?

The thought of separation from the boy tightened Lydia's throat. She should not have allowed herself to get so close.

But at Lydia's voice, Caesarion struggled free of the younger girl's arms and sped across the chamber, arms high.

Lydia caught him up in her arms. Tears sparkled in his dark lashes and ran rivers wide as the Nile down his cheeks. "Now there, what has happened?"

"I fell." He sniffed and pointed to a scraped knee.

"I was about to dress the wound." Andromeda's voice was buttery soft for Cleopatra's benefit.

Lydia set the boy down again. At seven years old, he was too big to carry. She needed to get Andromeda out before she mentioned what she had seen in the corridor. With a nod toward the girl, she said, "That will be all. I'm sure Banafrit needs your service downstairs."

Andromeda narrowed her eyes, glanced at Cleopatra on the far side of the chamber, oblivious in her wardrobe preparations, then strolled from the room.

For all the frenzied commotion of the lower-staff level, Cleopatra's multi-roomed chamber was an oasis of peaceful luxury, with flaming braziers scattered against the walls warming the rooms and heavy tapestries at the windows to block the winter chill. The rooms were spacious and high ceilinged, the walls frescoed in golds and reds by the best Alexandrian artists.

Cleopatra herself was a thing of beauty, draping herself in her signature eclectic mix of jewel-like Roman purples and crisp Greek whites, with the Egyptian's cropped black wig, striped *nemes* head cloth, and rearing gold cobra shimmering at her forehead. Indeed, the meeting of these two leaders was a blend of nearly all the world—the Greek pharaoh of Egypt now sought by Rome meeting the Arab governor of a Hebrew province.

Caesarion was still crying, and Lydia dropped to the floor beside a warm brazier and pulled him to her. "Let us look at this knee. There, now that is nothing. Look. A scrape, and only a little blood clings to it. How shall you be a fine Egyptian soldier if you wail over such a small wound?"

He snuggled closer to her, head on her shoulder, and she sang softly to him, a favorite tune that always calmed his restlessness. Her voice carried, pure and gentle, across the chamber.

"I swear by the gods, Lydia, that voice of yours could charm a monster." Cleopatra laughed coldly and inclined her head toward Caesarion. "Or a monstrous child."

Cleopatra still fussed with the purple-edged toga she was arranging, and Lydia left the boy to cross the room and help. With deft fingers she draped the toga in the Roman fashion, tucked the ends snugly against Cleopatra's slim figure, and turned the woman toward the bronze.

Cleopatra surveyed herself and smiled. "Yes, as usual, everything you touch grows more beautiful, does it not? How could we possibly manage here without you?"

The compliment should have warmed Lydia, but she knew better than to believe it was born of affection. Cleopatra never allowed anyone to feel secure. Though only ten years older than Lydia, since Caesarion's birth, Lydia had seen her order the murders of both a younger brother and sister. And her second brother's death—

Lydia tried to refuse the memory, the soul-suffocating memory that crouched in waiting if she was not diligent in breathing it away. Cleopatra had followed in her father's royal footsteps, having watched him order the execution of her older sister, Berenice, while Cleopatra was still a girl.

Lydia returned to Caesarion, still cradling his knee, and pulled him to herself.

Cleopatra turned to her, eyed the two on the floor, and tilted her head. "You always find a way to look prettier than your station should allow, don't you? Is that one of my dresses you have pilfered?" Her mood had turned sour suddenly, as it often did.

"What? No!" Lydia smoothed the white linen sheath dress embroidered with delicate threads of blue. "No, I sewed this myself."

"Hmm. Well, you look too elegant to be a servant. I am sick of you and your ideas. Perhaps it's that troublemaker you spend time with, Samuel. I've been meaning to get rid of him. He's far too old to do much good at the Museum any longer."

Lydia opened her mouth, but there was nothing to be said. Better to ignore the threat and pray it was spoken without much thought.

Cleopatra observed herself in the bronze once more. "Well, this should be good enough to win Herod as a friend."

Friend? As the only living Ptolemy left, besides her son, she was a shrewd and wary ruler and no friend to anyone. Not even Marc Antony, who had fallen victim to her charms two years ago, after the assassination of his mentor and her lover, Julius Caesar. She had nothing left of Caesar but his son, and she had quickly understood the need to ingratiate herself to the next man in line to rule all of Rome. Antony's twins had been born to Cleopatra a few months ago, and she had only grown more paranoid since.

The queen floated from the room on a wave of perfume, leaving Lydia hugging Caesarion all the more fiercely, the younger brother she would never have.

Often as a child she had pretended that she was a princess too. Stolen from her parents who even now searched the world for her. But such dreams were remnants of childhood, and there was nothing, no one, that was truly hers. No one to whom she belonged.

She buried her face in Caesarion's sweet-smelling hair.

It was best to keep some distance.